'Gilbert was the glue between the players and management and our performances on the field, and was a huge part in our successes. As a player, he wanted to push me to reach the stars, and his methods helped me every day. One of his strengths was to build a person's mindset so that they could believe anything was possible. I'd often come out of a meeting with him thinking, "Bloody hell, I'm the world's best. I can run through brick walls."'

Kieran Read, former All Blacks captain

'Gilbert had an incredible influence on the All Blacks story. After joining with the team in 2000 his methods became an integral part of our legacy, like the black of the jersey. While helping us to win two Rugby World Cups, he was a major cog in our wheel.'

Wayne Smith, former All Blacks head coach and assistant coach

'I used to go into Gilbert's room for a chat during the Rugby World Cup and when I looked around the place, there were sheets of paper everywhere with hundreds of notes scribbled on them. *Chat to this bloke. Do this. Do that.* It was like a five-year-old had scribbled all over the wall, but he never seemed under pressure, and he helped so many players to be at their best. He was the heartbeat of the All Blacks.'

Dane Coles, 2015 Rugby World Cup winner

'Gilbert Enoka had a huge influence on both my personal and professional life. The first challenge I presented to Bert was a tough one, having to reintegrate three young New Zealand cricketers that had been banned for smoking marijuana on a recent tour to South Africa. Not easy when some of the team had confessed and others had chosen not to. Bert was excellent. He was strong, yet pragmatic and empathetic on what to expect and how to deal with it. Problem-solving with Bert would become one of the most important aspects of our relationship and in my development as we both progressed our way through our Black Caps apprenticeship.
'My leadership was very much based on strong principles learned from Bert, either in the classroom or on the fly with real time problem-solving as I navigated the nuances of cricket captaincy. I still remember vividly one late night 'one-on-one' session with Bert where I was at breaking point with the team losing and me horribly out of form. We "pro" and "neg'd" a list of why I should or shouldn't continue the role. The list was heavily in favour of me

raising the white flag. I went to bed that night no longer captain of the NZ cricket team. By the time morning light had hit the curtains I had reinstated myself with a renewed purpose of turning things around. I informed Bert straight away and got the distinct feeling he already knew.

'Bert has a beautiful way of bringing a group of people together. To give them a purpose or a challenge to commit to something greater than oneself. He would use many different techniques to do this but his ability to "theme" a challenge was truly outstanding. To connect a common goal with an emotional attachment can be immensely powerful and Bert's ability to strike the balance and drive the process was brilliant. Making individuals and teams better than before will sit with me until I pass. Gilbert Enoka is an outstanding man, and I am very grateful that our paths crossed at the time they did. His contribution to New Zealand sport, as well as his work away from the sports fields, make him a truly great New Zealander.'

Stephen Fleming, former Black Caps captain

'After some disappointing performances in the early 2000s, the coaches realised there needed to be more ownership by the players in a leadership sense. Gilbert was key in establishing the player Leadership Group of the All Blacks and he helped the leaders understand what was required and how they could effectively lead in the direction the team desired. He helped transform the All Blacks from being mainly a coach-led team to a player-driven leadership structure.

'Bert also had an immense part to play in building and maintaining the culture of the All Blacks. We spent time understanding what the legacy of the ABs meant and what the expectation was for members of the current team. Bert helped us both as individuals and as a team, to allow this expectation to be positive and drive excellence in performances, rather than have it weigh you down and inhibit performance.

He helped grow the All Black culture day to day, week to week, and campaign to campaign. His consistent reinforcement of our values and standards was key to never letting our culture erode due to lack of focus. Each week Bert would help drive the tone and key priorities that both the individuals and leaders needed to address in order to maintain the consistent level of excellence the team were after.

'As a captain, it was always extremely helpful to be prompted by Bert about the areas of leadership I needed to think about each week. It helped me to get the best out of my other leaders as well as the group. This allowed me to maintain the focus I needed to get my personal performance right but also contribute to the wider team.

'When I became captain I had to learn a huge amount in order to have the tools required to handle the toughest situations. Some of these learnings came through experiencing disappointments such as losses. Bert's guidance in these situations was extremely useful. He helped me to maintain perspective but then dig into what could be learned during these tough moments. Bert's ability to bring the best out in both the players and management was hugely influential to our success as a team.'
Richie McCaw, 2011 and 2015 Rugby World Cup winner

'Gilbert Enoka stripped away the noise and showed me clarity – reminding me that my worth wasn't tied to the game, but to the person I am beyond it.'
Steven Adams, NBA basketball player

'I worked with Gilbert at Chelsea for a short period of time in 2023. In truth it was a challenging time for the club. Gilbert stood out for his calmness in every situation. He always had a positive word at the right moment. It was clear that he had worked at the highest level, and had been integral to all of his successful teams. He had a way of telling stories from his experiences that were always of great help to the task at hand. He was a huge support to me and I still recall his words in my working life now. I am very thankful to have worked alongside him.'
Frank Lampard, former Chelsea manager

'Gilbert offered invaluable advice to me and shared wisdom on navigating the emotional challenges that accompany high-performance teams, learning not to let individual athletes lose their sense of purpose. I was impressed by how relatable his delivery was, and he often emphasised the importance of authenticity. He brings a lot of heart and soul to his approach to the mental side of high-performance, which I loved, and he expresses it throughout this book.'
Emma Hayes, USA Women's National Soccer head coach

'How do you capture Gilbert Enoka's immense contribution to the All Blacks in just a few sentences when it truly deserves an entire chapter? His influence extended far beyond the field, helping to shape the team's culture and legacy. He was the secret ingredient in a golden era of New Zealand rugby, and a master at bringing clarity and composure no matter

the situation. It was no coincidence that the team attained unprecedented success during his time of association. His presence has left a lasting mark not only on the sport but also on those that shared this part of the All Blacks story with him.'
Steve Hansen, former All Blacks head coach

'Gilbert Enoka helped me understand the importance of dealing with the mental side of sport, he helped me deal with some issues from holding too much in and hanging on to bad performances to how I dealt with that. He taught me how we can control our emotions to execute our roles under extreme pressure at the elite levels of sport. I learnt this was the most important skill to have in the test arena and Bert made me appreciate this. So much so that I pass on the importance of mental skills to all the teams I'm involved in! He saw what was needed within the All Blacks when I was captain. We had to grow leadership and spread the load and not just leave it all up to the captain and vice-captain. I feel that Bert played a big part in the changes that we implemented around leadership and also creating a culture of ownership and accountability along with the coaches and leadership group that strengthened the legacy of the All Blacks!'
Tana Umaga, former All Blacks captain

'Gilbert Enoka was a major influence on the All Blacks and one of the key personnel that helped the All Blacks win back-to-back Rugby World Cups in 2011 and 2015. The way in which he provided our senior players with the knowledge and skills to take ownership was instrumental. It became the backbone to the success on the field. We couldn't have done it without him.'
Graham Henry, former All Blacks head coach

'Bert has had a massive impact on the New Zealand rugby landscape and the techniques he introduced in the All Blacks were cutting edge at the time. It wasn't just rugby stuff. It was life stuff, and we learned to cope with difficult situations, like having awareness of where your headspace is at, and how to bring it back to a place where you could think clearly and calmly. He was so valuable in the rugby environment.'
Sam Cane, former All Blacks captain

Become Unstoppable

Become Unstoppable

The Blueprint from the World's Most Successful Sports Team

GILBERT ENOKA

WITH MATT ALLEN

EBURY EDGE

UK | USA | Canada | Ireland | Australia
India | New Zealand | South Africa

Ebury Edge is part of the Penguin Random House group of companies whose addresses can be found at global.penguinrandomhouse.com

Penguin Random House UK
One Embassy Gardens, 8 Viaduct Gardens, London SW11 7BW

penguin.co.uk
global.penguinrandomhouse.com

First published by Ebury Edge in 2025

Copyright © Gilbert Enoka 2025
The moral right of the author has been asserted.

Penguin Random House values and supports copyright. Copyright fuels creativity, encourages diverse voices, promotes freedom of expression and supports a vibrant culture. Thank you for purchasing an authorised edition of this book and for respecting intellectual property laws by not reproducing, scanning or distributing any part of it by any means without permission. You are supporting authors and enabling Penguin Random House to continue to publish books for everyone. No part of this book may be used or reproduced in any manner for the purpose of training artificial intelligence technologies or systems. In accordance with Article 4(3) of the DSM Directive 2019/790, Penguin Random House expressly reserves this work from the text and data mining exception.

Typeset in 11/15pt Calluna by Six Red Marbles UK, Thetford, Norfolk

Printed and bound in Great Britain by Clays Ltd, Elcograf S.p.A.

The authorised representative in the EEA is Penguin Random House Ireland, Morrison Chambers, 32 Nassau Street, Dublin D02 YH68

A CIP catalogue record for this book is available from the British Library

ISBN 9781529146943

Penguin Random House is committed to a sustainable future for our business, our readers and our planet. This book is made from Forest Stewardship Council® certified paper.

To my wife, Michelle, and our children,
Ben and Jess —the greatest gifts in my life and
the reason my heart beats.

Contents

Foreword – by Wayne Smith   xiii

Opening Thoughts: One of One   xvii

PART 1
LEADERSHIP

Introduction: When the Leader Improves, Everybody Improves		3
1	The Seeds of Great Leadership	7
2	Three Laws For Leadership (And Life)	23
3	The Magic of Movement	37
4	The Lethal Cocktail	56
5	Leadership Accelerators	76

PART 2
CULTURE

Introduction: Better People Make Better All Blacks		95
6	Set Your Standards	98
7	Preserve the Core, Disrupt the Edges	115
8	We Trumps Me	135
9	The Belonging Place	154

PART 3
MENTAL PERFORMANCE

Introduction: It's Easy to Sweat		177
10	Pressure Is a Lifestyle	180
11	The One Guarantee	191

CONTENTS

12 The Four Rules of Engagement for Moments of Uncertainty and Ambiguity — 202

13 Managing the Moment Pt 1: Strengthening the Mental Game — 213

14 Managing the Moment Pt 2: The Duel Within — 228

15 Winning the Energy Battle — 242

Concluding Thoughts — 255
References — 260

Foreword

By Wayne Smith

Gilbert Enoka has made a great impact on my career, in both rugby and life. I worked with him at the rugby union team Canterbury Crusaders from 1997 to 1999, and during my three spells with the All Blacks, the first as head coach (2000–01) and then as assistant coach (2004–11 and 2015–17). But he's also had an incredible influence on the All Blacks story, and after joining with the team in 2000 his methods became an integral part of our legacy, like the black of the jersey. While helping us to win two Rugby World Cups, Bert, as we fondly called him, became a major cog in our wheel.

Much of this success comes from his unusual back story. Raised in an orphanage in Marton, Bert grew up with gratitude, empathy and a drive to better himself and others. This helped him to connect with people in a way that might not have been considered by many. I remember when he first started with the team, he gave everyone in the squad an exercise book, our *bible* as it came to be known, and we used it to write down our thoughts on leadership, team culture and mental performance – all of which he discusses in the pages of *Become Unstoppable*. Later, he introduced the concept of *the critical friend* to the All Blacks, a mentorship-style programme where we met with a trusted other once a week for advice on where we were headed professionally and what we might not have been doing quite so well. No matter what was going on, Bert always put the team first.

I first met him in 1982, while playing for the All Blacks and Canterbury. Rugby union was an amateur sport at the time, and I was then an unwanted schoolteacher who worked for a sports shop on the side. Luckily the owner was prepared to pay my salary whenever I was away with either rugby team, but my performances were underwhelming. Sometimes the ball felt as big as a pumpkin, other times it was as small as an apple. There were games where I scored for fun, and others when I seemed to be stuck down in a hole. Something was missing and I never understood why. At the time, my job as a sports shop assistant needed me to visit schools around Canterbury, where I peddled equipment and sports gear to physical education departments. One visit was to change my life.

When I shared a cuppa with a young PE teacher by the name of Gilbert in Hillmorton High's staffroom, I was set on a sporting trajectory that would last for 42 years. Bert was then playing volleyball for New Zealand and studying for a Masters in Psychology. But even then, he was clearly ahead of his time. I'd lived in a little town called Putāruru in South Waikato where I was taught from a young age that the 'top two inches' of my head were critical in rugby, but no one ever told me how to use them. My conversations with Bert gave me that knowledge. He enabled me to find new solutions to old problems on and off the field: a visualisation programme became part of my weekly training plan, where I practised the missing parts of my game in my mind. This work complemented the tough, physical team sessions that took place under inadequate lighting in rugby's amateur era, where the concept of stretching seemed otherworldly. Discussions with Bert around staying in the present, focusing on the next task, and not worrying about the scoreboard or past mistakes became a part of my arsenal. I felt steadier on the field. I became less error prone. And as my performances improved, my self-confidence soared. In the All Blacks' changing sheds, I felt like I belonged.

Bert had opened these floodgates for me and our friendship flourished. We were both family men and appreciated that our work couldn't happen without the love and support of our wives and kids, and as I moved into coaching, I was determined to take him with me. His ability to connect with players, his thirst for knowledge, and his expertise in teaching others became my secret weapon. But in an age where sports psychology was viewed as word salad and a sign of

FOREWORD

weakness, the good men who gave their lives to administering our sport had a blind spot. It seemed there was no place in rugby for the Gilbert Enokas of this world and they pushed back on his inclusion. So, when I was promoted as a coach to Canterbury B and sevens teams, Bert became my 'sports masseur', and we operated underground. The players were instructed to bring their *bibles* and pens to every training session and the first 20 minutes were spent reviewing our performances and working at getting better *at getting better*. Every exercise book had a glossary for any new words, plus a section for *what ifs* . . . Bert was readying the players to excel, and with their buy-in we became champions.

Then in the late 1980s word must have got out that, maybe, Bert wasn't a masseur. *That something else was going on.* A senior executive from the rugby union decided to find out for himself and travelled to a tournament with us. On his arrival, Bert panicked and rushed out to buy some massage oil from a convenience store next to the hotel. His plan was to rub down one of the players whenever the executive walked into view, but in his desperation, he'd picked up the wrong bottle. Rather than using a lotion suitable for deep tissue massage, he was carrying a bottle of peanut oil in his bag.

'Bloody hell, Bert,' I said, when I first spotted him rubbing the liquid into one of the boys' shoulders. 'I wanted them loosened up, not deep-fried.'

By 1997, Gilbert's impact on his teams had been validated, as was the fact that sports psychology was finding its place in top-level rugby. A new age was dawning, the top two inches were suddenly considered a resource for every player and Bert was leading the charge. When I became head coach of the Crusaders in 1997, a forward-thinking CEO called Steve Tew was running the franchise. But even then, it was a challenge to get Bert on the staff (and paid, to boot). That Steve was able to push Bert's employment past the board, in retrospect, was a pointer to how successful and famous this rugby club was to become.

As the Crusaders flourished, becoming Super 12 champions in 1998 and 1999, Bert's influence allowed us to stay calm in the fight and to find clarity during the chaos. His skills were soon recognised

FOREWORD

at an even higher level and the experienced All Blacks coach Graham Henry felt he could be a resource in helping the national team reach new levels of performance. The game was becoming professional. The stakes were higher. And other international teams had closed the gap on the All Blacks. Graham believed that by bringing Bert into the team as a mental skills coach and leadership developer, the All Blacks culture could be weaponised, taking us into areas of performance untapped by other sides on the world stage.

This was the start of Gilbert's immense influence in a 23-year spell with our national team. Through this time, the All Blacks – led by the incomparable Richie McCaw, Dan Carter and Kieran Read – won two successive Rugby World Cups, multiple Tri-Nations and Rugby Championships along with three Grand Slams and the Laureus Team of the Year Award. Gilbert's influence and career should not just be measured by these successes alone, though. His humility, honesty, affinity and respect for people provided a model for players and coaches alike. I never coached without Bert in my career, he was a part of my life, and he provided generations of competitors with the mental tools to succeed – both on the scoreboard and, more importantly, in life.

Now he can do the same for you.

Grab your exercise book and pen. Then get better at getting better . . .

Wayne Smith, 2025

Opening Thoughts

One of One

Off the field, through the tunnel, and into the All Blacks' shed at the Parc Olympique Lyonnais in France. It was here that one of the most momentous occasions of my career would take place. The men in black had just sidestepped a potential banana skin: a do-or-die group game against Italy in the 2023 Rugby World Cup. And we'd done it in style too, swatting aside our opponents 96–17, to avoid a shock elimination. A euphoric mood reverberated between the players and coaches, partly because of the result, but also because two important landmarks had been reached. The first involved Samuel Whitelock, the All Blacks' imperious lock, having become the first player in history to make 150 appearances in the famous jersey. The second placed me in the spotlight, as I made my 300th outing as the All Blacks' Mental Performance and Leadership coach, positions I'd held since 2000, when Wayne Smith, then the head coach, had brought me into the group.

Both Sam and myself were called to the front of the shed as the players turned to face us. An eerie moment of stillness settled in the room as everyone took up their positions, dressed in their official team suits and ties. And then Aaron Smith – the *kaea*, or leader – made his call and the haka began, the ceremonial Māori dance that was part of the team's pre-match ritual and a display that was engrained into our DNA like the black of the jersey and the silver fern stitched across our hearts. Before Test matches, its performance connected the players to their past while encouraging them to express themselves in the present. But the haka was also a message to the

OPENING THOUGHTS

world. It said: *We are here; we are one; and we are ready.* As a pre-match ritual, it often defeated our opponents before a tackle had been made in anger.

Sometimes, though, the ceremony was turned inwards, either to welcome a new player into the fold, or to commemorate an individual or a significant milestone, such as this occasion with Sam and myself. In such circumstances, the ritual became a celebration, one the recipients welcomed with honour because the haka was always delivered with authenticity and passion. This day was no different. My heart pounded with pride when the players moved and roared in unison and my sporting life seemed to pass before my eyes. I'd joined the All Blacks some 23 years earlier, at a time when my work, *performance psychology*, was very much the ugly duckling of the sports sciences. There were no peers or predecessors to lean upon when I'd first started working on the mental aspects of the game in the mid 1980s and I'd been forced to push through the headwinds of tradition and bureaucracy. But in doing so, I'd connected with athletes and coaches on a level that took them beyond the basic metrics of form, statistics and results, and into a space where they could hit unexpected levels and maintain consistency. And all while connecting with the most important thing of all: *Their soul.*

This work later contributed to the All Blacks becoming the greatest team of a generation, as we won two Rugby World Cups in 2011 and 2015, 21 consecutive Bledisloe Cups, seven Tri-Nations Series, and ten Rugby Championships. (The Tri-Nations, which featured New Zealand, Australia and South Africa, became the Rugby Championship in 2012 when Argentina joined the competition.) In striving to reach these targets, we encouraged the squad to *Dominate the Decade,* a concept we referred to as *DTD,* and we used this concept to raise our incredibly high standards even higher. The result of this psychological shift was 118 consecutive months spent at the top of the World Rugby Rankings between the years of 2009 and 2019. The evidence was undeniable: we were world beaters. No other collective I'd worked with in sport came close to the All Blacks squad, in terms of quality and innovation. This belief was confirmed when we won the World Team of the Year category at the 2016 Laureus Awards.

As the haka rampaged and roared around us, I felt a little conflicted. Being the centre of attention didn't sit easily with me. I wasn't a fan of the limelight and my work as the Mental Performance and Leadership coach had mainly been delivered from the shadows, away from the prying eyes of the opposition, media and fans. At the same time, I was humbled by the respect on show from the players, among them Sam Cane, Dane Coles, Codie Taylor, Rieko Ioane, Aaron Smith, and the Barretts – Beauden, Jordie and Scott. As their eyes focused on Sam and myself, every gesture seemed to rattle and echo through me, and the group became connected in a way that's hard to describe today. All I know is that any emotion in the moment felt doubly powerful; it penetrated deeply. And then as the noise died down and the players came by to congratulate Sam and myself, one of our wingers, Leicester Fainga'anuku, shook my hand.

'One of one, Bert,' he said, smiling. '*One of one.*'

I had no idea what he was referring to. 'What do you mean?'

'Well,' he said, 'as an All Black on matchday, you can only be one of 23 players, either on the field or on the bench . . .'

'Yeah?'

'And as an All Black, you're only ever one of over a thousand players to have worn the jersey. But you, Bert, are the only person to have been involved in 300 games. You're unique. *One of one.*'

Instantly, my personal journey seemed bonded to the team and the All Blacks legacy in a way I hadn't previously considered. My work, and that of my colleagues, had been groundbreaking and transformative for sure. I certainly felt privileged to have experienced such a remarkable career with such an incredible bunch of players, leaders and staff. But like Leicester had noted, I'd also made an indelible mark, and my story was so very different to anyone else involved with the All Blacks. As the crowd dispersed, I stood alone in the shed. *One of one.* As always.

*

You'll discover over the course of *Become Unstoppable* that my career has been an eventful one. But having started at the sharp end of sports psychology at a time when its undeniable influence was either mocked or ignored by those in positions of power, my value as a *one of one* saw me working with some of New Zealand's most powerful sports teams including the New Zealand cricket team (the Black Caps), the national netball team (the Silver Ferns), and the Canterbury Crusaders rugby union side. Later, I worked with the New South Wales Blues rugby league team and with the Premier League football side Chelsea, though the throughline in this CV was undoubtedly my role as the All Blacks' Mental Performance and Leadership coach as they became arguably the greatest sports team of their generation, if not of all time.

None of these achievements came easily though, and my first games with the All Blacks were real eye openers. After early fixtures against Tonga and Scotland, we were set to play Australia, then the world champions, in the Bledisloe Cup on 15 July 2000. The venue was Sydney's Stadium Australia, and a crowd of nearly 110,000 fans had shown up. At that time, head coach Wayne Smith and myself had begun developing some of the psychological structures that would later drive the All Blacks to success, but there was still a long way to go. Some work had been done on developing a shared vision and a set of values to guide the group in tough moments, but really we were just taking baby steps. It was obvious that there was a huge opportunity for growth inside the mental performance space.

In those days, rugby players, like a lot of professional athletes, were very macho. They couldn't see the benefit in using a Mental Performance Coach, like myself, or leaning into a programme of work that would focus their mind during moments of high stress. Yet what I witnessed in the changing rooms before the Bledisloe Cup game suggested that a dramatic change was required. As the All Blacks readied themselves in the shed, their agitation was visible. Some of them were so anxious they vomited in the toilets beforehand. Worse, this was accepted by everyone present as normal pre-game behaviour, though their unease didn't show on the field at first. We raced into a 24–0 lead during an eight-minute pulverising, before wilting under an extended period of pressure as the Australians drew level. In the second half, the game ebbed and flowed, Australia surged into a lead, and we were only able to save our blushes thanks to a last-minute Jonah Lomu try, which won us the game 39–35. This was a great result for a new coach in his first major outing, but it was obvious to Wayne and myself that significant gains could be made, and a lot of unnecessary heartache would be avoided, if the players managed the mental challenges that accompanied the biggest games.

At first, our progress in correcting this issue was slow and the team seemed unable to move forward, on and off the field. Wayne, by his own admission, struggled during his time as the All Blacks head coach and could only make changes in small increments. He left the position in 2001 and his replacement, John Mitchell, took up the mantle, but our progress remained slow until John was replaced by Graham 'Ted' Henry in 2004. Like his predecessors, Graham soon experienced a similar headache. This was illustrated by an underwhelming Tri-Nations Series in 2004, and then some misbehaviour among the players during our first Grand Slam tour of the professional era in the UK a year later.

In what was a widely reported event, a meeting had been called as we prepared for the first of our upcoming fixtures. But as the players gathered in the team hotel, it became apparent that three of our All Blacks had gone AWOL. The truth was quickly revealed. Having drunk too much on a night out, the trio in question made their way from Wales to London where they'd planned to meet up with a former teammate. After sobering up en route, they realised the error of their ways and made a panicked call to team captain Tana Umaga in which they begged for forgiveness. Tana, unimpressed, then made a specific request to the management group.

'I don't want you blokes involved,' he said. 'I want to deal with this and meet with them myself.'

God knows what went on during the 'discussion', but the guilty players looked rattled afterwards. 'I'll never do that again,' said one. 'I've never been as terrified in a meeting as I was with Tana.'

This was the final straw for Graham and the rest of his management crew. At the time, there were one or two bad apples in the squad and way too many episodes of hardcore drinking and bullying. Behind the scenes, a toxic and selfish attitude had developed, whereby the needs of the individual were taking priority over those of the collective. Something had to change, and it was against this backdrop that an intense discussion occurred within the management group. Eventually, the coaches settled upon a plan: to create an environment where talent could live, and excellence prevail. We wanted to make the exceptional *normal,* and to do so, three essential anchors were established:

1) *Leadership.* A high-performance environment doesn't emerge organically; it requires intentional design, clarity and alignment. To set a positive direction for the team, we first identified the 'right' leaders among the playing group and became very intentional about their development. We knew that a group of committed leaders would help define the All Blacks' vision and set the behaviours and expectations that would shape its performance levels. Once we established a leadership group – and all of them were committed to its ongoing growth and development – then the rest of the players would follow their command.
2) *Culture.* Leadership was vital when establishing a foundation for success, but it could only be built upon with a healthy team culture in place. This was an environment where a set of high-performing behaviours, beliefs and mindsets – or *culture* – could be embraced and accepted by all. This was vital if the All Blacks were to improve as a team because a culture that fosters accountability, a sense of belonging and high expectations would ensure that everyone wanted to give to the cause, 24/7.
3) *Mental performance.* These were the skills that would help our players and teams to thrive under pressure, while exerting maximum effort and performing to the highest possible standards. To achieve this, we curated a toolbox of

psychological techniques and tactics for the players to use in high-pressure moments and episodes of adversity.

The path ahead was very clear. The leadership programme would give us direction, as well as initiating and aligning the players to what was required. A solid working culture would sustain the group. And growth in the area of mental performance would enable the players to thrive and execute decisively under pressure.

Picking out the leaders was a straightforward process. Richie McCaw, Keven Mealamu and Dan Carter were emerging as powerful forces within the All Blacks group, and together they helped to drive the team to new heights. They, along with the other leaders, began to shape the attitudes of the players around them. For example, following on from the incident in Wales, we created a 'No Dickheads' policy, which, as the name suggested, encouraged the squad to root out any red flag personalities. There were no set guidelines. Whenever a dickhead was identified, or a dickhead trait came to the fore, it was on the group to police them.

In some cases, the offending players were pulled aside by one of the leaders and informed their actions weren't acceptable and that they needed to change. This was usually enough to inspire a course correction, and I can't recall any incidents that led to an immediate dismissal, nor can I think of anyone being sent home after several repeat offences. The most common outcome for a player unable or unwilling to rethink their attitude was an unfussy withdrawal, where they made themselves unavailable for selection going forward. This was a good outcome for everybody. It restored the productive vibes behind the scenes with minimal disruption, while allowing the leaders to drive the group forward unhindered.

Culturally, our changes were wide-ranging. We created a new haka through 2004 and 2005, after learning that some of the players had become disconnected from its Māori roots. (A handful of others felt it was a psychological burden ahead of big games.) To solve these issues, we deepened our understanding of who we were and what we represented by asking ourselves a series of questions. Among them: *Who are we as All Blacks and New Zealanders? What does it feel like to pull on the black jersey?* And: *What does it mean for our opponents when they're confronted by the All Blacks at our fiercest?* Over a series of conversations, we created a narrative that deepened the players' connection to the silver fern, the jersey, the country and to the warriors that had come before us. (And those that would follow.) The impact of these initiatives on our culture was massive. A sense of belonging and commitment was created, increasing our power on the field.

Alongside this work, psychological training became our *secret sauce*, and we used it as a form of preparation in the build-up to every Test match and competition. The players learned how to manage their emotional state and overcome moments of adversity; they discovered new tactics for recharging their bodies and minds between demanding events; and they learned how to mentally reframe any pressurised situations, so that they could come alive when the stress kicked in, as revealed by 2019 captain Kieran Read when I chatted to him recently:

> *We learned that pressure was a lifestyle, and we should feel privileged to be experiencing it. Once I'd crossed the white line, I told myself that the butterflies in my stomach were a sign I was in the right place at the right time. Rather than feeling scared, I had to walk towards expectation and pressure and then face it head-on – it was the only way to succeed. Once the ball was in play for the very first time, and I was making my first sprint, tackle and pass, those butterflies seemed to flutter away. Whenever a negative thought came into my mind, I accepted it – I knew that thoughts were thoughts, and they were impossible to shut out, so instead I sent them on their way and reframed them as a positive.*

The three anchors that powered the All Blacks' transformation between the years of 2004 and 2023 – leadership, culture and mental performance – and the lessons I learned throughout my career, make up the chapters in *Become Unstoppable*. When applied to everyday life they can help anyone to achieve greatness, regardless of age, experience or position. For example, it's not just the multinational CEO or the captain in an international rugby team that should sharpen their leadership skills, because at certain points, we'll likely have to drive the actions of others in our role as the supportive and inspirational teammate, family member, or friend. Equally, anyone can benefit from developing a powerful cultural model, and then sticking to it, whether they're at home, work or play. And all of us will experience moments of adversity and pressure, so it makes sense to master the mental performance skills required to handle life's toughest tests while still performing to our optimum. My hope is that by working through this book, you'll go from good to great. And in doing so, reach that most satisfying of benchmarks. *One of one.*

GILBERT ENOKA, 2025

AUTHOR'S NOTE: At the end of every lesson in this book is a story for consideration. Presented under the banner *Te Puna o te Kī*, this phrase, when translated from Māori, means 'The Wellspring of Wisdom', and has a very deep meaning in our culture. (*Puna* in the phrase is the 'collection point'; *kī* means 'to speak', and when put together the words are thought to deliver 'wisdom'.) The pursuit of spiritual wellbeing and nourishment in life is a worthy endeavour for everyone and locating sources for both can maintain a happy and fulfilling existence. The people of the Pacific find spiritual power in the mountains, oceans, rivers and a series of special places such as sacred sites and historically significant locations. It's here that people draw on one another's energy and the wisdom of their leaders, ancestors and historical events. This is one of the reasons why we're known as the *tangata whenua* – the people of the land.

All of us can take a similar spiritual path. A sports team, for example, will gain wisdom and spiritual insight from the places they visit during their journey – the matches and tournaments, the stadiums and geographical locations. As with my culture, there are many sacred spaces in which an individual or team can learn, among them: the training ground (a place of repetition and mastery), the changing shed (an inner sanctum), the playing field (an arena of battle) and the sidelines (a place where wisdom stands). The deepest lessons are learned here, but they can also shape a person's identity, forge resilience and reveal any hidden truths. Interestingly, these same environments exist for all of us, we only have to identify them. For example, an inner sanctum might be our place of work or *doing,* the family home, or a space of worship, whether that be for a spiritual service (temple), a practical discipline (studio), or physical exercise (gym).

To help reinforce the messages shared throughout *Become Unstoppable*, every chapter also comes with a *Wero,* which, in Māori tradition, is a challenge presented to an unfamiliar visitor to a village or home. Its original intent was to determine whether the stranger in question was approaching with peaceful intentions, or something more sinister. Under such circumstances, a warrior would advance and place a mānuka leaf on the ground, before gesturing to the approaching person to pick it up. If they accepted the leaf – and by extension, the challenge – with respect, it signalled a non-threatening intent. If the challenge was rejected, however, then the two meeting parties had a problem. In the process of completing this book, the leaf of the mānuka will be placed before you at certain times. I'd like you to accept each literal *Wero* as a test or process that will help you to reach your ultimate goals. Finally, every chapter concludes with a *Library of Learnings,* so that the key takeaways can be committed to memory.

PART I
Leadership

INTRODUCTION

When the Leader Improves, Everybody Improves

In 2004 the All Blacks were in trouble. Issues on and off the field had created an unstable atmosphere and our results were on the slide. Strong personalities and the desire for individual glory (the Disease of Me) were taking priority over the needs of the team, and the squad had stopped pulling together. Certain players were even suppressing the individuality of others by training or playing injured, just to prevent another person from making a claim on their jersey. Elsewhere, the group had become hierarchical, and their every decision was based on power and control rather than talent and contribution. But it was our behaviour off the field that was more concerning. Standards had slipped considerably, and the team were engaging in boozy events, known as *court sessions,* in which people were made to account for any slip-ups they might have made during the week. The *accused* were then punished with an alcohol-related forfeit.

This toxic culture reached rock bottom following a heavy defeat in our final game against South Africa in the Tri-Nations. The mood was poisonous. A lot of the ire during that night's court session was aimed at the management team, and some of the players picked on the staff. They were made to drink and drink and drink, and at the end of the night one half of the room had passed out on the floor, the other staggered to bed. Something had to give. In the morning, Wayne Smith slid a note under the door of head coach Graham Henry, and on the paper was a simple statement of intent.

'Unless things improve, I'm going to resign at the end of the year.'

Wayne knew a lot about leadership and man management. After working as the All Blacks head coach from 2000 to 2001, he'd moved to England and the Northampton Saints where, after three years, Graham had persuaded him to come back to the international scene as one of his assistants. But Graham knew a lot about management too, and like Wayne, he'd also become sick of the players' antics.

'Well, I feel the same, Smithy,' he said, when the two met later that day. 'I didn't come back for this either.'

What followed was a redesign of the All Blacks' leadership structure and programme. Over several days of discussions, a simple code was established, *when the leader improved, everybody improved,* and in a campaign spearheaded by team captain Tana Umaga, we embarked on a leadership reset that would prove defining for the group. The players were taught to put their personal ambitions aside for the sake of the team. Those that couldn't or wouldn't fall in line were left out of the squad. (Our mantra: You joined *us*, we didn't join *you*.) Meanwhile, a Leadership Group (see Chapter Three) was built around the players that we believed possessed either a) clear inspirational qualities, or b) the potential to develop them. On tours and during tournaments it was their role to meet with the coaches, grow as influencers within the group and empower the team. This was a politically tricky move. One of the unwritten rules of the All Blacks was that no player was promised a jersey, and in creating such a collective, this code was effectively being undermined. I could understand the concerns: a core group of leaders was being established and their place in the squad became almost guaranteed, regardless of form. However, after chatting to New Zealand's selectors, we were able to push the idea through for the greater good.

It takes a deliberate and targeted mindset to ensure that a Leadership Group such as ours can grow and develop. Over the next few years, we brought in experts from other fields to discuss the ways in which our standards and mental game could be improved. Among them were successful CEOs and company directors, managers from other title-winning sports teams, military experts, and even a neuroscientist. Those All Blacks selected for the Leadership Group visibly advanced through this work, and the players around them were transformed into competent deputies. But the coaches were advancing too, and as a result the All Blacks eventually became the world's greatest sports team, winning those trophies and accolades I mentioned earlier. Yes, there were one or two hiccups along the way, as we'll discuss shortly. But in striving to improve the leadership qualities within our collective, we'd embarked on a golden age.

The truth about leadership, as a lot of the teams I've worked with have discovered over the years, is that title and prestige count for very little. A large chair doesn't make a king, and just because someone has been given the status of captain, manager, CEO, chairperson, or president, it doesn't mean they're readymade for the job. That's why so many teams, companies, and even countries fail: the leader sets the tone for what happens in their environment; they drive the strategy, choose their support staff, and influence the mood. (It's the same for charity organisers, head teachers, project leaders, and even parents, because these people are required to manage a group, big or small.) Problems inevitably follow if the wrong person is in charge because, when unchecked, a bad leader can destroy everything with a flippant idea, one poorly thought-out decision, or, in the All Blacks' case, an inappropriate drinking culture. Picking the right people for the job is imperative, and following on from the dark days of 2004 we made it our priority.

Of course, there's a discussion to be had about leadership and the concept of nature versus nurture. *Are people born to lead or do they learn the relevant skills along the way?* My career taught me that both can be true, and the best leaders generally grow into the role regardless, with Richie McCaw, Dan Carter and Kieran Read standing as good examples of this process. All of them were part of the All Blacks' Leadership Group and team captains at one point or another. For some, like Richie, their growth came easily. For others, the work felt a little stickier. But with the right strategies and techniques, all of them were able to lead their teams in the right direction on the biggest stages. By following the strategies outlined in the coming chapters, you'll be able to do the same.

AUTHOR'S NOTE: The definition of *leader* in this section doesn't refer solely to the high-powered CEO or billionaire entrepreneur. All of us are required to inspire, support and motivate others at certain points in our lives, regardless of our position or experience. Taking onboard the lessons contained within the following section will help you to fulfil your potential and overcome challenges, big and small, independent of *who you are* or *what you do*.

CHAPTER 1

The Seeds of Great Leadership

During my life, I've worked and lived alongside a succession of inspirational leaders that seemed to operate at a higher level to everyone around them. On the list was Jock Hobbs, a former All Black captain and chairman of the New Zealand Rugby Union board. Jock was brave enough to re-hire head coach Graham Henry, and by extension me, following our disastrous Rugby World Cup showing in 2007 where we were beaten by the home nation, France, in the quarter-finals. In the previous five World Cups we'd never been sent home before the semis. Our embarrassment was an international talking point, but Jock's decision ushered in an era of unprecedented success. Graham would go on to become a champion in his own right, leading the charge when we secured victory in 2011. Elsewhere, there was Brian Lochore, who won the World Cup as coach in 1987, Wayne Smith, who helped the All Blacks to win the 2011 and 2015 World Cups as an assistant, and 2015 World Cup-winning head coach Steve Hansen.

On the field, Richie McCaw was arguably the greatest leader in All Blacks history. As captain for 110 matches, he drove us to World Cup success in 2011 and 2015, seven Tri-Nations wins and three Rugby Championships. Throughout his career, Richie led by example, fearlessly taking hits for the team, no matter the personal cost. He also carried a serious level of authority, having experienced some tough times in the first half of his international career, most notably that 2007 World Cup debacle. Richie learned from his mistakes, and whenever he was called to address the group in the sheds, or during a squad meeting, the room fell silent. His presence was so strong the All Blacks would have followed him anywhere.

Great leaders aren't always placed front and centre, though. For example, All Blacks assistant coach Ian Foster was an unheralded figure in our 2015 World Cup campaign. He then navigated us through the Covid pandemic before narrowly missing out on World Cup glory as head coach in 2023 where we lost to South Africa in the final by a single point.

Personally, one of my most inspirational influencers was my mother-in-law, Joan Lydon. She referred to me as her *fourth son*; I called her *mother*, and she had a profound impact on my life. I'd taken longer than most to grow into myself and a lot of who I became was down to the quiet influence of Joan and her husband Mike. There was real depth to our connection.

In living and working with these individuals, plus a roll call of legendary sportspeople, I discovered that great leaders generally displayed five traits – defining techniques or styles that acted as motivational rocket fuel. I've since named them *The Seeds of Great Leadership* and they are as follows:

- Great leaders know it's not about them. (But it's only about them.)
- Great leaders are Vikings with a mother's heart.
- Great leaders are masters of intuition.
- Great leaders power up the village.
- Great leaders are totally committed to personal growth.

These characteristics vary in size from person to person, but a leader must possess all five to some degree if they're to inspire the people around them. As mentioned earlier, certain individuals seem destined to lead, while others develop the skills. But by planting and nourishing the following seeds it's possible for all of us to guide our teams with authority, regardless of whether the act is a result of nature or nurture.

Great Leaders Know It's Not About Them (But It's Only About Them)

Picking leaders for the All Blacks was an easy process because they were generally identified on the field first, often without the specific individuals knowing the process was taking place. For example, when the team was under the pump, chasing a lead, or attempting to control momentum in a tight game, the men in black often turned to the same two or three faces for reassurance, instruction or guidance. Those individuals then became our designated leaders because in that moment, the group had chosen them to lead, rather than them choosing to lead the group. (Therefore: *It wasn't about them.*) However, once installed into a position of authority, those same leaders' character and behaviours had to set the standards for the rest of the squad. In effect, they made the decisions for the team, both consciously and subconsciously. (Therefore: *It was only about them.*)

This is where the hard work comes in. All of us can become unstoppable when we strengthen our mindset and character – the two things that other people can't take away from us. This is especially so if we're looking to lead in some way and it's vital we put the work in. To achieve this, I often recommend that a leader at any level carves out a *holy hour* for themselves every day – a window in which they can care for their body and/or enhance their character and mindset. If you're struggling for ideas on what to do, consider journalling (see *The Wero* in this chapter), listening to a self-development podcast, stretching and exercising, learning a new skill, or taking on a task that will enhance your worldview in some way, such as volunteering or donating. Who you are, and who you become after this work, can influence how others perceive you (and whether those others will follow you or not). I've never met a positive and inspiring leader with a poor character or weak mindset, so take some time to enhance yours.

> Go for a 20-minute walk with no distractions and think about the people you know with a strong character and impressive mindset. *What qualities do they possess and how could you apply them to your life?* Afterward, record a short voice memo with your main reflections.

Great Leaders Are Vikings with a Mother's Heart

Every team, whether they're sporting, corporate, or even family, needs a defined set of standards to work from – behaviours that, when modelled and followed consistently, can lead them towards their goals. One such standard would be the All Blacks' attentiveness to personal housekeeping: it was always our aim to leave an environment in a better state than when we'd arrived, and we fastidiously cleaned the team's training shed, eating spaces, bus and meeting rooms because it was our belief that a sloppy attitude off the field led to a sloppy one on it. Elsewhere, being on time was a non-negotiable and it was driven ruthlessly across the All Blacks environment. For example, there were consequences for arriving late to a team meeting, bus departure or commercial commitment. Most new All Blacks set their clocks 15 minutes fast, to avoid transgressing.

No one was immune from these standards, whatever their rank. That said, all the great leaders I've worked with understood the importance of showing leniency where appropriate, especially if a player was having problems in their life outside of the sport, which many did. All Blacks were human beings first and foremost. From time to time, we all had sick relatives, relationship problems, and other challenges. All the great coaches I worked with made a point of learning about their players' lives outside their immediate bubble because they wanted to stay dialled into any issues that might interfere with their performance. Whenever a problem surfaced, they'd assess the situation, connect with the relevant stakeholders (the player's inner circle, such as their partners, family members and personal management team) and release the individual from any commitments that might delay a speedy resolution.

To be a success in any environment, a leader should be both demanding and supportive, as detailed in the Stretch Matrix*. This is a chart where one axis denotes the level of challenge (or standards) faced by a team, or individual; the other axis denotes the support (or compassion) provided by their leader. The Stretch Matrix is then divided into four quadrants, with each one describing a specific management style.

1. The Zombie. These leaders rarely challenge others. They tend to lower their standards and do very little to support the individuals or the team. They spend most of their day occupying space without inspiring their people.
2. The Critic. A leader that knows how to challenge but is able to offer very little in way of support – often deliberately. Critics are aggressive and defensive. They focus on the

---

* This leadership matrix was originally developed by Ian Day and John Blakey, and I have taken the liberty of adapting this model to reinforce my position.

flaws and mistakes of others and rarely praise any successes. They're not good people to be around.
3. The Nice Guy. Deeply compassionate and forever seeking opportunities to offer support. The Nice Guy rarely challenges their colleagues, if ever, and demands very little from their teams. They are generally considered soft touches.
4. The Master Coach. AKA *The Viking with a Mother's Heart.* These leaders demand the highest standards while giving their team the weapons and structures to get there. Ambitious and approachable: this is the ideal position in the Stretch Matrix.

Joan Lydon was *The Master Coach* because she displayed very high standards. (Though she'd hate me for calling her that, such was her humility.) Powerful beyond measure, if she felt a person was wrong, or what they were doing wasn't right, Joan would tell them – no matter who they were, or what they did. Like Richie McCaw, her words and actions carried weight, and the way she went about her business was motivational. While our kids were growing up, she never missed a milestone, and she displayed a fierce loyalty towards her family. But Joan was also incredibly compassionate, a *Viking with a Mother's Heart,* and she softened those standards when a gentle touch was required. Elsewhere, Joan was my #1 All Blacks supporter (never loudly but always proudly) and I felt invincible knowing she was in my corner. Before games, she'd light a candle for the team and as we travelled towards the stadium, Wayne Smith or Steve Hansen would often lean over to my seat on the bus.

'Bert: has Joan lit the candle?' they'd say.

She also texted, and her messages always landed on the money, right up to the end when her hands were crippled with arthritis.

Dear 4th Son. Won't know the result till tomorrow, so go the ABs. Love, Mother.

Dear 4th Son. With you all the way, whatever the result. I'm excited. Love, Mother.

Hi 4th Son. Lovely day here. I thought of you and offered a prayer each time I woke last night. Need to win this one, Gilbert. All the best. Much love, Mother.

Joan was a powerful leader: she was a giver not a taker; she possessed a genuine sense of care for those people in her orbit, whatever the occasion; and she lived to an inspirational set of standards. No doubt about it, she was the complete package and the most remarkable woman I've ever met.

Great Leaders Are Masters of Intuition

Masters of intuition see beyond the obvious and anticipate the challenges and opportunities ahead because they can read a room with remarkable accuracy. Often these readings give them a sense of what will *most likely* happen rather than a definitive cue, and as a result their choices and actions can sometimes seem unconventional on the surface. Usually, though, their decisions are grounded in a deeper understanding: the intuitive leader has learned to rely upon gut instinct, which, while risky sounding, is a by-product of experience. As a result, they possess the confidence to act upon whatever it is their intuition is telling them.

This skill is found in many high-performance/high-pressure environments, such as the senior nurse working in an emergency ward who instinctively understands how to manage a person's condition before they've been thoroughly assessed. Likewise, a seasoned firefighter will know where to look for a victim trapped inside a burning building. During my career, Steve Hansen was brilliantly intuitive around player selection and in-game substitutions. During high-pressure fixtures, he didn't have the time to stop, check the stats, or ask for advice from his assistants. Instead, Steve backed his gut and made a call, trusting it would pay off in the biggest moments, which it often did.

When calling upon intuition, a leader must become an emotional detective. I learned this skill while working in my previous career as a teacher at Hillmorton High School, where I often arrived at the classroom early to assess the pupils as they arrived. (I later did the same thing at All Blacks meetings and on the team bus when we travelled to training or games.) My plan was simple. I wanted to observe everybody, whether they were a kid or an international rugby player, and identify any red flags, such as a heightened state of anxiety, changes in behaviour or a complacent attitude. I then made an appropriate intervention. Depending on the personality, I might step in for a quiet, kind or stern chat. On other occasions, I'd inform a connected teammate, friend or leader – someone with influence – in the hope they might trigger a course correction.

My first experience with this style of leadership took place as a primary school kid in Marton. I was no more than nine years old, and because of my upbringing in a care home, some of the other pupils referred to me as the 'home kid'. I was laughed at and made to feel like a second class person. But one teacher, Mr Pat Hayward, had recognised my discomfort and he always seemed to know when I was having a rough go of it.

'Gilbert, come with me,' he'd say, taking me out of class.

We'd then walk to the nearest store, where Mr Hayward would buy me an ice cream.

Not a lot was said during those trips. Mr Hayward never asked me directly about what was going on. *But he knew.* And this one act of kindness created a powerful connection between the two of us. Simply knowing that he cared was enough. (To think I can recall this event now, like it happened yesterday, speaks volumes.) You will forget a lot of things in your life but you never forget kindness. The experience later helped me as an adult, and I became very in-tune with the feelings of those people around me. I was able to spot a negative emotion or a troubled mind from a mile away.

As I progressed through my career, I was introduced to several techniques for developing and improving an individual's intuition. One of these was the hot debrief session, a military term for a quickfire meeting that took place in the aftermath of a battle. When working with the All Blacks, the Black Caps, and other high profile teams and individuals, these events were conducted during training, or immediately after a game or an event. The aim was to extract key learnings and this was done by asking three simple questions:

- What patterns or cues did you notice that signalled what was about to happen?
- Did any situation catch you off guard? If so, how could you better anticipate it in the future?
- In the critical moment, what options did you see and how did you decide which one to take?

The first question encouraged a person to consider any signals that might prove instructive in the future. The second helped them to identify any previously unacknowledged blind spots. While the third improved their ability to evaluate multiple options and improve decision-making during high-pressure situations. These questions are just as useful and applicable to any team or group setting we find ourselves involved in. For example, it might be that we've become entangled in a heated dispute with a teammate or a colleague at work or your partner at home. To prevent a similar event from taking place in the future, we should become emotional detectives, checking for any behavioural cues that might have indicated something was wrong ahead of time. We can then assess our reactions to the event. Recording these responses commits them to memory and sharpens our intuition going forward.

Great Leaders Power Up the Village

A poor or insecure leader will want to be master and commander of the group, refusing entry to anyone whose knowledge or authority might seem greater than theirs. These people generally surround themselves with yes-men/women, who generally won't challenge their ideas, causing the group (or village) to stagnate. A great leader, on the other hand, isn't worried about surrounding themselves with people that are highly skilled or well-informed because a) they're happy to park their ego, b) they don't feel threatened, and c) they appreciate that these people will help power up their team or organisation. This was the mindset we embraced inside the All Blacks. Whenever we were attempting to rebuild or plan, leading experts were brought in from the worlds of neuroscience, psychiatry, sport, business and the military. We understood that their perspectives and knowledge would educate our players and coaches on leadership, team culture and mental performance, *and power up the village.*

You can do the same for your team or colleagues, by first discovering what it is they need, and then powering them up by creating a series of supportive events and learning opportunities. (For example: how do they measure up in terms of team bonding, skill execution, decompression, and pressure management?) Take them to conferences. Introduce them to experts. Encourage them to conduct their own research. By building a powerhouse of capability around your group, you'll lead them to truly great things.

Great Leaders Are Totally Committed to Personal Growth

After a success, the great leader won't stand still or plateau – that's the behaviour of the good and the not so good. Instead, they'll break boundaries and redefine what's possible, while seeking feedback and self-development to stay ahead of the competition. The All Blacks leaders were obsessed with this attitude, and it was my job to help them to reach their targets because, as we knew all too well, when a leader improves, everyone improves. To achieve this, we asked our leaders to journal and reflect upon their leadership activity. At the end of each week, it was their responsibility to consider the following three questions.

- What did I lead? (It wouldn't have happened without me.)
- What didn't I lead? (I saw it, could have stepped in, but didn't.)
- What did I miss leading? (I didn't see it but should have.)

We weren't asking for essays, a couple of sentences were ideal and the leaders were encouraged to look for any trends in their answers. These reflections were then discussed with a trusted other and noted down on a Leadership Hit List – a one page document comprising a few things for the All Black to work on in the future. Some of the comments I can recall included . . .

1. Use your humour and personal touch to build connections and spirit.
2. Win the work rate contest and lead the numbers.
3. In meetings, lead by example and with mature behaviour.
4. Cultivate with insights rather than saturate with ideas.

By regularly reflecting upon their performances, the individual was able to negotiate their way through any moments of inertia and maintain a state of constant personal growth. The same technique can work for you too.

Te Puna o te Kī: The Growth of the G.O.A.T.

Richie McCaw's leadership aura came from his early World Cup experiences. In 2003, he was in his second full year as an All Black and considered by many to be a serious talent. Like a lot of athletes at the beginning of their international careers, Richie felt bulletproof, which was just as well because we were knocked out by Australia in the semi-finals. Four years later, things got worse when France sent us home in the quarter-finals. Ahead of the competition, the view among most people was that the All Blacks were the fittest and strongest team in the world – and we only had to turn up to win.

Everybody had bought into the hype, even the players, which created an unhealthy level of arrogance.

This flawed mindset soon manifested itself in our performances. In the quarter-final, we were 13–3 up at half-time and cruising, but then we fell apart. With only five minutes to go, the team was two points behind, and everyone seemed stuck in a hole. I watched the players staring at each other. *Could anyone offer us a way out?* At that point, Richie and the other leaders were out of ideas. Nobody knew what to do, probably because the thought that we might lose to France hadn't crossed our minds at any point. This was a massive mistake.

During the fallout, our arrogance was exposed, and when it was discovered that the team's luggage had already been sent to Paris – the venue for the semi-finals – ahead of the France match we were hammered for it, and rightly so. (One paper even argued the All Blacks were like a school bully who didn't know how to react once our victim had hit back.) In the backlash, no one was spared the rod, but Richie, by then the captain, copped the worst of it, and his credentials were questioned over and over. But he didn't let it crush him. He later used the experience as fuel, and in the years that followed, as the team was rebuilt and a cultural overhaul took place ahead of the 2011 World Cup (which we'll explore in Part Two), Richie found a new sense of authority and a connection to the All Blacks' legacy. The tournament was being held on home soil, and as we reflected on our flaws and vulnerabilities, his spirit was ignited. In this time, Richie grew into The G.O.A.T. – *the greatest of all time*. And he achieved this by sowing The Seeds of Great Leadership in the following ways . . .

It wasn't about him. (But it was only about him): When Richie became full time captain in 2006, he was inexperienced as a leader but spent a lot of time understanding and developing himself. He soon grew into the role and worked on his mindset and character. As a result, he became uncompromising on the little things that made a difference. He was always first to the training field. If there were sacrifices to be made for the team, Richie would volunteer immediately. He challenged others when the team's standards weren't being met; he challenged the coaches on their decisions and tactics; he challenged himself to improve for the good of the team. And he was never afraid of a difficult conversation.

He became a master of intuition: I remember watching Richie as he made a powerful covering tackle in a match against Australia in the Bledisloe Cup. He seemed to go around the houses, moving halfway across the field to meet with an opponent who was suddenly in possession and bearing down on our goal line. Nobody else had read the Australians' play, and everyone in the team had been caught flat-footed – everyone but Richie. He lined up his man, and out of nowhere, brought him down. In doing this, Richie killed a potential match-winning opportunity for Australia.

Afterwards, head coach Steve Hansen turned to me and shook his head. 'No one else in the world would have made that tackle.'

He was right too. That's because, as a player and captain, Richie worked on his intuition every day by debriefing and analysing his performances and his leadership choices.

He was a Viking with a mother's heart: Richie knew that to win the World Cup in 2011, the All Blacks needed to show honour, and to expect sacrifice and discomfort. Nothing was to be taken for granted as it had been against France in 2007. He then tackled the most important and frightening question a leader could ask of themselves: *Do the others trust me?* This was a big deal for him. When the team was under pressure in a big game, most All Blacks wondered whether they could rely upon the bloke on either side of them. Richie went one step further and ensured that he could be trusted by *everybody* on the field. This was done by being where he needed to be – every time, and executing accurately – and making physical sacrifices no matter the cost. This became a personal standard and it helped him to create an enduring bond with his teammates.

Throughout this process, Richie led by example. He stayed resolute under pressure and acted with integrity in everything he did, standing tall to care for his teammates during the most challenging moments, no matter the cost to himself. And the cost was huge. As the tournament approached, Richie was nursing a fractured metatarsal in his right foot and underwent surgery in January 2011.

The rehab process proved painful, but he didn't complain. Instead, Richie managed his hurt throughout the tournament, only missing pool games against Canada and Japan. When his metatarsal flared up again before the quarter-final against Argentina, he decided not to have an X-ray and played through the pain to help the team lift the Webb Ellis trophy as we defeated France 8–7 in the final.

He powered up the village: Richie's ego wasn't an issue when it came to seeking expert advice. He wanted to grow in all aspects of the game and understood that occasionally listening to an outside perspective was the best way to develop. He regularly met with other people who had embarked on similar campaigns, former captains that were both inside rugby and outside of it. All of them shared useful lessons that he later drew upon. He was thirsty for any knowledge that might help him, or the team, to succeed on the big stage and in the big moments.

Meanwhile, Richie supported the people around him because he loved them. I appreciate that 'love' is a hell of a word to use in the context of leadership, particularly sports leadership. However, when I've been in the toughest of situations with a team, the greatest coaches and captains have stood up and expressed their love for the people around them. Richie did just that. He cared deeply and showed it every day by working hard and suffering to ensure the team was successful. It sat at the heart of everything he did.

He was totally committed to personal growth: In 2011, we prepared for all possible scenarios on the field and ensured that everybody, including management, was ready. There were plans in place for when we needed three points to win a game; there were plans in place if we were ahead and needed to close a game down; there were plans in place to arrest opposition momentum. No stone was left unturned. Put simply, we were ready for whatever situation turned up come game day.

Richie led the way in all of it and became insatiable in his search for self-improvement. For example, when closing out the 2011 final against France, he'd prepared for such a tight situation by practising his body language and communication style. (Both of which we'll discuss in the Mental Performance section of the book.) Meanwhile, we changed our game at the macro level by innovating tactically, and on the micro level by improving our skillsets inside specific game phases across the team. That year, we were transformed. Rather than shrinking under the pressure, we welcomed it, hunting for the big moments so we could thrive inside them.

The Wero: Embrace the Bible

While I was a player with the Division One volleyball club Pioneer in Christchurch during the 1980s, mental performance sessions were held every week. At the time, I was developing my passion for sports psychology and introducing new practices to my teammates. One of the first processes we introduced to the group was the concept of journalling. Everyone in the squad was given a book of lined paper, nicknamed a *bible,* and they were asked to record their feelings on the latest performance, our forthcoming opponents, key goals, learnings and any challenges we might have been facing, either as a group or individually. These books were then brought to every training session, camp, assembly, or game, and a player was fined if they forgot. Wayne Smith and I later took this process to the All Blacks, where it helped the players to grasp the concepts, structures and strategies we were introducing, with the aim of transforming them into the greatest sports team of a generation.

Every journal was personal – one size fits one – but each book contained a handful of components that were universal to every player.

- A glossary of terms that everyone needed to learn. These were vital for improving in the areas of leadership, culture and mental performance. For example, '*Coping Strategies*: a series of planned responses to events that are beyond our control.'
- The identification of key performance moments: a list of cues on how to behave in incidents of high pressure or emotional flashpoints. (All of which will be detailed throughout this book.)

- Sections for writing notes, ideas and plans. *Because how will you remember anything if you don't write it down?*

Whenever we held a team meeting, or I had a one-on-one session with an individual, the *bible* was a key tool in everything we did. I'd like you to take the same approach as you read this book. Buy a notepad. Scribble down your thoughts as you move through the chapters. Answer the questions, analyse your answers, and build exciting strategies for yourself. Some of the lessons contained here will require you to plan or review. Others will need you to check in with your mindset and character for the coming days, weeks and months. The All Blacks embraced these books, and they enhanced our legacy, helping us to become unstoppable. My hunch is that a similar resource will work wonders for you too.

The Library of Learnings

- There are good leaders and there are great ones. The greatest have presence under pressure and are masters of intuition; they are Vikings with a mother's heart; they are committed to personal growth; they know how to power up the village.
- Every leader should ask themselves three questions every week: 1) What did I lead? *It wouldn't have happened without me;* 2) What didn't I lead? *I saw it, could have stepped in, but didn't;* 3) What did I miss leading? *I didn't see it but should have.* Note any common themes and use them to improve your performance.
- Work on your *holy hour* every day – a window in which you can care for your body and/or develop character and mindset.

CHAPTER 2

Three Laws For Leadership (And Life)

Gilbert is in the bottom row, fourth from the left.

The route to my 300-plus All Black matches was a turbulent one, and it began in 1958 in Palmerston North, where I was born the youngest of six boys. I don't remember too much about my early life. My father, known as 'Jimmy', had been raised in Rarotonga and didn't speak a lot of English. But when he'd met my mother, they fell in love, had six boys, and not long after I was born, he returned to the islands. My mother carried a disability that affected her mobility, and at the time she was unable to provide the stability our family needed. The six boys were placed into care at different facilities in the central North Island of New Zealand, and my brother Tony and I ended up at a children's home on Tutaenui Road in Marton.

The photo on the previous page is taken from that time. I'm in the front row, towards the left hand side. You can lose yourself in this photo and the faces, the spaces between the faces, and the spaces behind the faces. There were 30 of us, and while we were physically together, all of us were lost and felt very alone. Don't get me wrong, we were well cared for by the staff, who were known as 'aunties' and 'uncles', but what was lacking was love – the type experienced between a parent and their child; the kind that filled the heart and acted as an emotional umbilical cord. If you want to see what a human being looks like without nourished love, you can see it in this photograph. I lived with an emptiness: I missed having someone to tuck me in at night with a bedtime story. Someone to cuddle me. Someone to talk to me about what was going on in my mind. And someone to understand my pain when I was getting bullied or feeling left out.

I remained at the institution until I was 12 years old and during that time the feeling of being *less than* was sometimes overwhelming, even at the age when I didn't really understand what had happened to me. I viewed everyone else in the world as being normal, whereas I was damaged goods, and it was hard not to believe that I'd been placed in such a situation because of some crime or misdemeanour on my part. That thinking was all wrong, of course. Life had dealt me a rough hand for sure, but none of it was my fault. Still, there's no telling that to a little boy and the resulting emotional anguish became a theme throughout my younger years.

The separation soon turned me into an *emotional detective*. I became receptive to the hidden discomfort in others, and I had a knack for spotting upset in my friends and classmates, even when they were doing everything to hide it away. (This understanding later helped me immensely whenever I had to break through the psychological walls in an All Black or pro footballer.) But my personal struggle also became an internal battle as I moved forward with the rest of my life, especially when I stepped towards the forefront of sports psychology in the 1980s, at a time when people were dismissive and critical of my work, and resistant to my presence, even though I'd been asked to contribute knowledge and experience to their rugby, cricket or netball teams. The knockbacks, in life and work, toughened me up, but it wasn't easy. Although I had a tough exterior, I was soft on the inside. But after a while, I used the negativity as fuel, and in doing so, I learned three life-changing laws that I've since used as a way of pushing aspiring leaders to success, and to assist those people hoping to improve in some way, regardless of their circumstances . . .

LAW #1: *You'll never rise above the opinion you have of yourself*

During life, we go through good and bad experiences. The bad experiences, for some reason, tend to stick to us like Velcro, or become shackles that we drag around with us, sometimes for decades. This was very true of my backstory. Marton was a brethren institution, and our aunties and uncles lived off the land. Once we were old enough, the kids were expected to muck in with the chores and the work was never-ending: I washed the dishes, milked the cows, stacked the firewood, and weeded the garden. From time to time, my mother came to visit me and my brother Tony, but really, we were strangers. She had met another man, they were living together in Palmerston North, and when the day came when I could return to the family home, I was in tears. A big part of me wanted to return to the *idea* of a nuclear family life and its imagined sense of safety – my utopian castle in the clouds where I was loved and cared for – but I also wanted to stay at Marton because the brethren system was familiar. It felt safe and secure, and it was all I'd ever known. *I could survive there.*

When I arrived at my mother's home on Broadway Avenue, my older brothers had discovered a newfound sense of freedom and were cutting their own tracks. I never begrudged them for that, but this period of my life was particularly difficult. That had a lot to do with my stepfather: he was an alcoholic, and the dysfunction that accompanied his disease was disorientating and unsettling. Sometimes he was nice and kindly. On other occasions he could be vicious and evil. Our mother did her best, but the two of us could never close the gap between us because our stepfather was alienating and divisive. Those four years under their care, between the years of 1971 and 1975, felt harder and more uncertain than anything I'd experienced in the care home.

School was the nearby Queen Elizabeth College, which was the only institution willing to accept Tony and myself – a couple of care home kids that were considered 'bad eggs'. I was determined to prove everyone wrong, and though I found myself in more than one or two playground fights, I applied myself diligently to the work during my teens, later passing my university entrance exams (just). Suddenly, I had options for the very first time. And only one thought: *I've got to get out of here*. I didn't have a mentor, no one told me to go, I just knew that Palmerston North was not the place for me. Yes, I'd had a tough upbringing and felt rejected. And yes, that same sense of rejection was taking place in my school life too, where I'd been judged and bullied because of my care home experience. But those things didn't necessarily mean I was a bad person, a lost cause, or someone that was incapable of succeeding.

This experience, though painful, was educational and I'd realised that the only opinion worth considering was my own, especially when it came to my sense of self. That's because we all have critics, and the most savage ones are often inescapable because they're our innermost thoughts.* However, no one – leader or

---

* As a father, I made sure to instil this knowledge in my kids and after a long, tough tour with the All Blacks, towards the end of my career, my son Ben wrote the following note: 'Watching you inspire, motivate and lead day-to-day has been a true privilege. Thank you for always wearing your heart on your sleeve, for showing us the importance of family and good friends and for showing us how to step up when it matters most. You've instilled within us the confidence to navigate anything that life throws at us, whilst being able to have a good laugh along the way. Every day, near or far, you've been in our corner. Know that we will always be in yours.'

otherwise – can ever rise above the opinions they have of themselves, because they're our personal benchmark, and each one is marked upon us like tattoos, no matter how misguided some of them might be. Sadly, this is a dangerous situation for anyone, because the negative views, if left unchecked, will act like a self-made prison. I've learned that if someone believes their pessimistic thoughts (for example: *I'm bound to fail*) a self-fulfilling prophecy is created. Unable to rise above the opinions of the inner critic, they'll lose all confidence and fall short. As I worked through my teenage years, I'd worked out that to succeed it was vital I maintained a positive opinion of myself, even when the people around me wrongly assumed that I was a bad apple or broken in some way. That mindset acted as a pathfinder, even during the toughest moments.

> It's time to let go of your negative self-beliefs. Take two minutes to reflect on the following question in silence:
>
> What <u>opinions</u> do you have that are no longer serving you well?
>
> Pause here to really consider this. Opportunity doesn't shout, it whispers. *So, did you hear anything?* Record these thoughts in your journal so you can revisit them later.

LAW #2: *Choices not chances will determine your destiny*

Our lives are controlled by one dominant force: choice. And our chosen actions usually prove to be a far more potent driver than any opportunity or lucky break. That's because the decisions we make are more powerful than the conditions we face, and I came to this game-changing realisation in my teens. Whenever I struggled at home or in school, and later, if things weren't working out in my career, I'd take some time to reflect upon the thoughts I was having and the decisions I was making. Day in, day out, this process developed my resilience. It helped me to self-correct in many challenging moments, and I became determined to stick to my belief that the options I took moving forward – in body and mind – would determine whether I was successful or not.

This was really embedded at the age of 16, having decided that a life in Palmerston North was not for me, and I left home, catching the bus to Wellington, and then a ferry to Lyttelton Harbour where I eventually settled in Christchurch. I had no place to live and barely any money in my pocket, but I did have just enough grades to enrol at the Christchurch College of Education in their three-year physical education programme. Having also qualified for a government studentship – a regular grant that paid an equivalent amount to a dole cheque – I scooped up some part-time work, which allowed me to pay rent. Then I knuckled down. In those days, I was a hard worker but not a smart worker, and I found studying difficult, but by 1978, I'd done enough to earn a Teachers College Diploma in Physical Education and a BSc in Geography at Canterbury University.

It was there that I first played rugby. I was good, talented enough to earn age-grade provincial honours while playing for the university's Under-20s team, but the physical side of the sport wasn't for me. At that time, the game was known for its thuggery, and once a team had stepped over the white line and onto the playing field, the rules of society were seemingly tossed aside. I remember taking the ball cleanly at a lineout, only to be smacked about the head moments later – I soon learned that this was a warning from my opponents not to be such a thorn in their side. Eventually, I swapped the rugby field for Canterbury's volleyball court because the sport had everything: power and speed, skill and precision. It soon became my passion.

Eventually, I was considered good enough to play for the Division

One club Pioneer in Christchurch, which was regarded as one of the best on the South Island. I then impressed New Zealand's national selectors enough to represent my country from 1979 to 1984, where I was named Male Player of the Era for the 1980s by New Zealand Volleyball, an award that filled me with a lot of pride. I suppose I was easily identifiable on the court because I played in bare feet, a choice I'd originally claimed was self-styled and borne out of comfort. The truth, however, was that I hadn't been able to afford any trainers during the early days of my career, and my story made for an effective deflection. The habit stuck too. These days, I'm most comfortable when moving around without shoes, either at home, on tour with a team, or when delivering planning sessions to a group of people that know me well.

My performances with Pioneer and New Zealand triggered an interest in sports psychology. At the time, I'd wanted to improve my personal performance levels, and the levels in those players around me. The best way to do this, I reasoned, was by entering into the mind, the *final frontier,* and learning how the mental game might help or hinder an athlete. An enlightening journey began, and I read every book on what was considered a fringe subject, even attending symposiums all over the world when I could to gain an edge in the space. Then I applied the innovative methods, techniques and skills I'd picked up on my travels to the teams I was working with. At first, a lot of my ideas felt new and maybe a bit *out there* for many of the traditionalists (and sport was full of traditionalists at that time). But their resistance didn't deter me. Knowing that I was operating in a results-based business, where wins and trophies would serve as my barometer, I pressed ahead.

Pioneer Volleyball at the time was coached by Tony Barnett, a forward-thinking leader and someone who was well ahead of the curve. He understood my enthusiasm and our first step into the *final frontier* was to push the idea that mental performance was a development tool, one the players could use to their advantage, a bit like weight training or cardiovascular work. The suggestion that it might give us an edge over our opponents also quietened any dissenting voices and together Tony and I conducted weekly mental performance sessions. Among the subjects for discussion were team-building methods and the concepts of brotherhood, mind management and visualisation. Elsewhere, we introduced the squad to the ritual of journalling, and everyone was given those exercise books I mentioned earlier. The players were then encouraged to write down their thoughts on any new mental skills we might have discussed. It was also their responsibility to review their performances while noting any identifying challenges for themselves and the team.

With hindsight, this was a trailblazing move, and my progress proved addictive. A fire had been ignited within me and with every Pioneer win, my cravings for success increased. Managing the mind was a new cause and I became determined to take my ideas into the wider world of sport, a place where its potential had been widely ignored. Most importantly, every step of the journey was being determined by that one powerful force. *Choices*. Not chances.

I wasn't leaving anything up to fate.

LAW #3: *Your past does not have to determine your future*

While moving into sports psychology, I'd also been carving out a career for myself as a PE teacher, having graduated from Canterbury University in 1979. This began when I'd spotted an advert for a position at Hillmorton High School in Christchurch and having applied, their head of PE, Ron Hair, called my tutor from the Christchurch College of Education for a reference. He received a less than enthusiastic response.

'I wouldn't touch him with a ten foot bargepole,' said the gruff voice on the other end of the line.

Most people would have given me a wide berth at that point, but Ron was built differently. Hillmorton was a 'low-decile' school with a number of challenging students. In such an environment, Ron sensed my difficult past would likely become an asset because I'd be able to connect with the pupils on a different level, through empathy, which would hopefully shape them effectively. He wasn't wrong. I loved my time at Hillmorton – the students and the staff were the right people at the right time for me and I worked there for ten years, eventually swapping roles with Ron as I was promoted to the position of Head of PE, and he became my assistant. Because of his ego, or lack of, Ron wasn't bothered at the shift in hierarchy, and I was encouraged to carry on with my studies into sports psychology. I also led the volleyball programme at Hillmorton High, with the girls winning one national title and the boys' team twice finishing in second place. This was especially impressive given we were competing against the powerhouse private schools across New Zealand.

During this time, my hunger for sports psychology proved insatiable and I discussed the subject with any like-minded people that crossed my path. Leigh Gibbs, the former international netballer and then coach for Canterbury's netball team, was a colleague at Hillmorton High, and we often talked about mental performance and its role in the sporting arena. (In fact, Leigh was so enthused by my ideas that she brought me into the fold at Canterbury as her assistant coach in 1991 and later the Silver Ferns when she stepped up in 1994.) Meeting someone with a similar appetite for self-development always energised me. It made me feel less alone. And this sense was amplified in 1982 when the All Blacks player Wayne Smith walked into the Hillmorton staff room. Rugby union was an amateur sport at the time, and Wayne earned his money selling PE gear and equipment to schools for a company named Canterbury Sport. The pair of us soon began exchanging ideas on the power of the mind – or, as we called it *the top two inches* – and he admitted to struggling with his own game. When I shared some of the work we were doing inside our Pioneer volleyball team, a long-lasting relationship began, one that progressed into a great friendship and ultimately a brotherhood.

As an All Black, Wayne had a great deal of pulling power. He suggested I meet with the Canterbury rugby coach Alex 'Grizz' Wyllie because he felt my teachings could offer something to the team. After an initial meeting, Grizz invited me to present to the Canterbury squad, something that was unheard of back in the 80s. Around the same time, I began working with New Zealand's national cricket team, the Black Caps, and would do so for over a decade. The cricketers were an interesting bunch: talented but individually focused and our work in the mental space tuned them in to the idea of creating a shared vision for success alongside a series of connective values (the concept of which we'll discuss in Part Two). We also established a number of routines and structures to help them during high-pressure moments, knowing that with camaraderie, the team would play for each other and win, which they did, famously beating England at Lord's for the very first time in 1999.

Sadly, the selectors and board members at these teams were not so enthusiastic, and often I had to mask the true nature of my work. (As Wayne explained in his foreword, I was listed as 'massage therapist', which forced me into one or two panicked rub downs whenever a club official dropped in to see us.) These escapades represented another form of rejection and felt like a throwback to my days in the brethren home, as did the threatening letters from the New Zealand Psychological Society, who took issue with the fact that I didn't possess, in their view, the right level of qualifications to be an official sports psychologist. This treatment lasted for over a decade, as evidenced in one letter that was dated back to 2007:

> *Dr Mr Enoka,*
>
> *It has been brought to my attention that in a recent article in the* Christchurch Press, *you were once again referred to as a 'Sports Psychologist.' As the Board have previously corresponded with you on this matter, this causes me some concern.*
>
> *Can you please advise how you presented yourself to the 'Press', and/ or what steps you have taken to ensure the correct information is given to them?*

THREE LAWS FOR LEADERSHIP (AND LIFE)

Please note I will also be contacting the 'Press' for comment and clarification.
Yours faithfully,
Psychologists Board

While their intentions were honourable, I'm not so sure their methodology was.

Wayne Smith wasn't bothered by the negative feedback from my past, however, and he utilised my skills during his early coaching career – first at Canterbury B, and then with both the Canterbury and New Zealand Sevens rugby teams. When he became head coach at the Crusaders in 1997, he brought me in as his full-time sports psychologist and together we helped the team to win two Super 12 titles, in 1998 and 1999. Meanwhile, I continued with my studies, returning to university to earn a BA (Hons) in Psychology, while travelling the world to conferences and seminars where I realised that many of the theorists and so-called experts were miles away from coming to grips with what actually worked inside the cauldron of competitive sport. I decided to make my own way forward: my methods were simple, they were easily grasped by the players and coaches at the Crusaders, the Silver Ferns and the Black Caps, and they were yielding results.

The painful knockbacks, when they came, toughened me up and taught me that I had to look ahead to the future, not behind me to the past. Worrying or tripping over what had happened to me previously – the rejections, the feeling of being an outlier – wasn't going to get me anywhere. Whereas moving forward and working positively would likely bring results. There was little doubt that I was swimming against the tide, though. Sports psychology was still finding its feet, and as one of its proponents I made for an easy target, but I could only make one of three choices: 1) To bend to the will of governing administrators, board members and selectors, and do things *their way*. 2) To give up and work in another field altogether. Or, 3) To give it everything I had, *and win*. I went for option #3 knowing that by working on my mindset and character – the two things that couldn't be taken away from me – I would progress.

And then the All Blacks came calling.

Te Puna o te Kī: Outgrowing the Master

If ever a time summed up the law that choices not chances determined a person's future, it was the closing stages of my international volleyball career. Initially, my coach, Ctirad (Ben) Benáček had been my greatest advocate. A talented sportsman in his own right, Ben had seen and done it all internationally, in both basketball and volleyball, having competed in the 1948 Olympics for the Czech basketball team. He had tonnes of resilience too. During World War II, Ben had walked from Prague to Paris to escape the Nazis, and he worked his teams from inside that same gritty paradigm. Under his watch we endured mammoth training sessions – a combination of brutal physical work and powerful life philosophies that, while interesting, had very little grounding in the sports sciences.

I learned a great deal from Ben in that time. But whenever a player grew in stature or ability, he tended to hold them back. I'm not entirely sure why, but before long, Ben was both my best and worst coach: the best because he helped shape many of my philosophies; the worst because he hated the thought of others becoming better at the job than he was. Once I'd developed an interest in coaching, and the teams I was helping, like Pioneer, became increasingly successful, Ben blocked my route forward at international level. Some of this was done covertly by excluding me from team discussions. On other occasions, I wasn't selected for a camp or tour. No reason was ever given, but I wasn't alone in this regard. Several other players had seen their paths cut short in a similar style and I found the situation quite sad. Had Ben taken our enthusiasm, commitment and growth for what it was – the result of *his* work – we might have pushed our teams to even greater heights.

Not that I was too bothered. Rather than worrying that my chance at international level had gone, I instead decided to view the experience positively. Ben's attitude had been a sign that I was on the right path. And my choice to press ahead with my work inside the sporting arena – and then into the business and corporate landscape – would ultimately yield positive results. The world was readying itself for structured intervention inside *the top two inches*. And I was waiting at the door.

The Wero: Conduct an Identity Audit

What's the one opinion you have of yourself that might be holding you back?

All of us are guilty of clinging onto negative self-beliefs, though they're usually grounded in past moments of failure and rarely take into account any progress we might have made over time. Examples can include:

- *I can't succeed because my family is full of failures.*
- *We won't win, because we've been unlucky so far.*
- *I'm rubbish at this. I don't know why I bother . . .*

Negative thoughts of this kind shouldn't be taken as predictors of a future event. Remember: *Our past does not determine our future.* Meanwhile, when it comes to the opinions we hold about ourselves, the people around us often view our characteristics and performances in a way that differs wildly from our own. For example, we can sometimes feel as if we've put in a bad performance at work or within a creative or competitive environment. But having spoken to our teammates, we might learn that everyone else has taken the opposite view. (This is particularly true in fields that are subjective.)

My advice would be to conduct an *identity audit.* Write down any opinions that you have of yourself that aren't serving you well. Then ask three people (family members, teammates, colleagues) to describe what they believe your greatest strengths are, or what you're capable of. My guess is that you'll be pleasantly surprised by their views and less concerned about your own.

The Library of Learnings

- Bad experiences can stick to us like Velcro. If we don't shake off the negative opinions that we hold about ourselves, they'll act like shackles and slow our progress, sometimes for decades.
- Our lives are controlled by the choices we make. And these choices usually prove to be a far more powerful driver than any opportunity or lucky break.
- The past doesn't have to be your undertaker. Look to the future rather than worrying about the mistakes or circumstances that have arisen from your backstory.

CHAPTER 3

The Magic of Movement

Every great leader recognises a simple reality about team dynamics: to succeed, a group of individuals, whether they're in sport, business, or even family life, must have a clear and identifiable direction of travel. In the All Blacks' case, our destination, or goal, was to win Test matches and major tournaments, like the Rugby World Cup. Meanwhile, a business will want to position themselves as market leaders, and a family might strive for educational and/or future vocational opportunities for their children. Each of these groups have a clear and definable direction that's known to everyone inside their circle, plus an agreed strategy and a list of required behaviours to succeed. When everything is aligned, the team will move with velocity, as illustrated in Diagram A below. When it doesn't it will most resemble Diagram B. (In both cases, think of the big arrow as the direction of travel and the smaller arrows inside as the players or people working for a cause.)

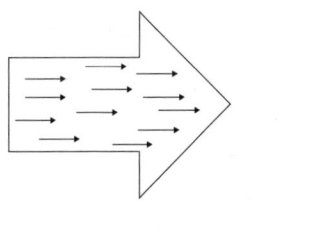
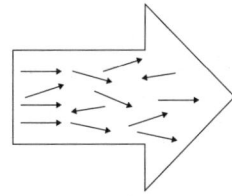

DIAGRAM A   DIAGRAM B

The All Blacks from 2008 onwards were typical of a Diagram A team. The coaches, leaders, players and support staff – after considerable reflection and discussion – had recognised an inspiring target, *to win the 2011 Rugby World Cup*, and the group worked tirelessly to get there. However, if those same people had not aligned, or bought into what was required to succeed, then a serious tension would have developed inside the group. Any conflicts would have significantly impacted our direction of travel, causing us to pull in different directions, creating friction and drag. In such a scenario, it's unlikely the All Blacks would have been anywhere near as successful.

Diagram A, sadly, is an outlier. Often, it's very difficult to convince a group of individuals to commit to a cause or pull in the same direction for long periods of time. That's because teams are made up of different people with conflicting personalities, beliefs and motives, which can fluctuate wildly from day to day, and challenge to challenge. For example, the workers in any given company will have signed up for a variety of reasons: some people are motivated by money; others are driven by position, status, or the hope that their role will act as a stepping stone to something bigger down the line. There can be clashes in a family environment too, and one parent might have a very different idea on their child's education, or healthcare, to their partner.

This concept was highlighted to me in 2023 when a corporate organisation I work with visited the Ritz-Carlton Leadership Centre. While there, the crew from Ritz-Carlton presented a recent engagement study that highlighted the way people worked in teams. Their results noted three identifiable categories.

GROUP ONE: *The Superstars*. These employees are committed and fully invested in the vision and direction of the group, giving their all in both energy and spirit. The study claimed that this group usually makes up around 32 per cent of a team. A collective dominated by Superstars is a beautiful thing to see, but this environment takes a lot of effort to build and maintain.

GROUP TWO: *The Undecideds.* These individuals like the leader, and they're also intrigued by the direction of travel, but they're yet to be fully convinced. Yes, they possess Superstar potential, but they could just as easily go the other way. Until they've committed to a mindset, The Undecideds will show up on time and do what's required, without ever going above and beyond. The challenge for any leader looking to create forward momentum is to nudge these personalities in line with The Superstars because they make up around 50 per cent of a team.

GROUP THREE: *The C.A.V.E. Employees.* So called because they are (C)onstantly (A)gainst (V)irtually (E)verything and easily identifiable due to their negative attitude. These individuals will undermine any attempts to generate a positive direction of travel with their lack of enthusiasm, grumbling and bad vibes – and they can destroy relationships over time. In a team of ten, one or two will be C.A.V.E. Employees, and when identified, they should be coached, communicated to, and aligned with the group's forward momentum through clear instruction. If that fails, the C.A.V.E. Employees should be jettisoned from the collective.

Sports teams aren't immune from the forces identified by the Ritz-Carlton Leadership Centre. While a group's direction of travel might seem obvious at the outset (to win the league, gain promotion, or make the playoffs), convincing the athletes inside the arrow to stay on target can be very difficult at times. External and internal forces can destabilise the group if they're not managed effectively, among them: selection and non-selection issues, results and performance levels, a life in the media fishbowl, and the challenges of family life, especially when long periods abroad are common. These issues aren't exactly new. They were in play when I first arrived with the All Blacks in 2000, and I've learned that Diagram B is often the likeliest reality for those who live a life in the fast lane, unless a special harmony can be created.

However, to establish a Diagram A team, it only takes three simple steps.

Step One: Create an Emotional Connection

When a player or person is emotionally connected to the *external movement* of a team, their *internal movement* will become aligned, shifting them from an Undecided to a Superstar. To get an idea of how this process works, imagine the big arrow in Diagram A as an individual rather than a team. The smaller arrows floating around inside represent their motivation and commitment levels, and they behave much like the engine in a car. If the individual has been inspired by an idea or challenge, every arrow will point in the same direction. The engine will then switch on, committing fully to the cause or challenge, smashing through any obstacles in its way. If the same person is unconvinced or demoralised, their engine will splutter and stall before the car has left the garage.

I watched a successful version of this process take place while working with the New South Wales Blues rugby league team during the 2024 State of Origin series – the annual clash between the Blues and Queensland in what is a best-of-three series. The Blues coach, Michael 'Madge' Maguire, brought me into his full-time management team to help him with the issues of leadership, culture and mental performance. At the time, the Blues were facing a third straight series defeat, and in preparing for the series, Madge met with a long list of former Blues players from around the state. His aim was to draw any information that might serve the team well in the upcoming series. During every discussion, Madge pulled out the team jersey and asked a simple question: *What does this mean to you?* His objective was to record the responses for a motivational video that he hoped would create an internal shift in those players selected in 2024. In an ideal world, the messages would help develop a *whatever it takes* mentality.

The responses were incredibly moving. Some of the players, long retired, talked fondly about their former teammates, the Blues' greatest moments, and any events where the group had triumphed over adversity. Madge edited the best stories into a short video and when the final squad selection was announced, he invited every player to a 'True Blues Night' – a get-together with a few beers at the beginning of the six-week State of Origin campaign. The room was packed, and a lot of the Blues legends from the film had showed up in what was a record turnout. When Madge's video was played on a big screen, the mood in the room shifted dramatically. He then invited several Blues legends to talk through their experiences of representing the state and the jersey and their emotional connection to the team. You could have heard a pin drop.

Something shifted inside everyone in the room. As expected, the Superstar-types were right there with Madge. But the emotional weight of what was being said had also inspired The Undecideds to step up. Meanwhile, if there had been any C.A.V.E. players in the squad – egotists with their own agendas – they remained hidden. In producing such a powerful video, Madge had created that rare and wonderful thing: a team so connected to their defined direction that their commitment had been locked in. To build on this development, the squad drove up to the Blue Mountains the next day and the players and staff were asked about their experiences from the 'True Blues Night'. The key themes that emerged were then distilled into a charter called 'The Blues Way', which became a compass for the group. Wherever we were, or whatever the team was experiencing or doing, 'The Blues Way' was a reminder to maintain our desired direction of travel.

Some of the outlined themes focused on mindset. Throughout history, the New South Wales team was known for producing some incredibly talented players. However, they tended to fracture when the heat came on during Origin games, and certain individuals had been known to ignore tactical instructions to do their own thing and go their own way. To observers, the Blues appeared flaky and dysfunctional; they rarely pulled in the same direction. The running joke was that their teams could always be trusted to find new and imaginative ways to lose. As a result, their record against

Queensland was underwhelming. Prior to the 2024 series, we had won 16 titles, compared to our rivals' 24. With 'The Blues Way', it was our aim to create a robust sense of unity, that kept everyone pulling in the same direction, no matter what was happening on and off the field.

Part of this effort involved us invoking the 'Spirit of Turvey' – a famous sporting narrative named after the celebrated Australian halfback and National Rugby League Hall of Famer, Steve 'Turvey' Mortimer. (The nickname had come from his time playing as a junior at Turvey Park.) A Blues player during the 1980s, Mortimer had built a reputation for being one of the team's most passionate players and his standout moment arrived in 1985, when, as captain, he stopped the team bus ahead of the first game against Queensland as it drove towards the stadium. Mortimer had noticed that some of the younger players seemed overawed by the scenes on the streets outside, which were packed with rival supporters.

'Look at all those bastards,' he said, pointing to the crowds. 'They hate us.'

Then he pointed to the bus driver. 'Even *he* hates us.'

Mortimer then walked down the aisle and delivered a stirring speech to his teammates. The Blues went on to win the match 18–2, securing a valuable first game win away in the 1985 series. This laid the path for their first ever State of Origin series victory, and his efforts on the field that day, his body bloodied and bruised, became a symbolic trigger for the 2024 squad, mainly because it echoed the mood we wanted to take to the field. Whenever the Blues needed to dig deep, the players shouted out 'Turvey' as a trigger. The 'Spirit of Turvey' became yet another connective factor, and we eventually took the series, winning the decider, 14–4 at Suncorp Stadium in Brisbane. Madge's work in creating an emotional connection between the current crop of Blues and the legends of the past had ensured a unified direction of travel. He had generated the necessary internal movement to shift what was required externally. And in doing so, we became memory makers ourselves, writing a story that entered us into State of Origin folklore.

Step Two: Building Teams Within Teams

A leader or manager can take sole responsibility for directing the internal and external movement of a group, as evidenced by Madge during the 2024 State of Origin series. Alternatively, that responsibility can be shared, because when a team is packed with leaders, each of them committed to a designated direction of travel, their chances of success are greatly increased.

The All Blacks did exactly that following the disastrous campaign of 2004. Amid the scrutiny that took place in the aftermath, no stone was left unturned as we tried to figure out why and how things had gone so badly. At that time, most teams were following a traditional leadership model which generally revolved around one charismatic captain and a head coach. But within the All Blacks, such a dynamic had created cliques and division (as evidenced by those toxic court sessions) and we decided to reject this set-up in favour of a shared leadership programme. The idea was that a high level of responsibility and accountability should be decentralised among a small, dispersed group of players who could then motivate and drive the team from within. This is currently a common practice within professional sports teams, but at the time it felt like a revolutionary tactic.

A strong, like-minded group of individuals were selected for the Leadership Group through the mantra that an All Black didn't choose to lead the team; *the team chose the All Black to lead.* (See Chapter One.) But certain individuals were also picked so that the various groups within the squad could be reached – players of different ages, backgrounds and religions. For example, some leaders were selected because they were rocks in the heat of a battle; others because they connected with a specific cultural unit, such as the Pacific Island players. Being able to speak with every faction within the collective soon aligned the All Blacks' arrows and our direction of travel.

In total, around ten players made up the Leadership Group. Then we worked the socks off them. Every two or three weeks, usually during the Super Rugby season, our selected leaders came together to work with education and performance experts who improved their abilities in areas such as public speaking, leadership techniques, the understanding and development of self, and pressure management. Our hope was that by developing this group, they would then help the rest of the squad grow into capable and committed deputies. (Remember: when the leader improves, everybody improves.) Meanwhile, the Leadership Group met regularly with our coaches on matters of importance, such as the team's overall vision, the maintenance of team standards, and the incorporation of any new routines and training techniques, as well as discussing general 'housekeeping' issues. They became a connective link between the players and coaching staff. Likewise, we encouraged them to be the best players in their position on the field.

Dan Carter recounts his experiences of the Leadership Group as follows:

> *I started with the All Blacks' Leadership Group in 2007, around three years after its formation, and my performances accelerated from there. This was important because when I'd made my debut in 2003, I was a quiet and shy boy. Sure, I wanted to learn from everyone and earn my teammates' respect through my performances. But I was also scared to ask questions or make mistakes. Despite this, the likes of Bert and Graham Henry had spotted some potential and brought me into a future leaders' group. I sat in on meetings and learned about the sacrifices I'd have to make going forward, which helped me grow as a player and a potential captain. Having got there, I never had to play catch-up.*
>
> *This mentality empowered us. After establishing a strong Leadership Group in 2004, the players learned to call the shots on and off the field. We delivered the attack strategy. We delivered the defence strategy. We delivered the mental performance strategy. We even self-policed and enforced the team's standards and disciplines. If gear was left behind on the bus, or if a player hadn't given their all in training, one of the other guys would call them out. Keven Mealamu, one of the world's nicest guys, would come down hard on us for not picking up the rubbish. 'This is not the All Blacks way,' he would say. We also drew on our different*

> backgrounds and cultures. Richie McCaw delegated various leadership duties to his teammates. Brad Thorn checked in with the younger players to make sure they were OK. And everyone was encouraged to connect with honesty.

One important responsibility of every leader was to head small, but distinct teams within the squad that we hoped would take everyone's attention to detail to another new level. Named Independent Operating Units, or I.O.U.s, these groups were first established in 2007, during the fallout from the Rugby World Cup. The idea initially came from a comment made by our head coach, Graham Henry. He'd believed that one of the issues hindering the players' growth and performance was that not enough of them were studying or even talking about the game enough.* The I.O.U.s were designed to create an educational and supportive framework for every member of the squad, and their work featured several guidelines.

- There was an I.O.U. for every key unit across the field of play, including the outside backs, midfield backs, the insides, the loosies, and the second and front rows.
- The key objective was to make ownership, responsibility and accountability real.
- Each I.O.U. was headed by someone from the Leadership Group.
- The leadership expectation was simple: come game day, ensure you are the best player in your position on the field and that your I.O.U. dominates your opponent's equivalent unit.

---

* After winning the 2011 and 2015 Rugby World Cups, these I.O.U.s were renamed P.O.D.s, or Pockets of Dominance. We'd wanted to freshen things up and create forward movement in our leadership. The expectation of the leaders was for them to become energised as individuals and to then energise their P.O.D.. This would then energise the team. It was also important that each P.O.D. dominated their opposite numbers on game day. There were never any outs on that.

Our work in this area was relentless. The I.O.U.s came together several times a week (without the coaches) to discuss game specific strategies, matters relating to our performance under pressure, any looming challenges, and anything that might have been on the players' minds. Nothing was off the table. As the I.O.U.s worked, the players within them grew, and the team's forward momentum gathered pace.

> Imagine you had to explain the concept of an I.O.U. to a teammate, colleague or friend in 30 seconds. *How would you phrase it?*

Step Three: Create a Library of Lessons

Losses were lessons; victories were benchmarks. But for a team to maintain their upward trajectory, any educational moments must be absorbed and recorded. That's because unpleasant history, when ignored, has a habit of repeating itself. To avoid this issue, the All Blacks' Leadership Group decided to become the fastest learning team on the planet. Every match, Test series or tournament was considered a reconnaissance mission, and we extracted as much information as possible, by gathering everyone's thoughts and observations as quickly as possible afterwards in a hot debrief session. Any significant discoveries about a team, player, event, or even ourselves, was written down on a poster and added to a vault of knowledge we called The Library of Lessons. Some of the learnings focused on the psychological aspects of the game. (You only own cups when you can touch them; if you play the same team two weeks in a row, expect the tension to decrease ahead of the second game.) Others focused on the Leadership Group itself, and/or our newly established I.O.U.s (All Black leaders create an edge: if the edge is there, focus it; if it isn't there, call it and correct it). These posters travelled with us on tours and during World Cups or Rugby Championships, and were usually placed strategically in the team meeting rooms.

Importantly, the Library had several rules:

1) If we're not looking for the lesson, we're too comfortable.
2) If we can't connect the lesson to an actual moment of preparation, training or a match, it's not real.
3) If we don't write the lesson down, we'll forget it.
4) If we can't write the lesson down in a way that <u>everyone</u> understands, it will be lost.
5) If we don't make the lesson visible, it will be lost.
6) If we don't remember the lesson, we will repeat it.
7) If we don't read the lesson again, we'll forget it.
8) If we don't share the lesson, we're not a team.

The All Blacks conducted this same exercise in the aftermath of 2007 and created a Library of Lessons that specifically focused on Rugby World Cups and the mental, physical and logistical turbulence they tended to create:

#1 One moment will decide everything

Whether we like it or not, four years of preparation will inevitably come down to one game. One game is often defined by one moment. And that one moment is often decided by one skill execution, and often by one individual. To the players: Do you want that individual to be you? If so, how will you prepare for this moment when it arrives? And how privileged will you feel if you're the one in that moment? Make sure you're ready.

#2 World Cups are different

A Rugby World Cup player will experience a change in 1) pace, 2) physicality, 3) tempo, and 4) expectation, simply because of the environment.

In each match they'll face an opposition they've never encountered before. <u>It's not France; it's France at a Rugby World Cup.</u> And the challenges will be very different. (<u>It's also not the pressure of being an All Black, but the pressure of being an All Black at a World Cup.</u>) When a player understands this, they can approach these challenges like any other: Embrace them. Use them as motivation. Walk towards them. Everything will be on the line and every team will be at their very best, so remember a simple truth: win and we get another week in the competition; lose and we're on the long flight home. The great players learn to love this space.

#3 The pressure is everywhere

Before the World Cup in 2007, we shied away from pressure. Sure, we knew it existed because pressure was a given for every All Black, but we didn't embrace it in a way that magnetised us to our desired goal. In 2011, the time has arrived to accept that World Cup pressure hits differently. It's bigger. Louder. It means more and it's everywhere. The big question now is this: What do we do under pressure? The way forward is to reframe it. Yes, there will be discomfort. And yes, there will be unpleasant feelings accompanying the big occasions. But they are to be enjoyed. High-pressure moments are places we want to visit and excel in. Dreams come true when performing on the biggest stages and reputations are either enhanced or weakened. Embrace the opportunity to enhance yours and that of the team. Like Richie McCaw says: 'Pressure is like water. It always finds the cracks.'

#4 In the big moments, do the basics brilliantly

Prior to 2007, the belief among many All Blacks was that the big plays often decided the big moments. But in the pressure cooker of a Rugby World Cup, this paradigm doesn't stand up to scrutiny. When we're under the pump, or things are going against us, we shouldn't have to rely on rabbits being pulled from hats. In the biggest moments, the great players execute the basics brilliantly. The team then seizes any resulting opportunities as they present themselves. Be the great player; become the great team.

#5 There are no outs in a Rugby World Cup

The 2007 version of the All Blacks contained several players who were coming to the end of their careers. Naturally, their minds had drifted to a life after the Rugby World Cup. Many were reflecting on what they were going to do next; where they were going to play or work; and what their life might look like beyond France. We witnessed players meeting with their agents in the team's hotel lobby when their focus should have been elsewhere. A number of others had sulked when they weren't selected. This created a major problem for the team, because a lot of them were looking for 'outs', and in essence, they became part-timers when what we needed were 24/7 players committed to doing the business on game day.

From that tournament onwards, everything changed. The lesson: *Today, the leaders will drive a standard of no 'outs', no exceptions, and everyone needs to have both feet in the game. That's because in the heat of the battle, a player imagining their life beyond a Rugby World Cup Final becomes a liability. They must be fully committed to the here and now. Those that can't, or won't, will be dealt with swiftly.*

#6 In a Rugby World Cup, the mindset must be right

In 2007, too many players felt burdened by the pressure of the Rugby World Cup. There was an expectation that the All Blacks would sweep to victory and that created a fear of failure within the group. The 2011 All Black wants anticipation and excitement; they need to feel invigorated by the challenge, not cowed. To achieve this, let's flip the language we use throughout the competition. Rather than thinking, 'What if we screw it up again?' or dwelling on a negative thought, switch the narrative. Say: 'Well, what if we win? Then what?' Take the burden mindset and transform it into a mindset of opportunity. Find the hunger to get it right. This will excite and energise you.

*

Bringing emotional connectors, I.O.U.s and Leadership Groups, plus a Library of Lessons into any working environment can prove game-changing, regardless of context. With these tools, it's possible for a leader, or leaders, to drive their team forward, while ensuring the players (those little arrows positioned within the larger one in our diagram) stay pointed in the appropriate direction, transforming any Undecided or C.A.V.E. personalities into Superstars.

For example, in a setting such as a construction firm, the I.O.U.s could bring together co-operative mini teams made up of builders, carpenters, project managers and even architects in a series of supportive or educational workshop-style hubs. An emotional connector, or Leadership Group, would work in a public service such as the Fire Brigade, where senior figures and galvanising/inspirational personalities could come together to help steer the watch towards a chosen direction of travel. And the Library of Lessons would prove invaluable in a fast moving environment, where data has to be processed and acted upon rapidly, such as in a tech start-up. These strategies helped to keep the All Blacks on course as they worked to become one of the greatest sports teams of all time. There's no reason why they can't help you and your team too.

Te Puna o te Kī: Using the Past to Power the Present (The Human Library)

During the build-up to the 2023 Rugby World Cup, one thing kept me awake at night. None of the players in the squad were veterans from the 2007 tournament. This was a problem, because having a handful of individuals with personal connections to our historical pains kept them in our thoughts – in 2011 and 2015, the old guard had been living reminders of what happened when a team took their eye off the ball. Without those personalities and their experiences in place, I worried that complacency might creep in and the lessons from our previous campaigns would lose their power.

We realised that one of our challenges was to bring these learnings to life, and in a way that was both meaningful and impactful for the class of 2023. Our first step was to gather inspiration from people who had previously walked the Rugby World Cup journey, though short but motivational messages delivered via video link wouldn't do. Instead, we introduced a Legacy Group – a five-man *Human Library* comprising individuals that had famously experienced the unique pressures of a Rugby World Cup. Our hope was that they could bring a tangible sense of the past to inform the present. In the end we selected several former All Blacks and they joined the group as we prepared, sharing lessons, ideas and stories in a timely and authentic manner. On the list were . . .

Richie McCaw: A player who was more than familiar with the strain associated with being an All Black leader. His reflections, learnings and lessons provided wise counsel in all competition phases, from our preparation and pre-tournament camps to the knockout rounds.

Dan Carter: A legend of the sport, Dan instinctively knew how to deliver in the big moments and his greatest moments couldn't be scripted. His experience was expected to bring value to the players hoping to execute in the biggest moments on the biggest stage.

Keven Mealamu: The most capped All Black player off the bench, Keven often stepped in from the shadows to influence the game hugely. He was the epitome of what it meant to be an All Black and his *mana* created a super respectful aura that was unmatched in my time inside the team. Meanwhile, his experience would serve as wise counsel for the players that couldn't make the starting XV but had a crucial and determining role on the sidelines.

Conrad Smith: His passion for the jersey was unheralded. Conrad was intelligent and articulate. He'd also connected with the legacy and the game in a special way. Conrad's knowledge of the game and its intricacies served as a special cocktail for many of our players.

Liam Messam: Liam had a huge influence on the group in 2015, despite not playing many games. His unselfish dedication to the team was an inspiration for all. He galvanised the All Blacks off the field, allowing them to be inspirational on it. No team wins a major event without a Liam Messam figure. His presence in the Legacy Group sent a message: you don't have to take part on the field of play to be a significant contributor to a legacy. Our feeling was that Liam would sway any Undecideds in the group, especially those players feeling frustrated at their lack of playing time.

This Legacy Group worked magnificently. Over the months leading up to and including the tournament, we scheduled their visits strategically. They attended camps, travelled on the team bus to training and games, and immersed themselves in our culture. During visits they shared their experiences (mostly through storytelling) and revealed what it took to win a Rugby World Cup. They had been there before. They knew the sacrifices required to win. Their past powered up our present and I often watched the players of 2023 as they left the bus having spoken to a Richie or Keven. It wasn't uncommon to see some of the boys looking emotional at what they'd heard.

Once the tournament was underway, the Legacy Group continued to have a significant impact. We created a Legacy Group Corner inside the team room where we quietly continued its influence. All five members of the *Human Library* provided ongoing messages of support and offered key insights at important times. The library soon became a vibrant, active and influential hub. Richie McCaw even sent a powerful note to the team ahead of the World Cup quarter-final against Ireland in Saint-Denis.

Hi Men,

This is a message to wish you all the best for this weekend.

How great it is to be at the start line of the game you will have all been looking forward to for so long. A quarter-final against the Irish is exactly the game you would have wished for. A game where the stakes are the highest is where the best step forward and take the opportunity that it presents.

To be successful in these games, it doesn't require magic. It requires a level of intent that they can't handle. This must be right from the first minute. They need to feel the shock of it. Whoever gets the chance to make the first hit, make the first clean, make the first carry . . . MAKE IT COUNT!

Along with intensity, it is everyone doing their job and executing the basics that will ensure the performance you are after. This will mean when that one opportunity opens up, you take it. It will require 23 players to play like men and leave nothing in the tank.

Go well men.

Right behind you.

Richie

This message, and several similar notes from Conrad, Keven, Dan and Liam arrived throughout the Rugby World Cup. Each one was placed into the Legacy Group Corner, and catalogued and referenced as they would have been in any other library. Every note was a resource. All of them were motivational pep talks. Whenever I walked into the corner, I always spotted players reading quietly on their own. They were extracting their own pieces of power from these most special pieces of dialogue – and they took us so close to yet another tournament win. The journey saw us defeat Ireland and then demolish Argentina before losing narrowly 12–11 to South Africa in the final.

In a sport of fine margins, the All Blacks had come as close as you could imagine, but that's because our past had fired up the present, and all thanks to the Legacy Group. Their history, good and bad, had taken us to within a whisker of winning the greatest prize of all.

The Wero: Create your own Legacy Group

Every environment could benefit from creating their own Legacy Group – a person or a pool of people in place to act as consultants, sounding boards and reassuring voices of reason for those individuals not used to dealing with high-pressure situations or the complex mechanics of a job or role. Imagine a sports shoe company with a former Olympic athlete in place to offer support. Or a start-up company with a successful entrepreneur on standby to lend advice. Or a power plant with the individual who designed a component part of their system to step in when a technical issue takes place? While idealistic, these scenarios paint a picture of what can be achieved with a Legacy Group in the house.

It's not enough to shove some old faces into a corner of the office, though. The 2023 All Blacks Legacy Group was carefully curated, and each member was brought in because of their unique perspective on a particular aspect of the game. Richie because he was the G.O.A.T. and had once been under fire from the media. Keven because he'd impacted the game from the bench and his *mana* was generational. Dan because he'd shown up in big moments and delivered in big games. And so on. In the case of a new business, a good legacy adviser might be someone that has launched a company and failed, only to succeed later in their career. There will be plenty of lessons in the mistakes, as well as the victories, and their dramatic past will power the present.

The Library of Learnings

- To succeed, a group, whether they're in sport, business, or even family life, must have a clear direction of travel. A destination that is obvious to all inside the group. To gain momentum, every individual must be aligned so they can move in the right direction.
- Teams are generally made up of three distinct categories: 1) The Superstars – those individuals prepared to follow the leadership into battle; 2) The Undecideds – the neutrals who will do the bare minimum; 3) The C.A.V.E. Employees – the (C)onstantly (A)gainst (V)irtually (E)verything types who are negative and bring a bad vibe. Type 2 and 3 will hold your group back.

- To bring everyone into line and enhance a positive direction of travel, it helps to give responsibility and ownership to key individuals within the team. This can be done by creating Independent Operating Units/Pockets of Dominance (I.O.Us/P.O.D.s) and Leadership Groups (with a Library of Lessons). External assistance can be provided by a Legacy Group. When combined these mini teams pull everyone together.

CHAPTER 4

The Lethal Cocktail

Saturday, 1 October 2011

Kick after kick, after kick. Ball after ball, after ball. Dan Carter launched a series of conversions, drop kicks and penalties from all over the training field at the Rugby League Park in Wellington, each one soaring through the goalposts. My job was to catch and gather the balls, returning them to Dan so he could continue the process all over again. Conversions. Penalties. Drop kicks. Strike after strike, after strike. Ball after ball, after ball. Dan's accuracy was undeniable, which was one of the many reasons why he was regarded as the greatest Number 10 in the game, and a fan favourite. When kids played rugby in the backyard, they either wanted to be Richie McCaw or Dan Carter. Mainly they wanted to be Dan Carter.

That's because he played the game differently to other players. *He read the game differently too*, spotting opportunities many of his opponents couldn't see, in pockets of space that others couldn't imagine. His speed and agility were off the scale. He was a freak, a gift to the game of rugby and to sport in general. Meanwhile, my role as designated ball collector was part of his preparation. When it came to kicking practice, we did it together, rain or shine. Dan kicking, me chasing. Ball after ball, after ball. Fetch after fetch, after fetch. Our relationship was so symbiotic I'd been nicknamed *The Golden Retriever*.

Suddenly, I heard a shout. When I looked over, Dan was laid flat out on the grass and appeared to be in serious pain. Although I was only ten metres away, I held back from rushing over because it wasn't the All Blacks way for a coach to tend to an injured player, that work was left to the medics. And full disclosure: I thought he was kidding at first. Dan was the ultimate pro, but he was also the team's joker and known for making light of situations that might have otherwise bothered the group. At the time, we'd been working through the final training session before a pool match with Canada (and Richie McCaw was already struggling with a foot injury that was putting his full participation in the tournament in jeopardy). It would have been just like Dan to put the frighteners on everyone – just for a laugh.

It quickly became clear that Dan wasn't playing, and that the situation was serious. He was in agony, clutching his inner thigh, with his face pressed down in the grass, and before long the absolute worst case scenario was laid on us. Dan's groin adductor had been torn in a freak injury and there was a chance his Rugby World Cup was over. It was hard not to think about the pain of 2007. Back then, he had left the field injured during that horrendous game against France and we'd subsequently fallen apart. Given Dan's importance to the team, there was no doubting the gravity of the moment.

Graham Henry, a great head coach and a beautiful man who always wore his heart on his sleeve, looked dazed. His worst nightmare had come true.

'What are we going to do?' he said. 'He's the best Number 10 in the world . . .'

The apprehension soon spread and when the players got together in the training shed, a heavy mood filled the space. *Not good.* To prevent the group from becoming 'stuck' on the eve of a vital game – a state of psychological paralysis where an individual or team is overwhelmed by the emotions of a negative event – we had to act quickly. This was done by activating a formula I came to call *The Lethal Cocktail*: a recipe comprising only two ingredients, *structure and discipline,* that required a team or person to lean into a series of pre-planned and easily understood processes for a wide range of situations or events. The circumstances requiring their use was varied and included tactical instructions, the team needing to score a drop goal to save the game, a player's partner or family member being taken seriously ill, a public scandal hitting the team, or a star player being seriously injured.

Each event came with a pre-planned strategy that enabled the leaders (and everyone around them) to function and thrive without panic or confusion, especially when the pressure was cranked up, as it had been following Dan's injury. But it wasn't enough to simply prepare a set list of actions for a series of events. Each structure had to be executed with unrelenting discipline. In the military (and other fast-paced industries, such as the emergency services) these frameworks are called Standard Operating Procedures (SOPs) and they readied a soldier, police officer or firefighter for just about anything, from battlefield communication to casualty evacuations. These institutions had learned that cutting corners in warzones, riots and burning buildings put lives at risk, so nothing was left to chance. The same attitude would work for us too.

Really, any job or industry can rely upon SOPs. For example, the front of house server in a restaurant could apply the following actions:

- Greet the arriving customers.
- Check their names, dates and times are correct on the booking system. (Congratulate them if they're celebrating a special event.)
- Ask if they have any allergies or dietary requirements.
- Grab the appropriate number of menus and escort them to their table.

Prior to the 2011 Rugby World Cup, the All Blacks had been ignorant to *The Lethal Cocktail*. Yes, we had processes in place, on and off the field, but we were over-confident and believed that pure talent would be enough to propel us through, unchallenged. Our lack of structure and ill-discipline – plus a refusal to contemplate the possibility of a bad day at the office, some stroke of rough luck, or an unexpected outbreak of poor form or fatigue – meant we didn't contingency plan.

As a result, the players were caught off guard at the worst possible moments, a truth summarised by those confused final few minutes against the French in 2007 when we'd trailed in a quarter-final that many people had expected us to stroll through. When the heat came on, we all assumed a winning rabbit would be drawn from a magical hat – some piece of individual skill or bravery. Because that's what the All Blacks did: we created something from nothing. But the something never arrived. The nothing was all we got.

We weren't going to make the same mistake with Dan's injury.

The first phase in our *Lethal Cocktail* was to bring the time horizon forward. When a team finds themselves under pressure or experiencing extreme stress, as we were, it can help to focus on the immediate future: the next task, the next minute, the next discussion. Worrying about the medium- to long-term view (in our case the Canada game, or the Rugby World Cup as a whole) is generally counterproductive and often results in catastrophising. After Dan's injury, we knew not to look past the medical results, which would arrive once he'd been fully checked over by doctors. Any details about his recovery time, and whether we needed to consider a replacement, could wait until then. In the meantime, worrying was viewed as a waste of mental calories and so we put a positive spin on every conversation.

It takes discipline for a team to manage their thoughts and actions in such difficult times, but we stayed true to our plan. When the worst case scenario was eventually confirmed, and a series of scans and tests revealed that Dan was out of the tournament, we were able to operate from a position of calm. Our next time horizon was created, and Graham Henry readied his possible replacements, which in this case were Colin Slade and Aaron Cruden, who had only made his All Blacks debut a year previously. Given the way these players had trained with the group, they knew their roles and how to execute them. Both players also understood what was expected of them tactically and psychologically. Despite losing one of the game's greatest, we were still in good shape – for the time being.

Sport can be a cruel mistress. Dan's injury wouldn't be our last and when Colin was injured in the quarter-final game against Argentina, Graham brought in Stephen 'Beaver' Donald (nicknamed because of his resemblance to a character from the kids show, *Leave It to Beaver*) as our emergency replacement.*

At that point, Stephen's history with the All Blacks was patchy. He'd famously missed a penalty in the 2010 Bledisloe Cup after coming on for Dan. Then, having failed to kick the ball out of play towards the end of the game, we handed possession back to Australia which helped them to close out the game and inflict a painful defeat. The blame was unfairly dumped on Stephen, and he fell out of favour with the fans and selectors. But after Colin's injury, he was the next player on our list. Graham was desperate and opened his pitch to Beaver with a simple question: *Do you want to win the World Cup?*

At the time, Stephen had been fishing for whitebait on the Waikato River, and jumped at the chance, though he later admitted to having one or two reservations.

'I took the call and there was five minutes of bravado,' he said. '*Yeah. Sweet. They've finally got me back in there.* And then you're driving up there on the motorway and you realise, "Oh shit, I'm actually going to have to play rugby. You haven't run for about seven or eight weeks. You haven't kicked a ball for seven or eight weeks. And it's going to be quite serious when you get in there." There was a reality check . . . I didn't know what I was walking into.'

Hindsight always arrives 20-20, in Technicolor Vision and Dolby Surround Sound, but Stephen's involvement in the Rugby World Cup now feels scripted, almost Hollywood-style. Aaron started the World Cup Final against France, but 34 minutes into the biggest game of his career, he was carried off with a hyperextended knee and Stephen was thrust into the limelight. Talk about seizing the day. He kicked a penalty in the 46th minute, which proved ultimately decisive in our 8–7 victory. (France scored a converted try.) *Beaver Fever* kicked in shortly afterwards and the ground of his local club in Waiuku was renamed Beaver Park. A few years later, the story of his life was immortalised in the film *The Kick*

---

* During Rugby World Cups, a player not already in the squad can be brought in during times of injury crisis.

and he appeared in an episode of *The Masked Singer*. Everything about the story seemed sprinkled with fairy dust. Stephen had written his redemption arc, as had the All Blacks. But there was an equally important narrative beneath the headlines that wasn't being written.

The Lethal Cocktail had helped to get us there.

The Performance Triangle

STRUCTURE IS KING, DISCIPLINE ITS QUEEN

Structure + Discipline = Success.

It seems so obvious, doesn't it? But the truth is that very few leaders consider this formula as a powerful resource when team building or managing personal routines. In the All Blacks, we used a simple concept called *The Performance Triangle*, a model comprising three sides of equal length, each one marked by a key attribute required for optimal performance.

- Skillset: The techniques we brought to our specific domains of expertise.
- Mindset: Our attitude in any given moment or situation.
- Structure: Frameworks that guided our thoughts and actions, and/or routines and rituals that supported performance.

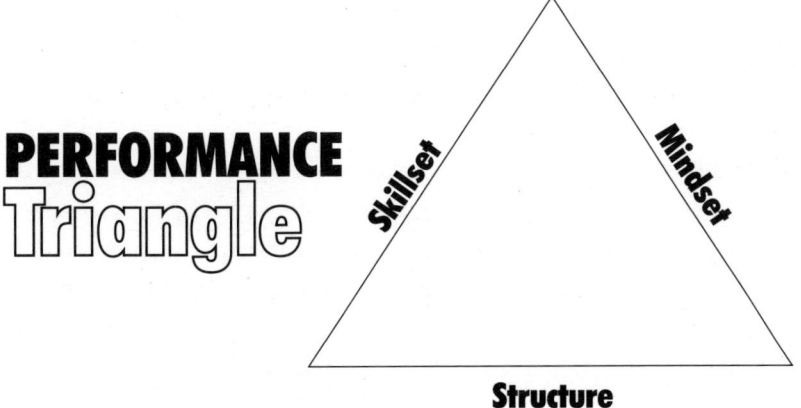

To achieve real and sustainable progress, every side of *The Performance Triangle* must be nourished. However, one of these components is a game-changing force that's powerful beyond measure, but it's the side people instinctively consider to be the least important. This oversight plays out whenever I stand in in front of a group of CEOs, construction workers, or even a class of young sports coaches. I'll ask someone to identify the element in *The Performance Triangle* I regard as a superpower and most voices will opt for 'mindset', though one or two outliers might suggest 'skillset'. I've now given these presentations all over the world and not too many people offer 'structure' as a performance enabler. But that's exactly what it is.

And here's why.

When a player joins the All Blacks, they're often driven by a powerful intention – they want to play 100 Tests and represent the jersey for ten years. They want to become a great – the next Dan Carter, Richie McCaw, or even Stephen 'Beaver' Donald. This desire is often unspoken, it exists at the subconscious level, and in my view, there's nothing wrong with that. After all, an All Black is expected to possess a huge amount of hunger and passion, and they'll already have a lot of the skillsets required to compete at the highest level. (It's what led them to being selected in the first place.) However, while these components are important, without structure and discipline, all the talent and passion in the world becomes irrelevant. That's because if a player isn't sticking to a programme of solid routines in training, while attending their rehab and prehab sessions, practising consistent nutrition habits, engaging in performance analysis and the like, things tend to break down before they've even crossed the white line to play.

A leader and their players must have a framework for managing the competing demands on their time, tasks, energy and efforts across every facet of their operation. In doing so, they can more reliably manage their roles and direction of travel. In rugby, these will include the things a player does inside their pre-match preparation, plus their in-game performance, post-match analysis, and mental skills training. For a high school head teacher juggling the stresses of exam season, there will be structures for homework marking, staff rosters and parents' evenings. Once in place and practised efficiently (like Dan Carter's drop kicks, conversions and penalties) these workable structures interlock and support the intense demands of any job or challenge.

In many ways, these processes act in much the same way as the wooden pieces in a game of Jenga. Each block is there to perform an important role. When one is removed, the overall tower might wobble a bit, but 99 times out of 100 it will remain upright. Remove four, five or six pieces, though, and the whole lot comes tumbling down. It's the same in any team. If an All Black works on their strength training, pre-match routines and media commitments, but neglects their sleep, nutrition and timekeeping, they're unlikely to last long. Likewise the head teacher that diligently preps their staff's schedules and maintains classroom harmony but becomes exhausted because they're unable to decompress effectively. In such situations, cracks are bound to appear, and performance breaks down. It's very clear that in environments with high demands, *structure is king*.

But if structure is king, then discipline is its loyal queen.

On the face of it, this might feel like a basic concept to a lot of people: *it's doing the right things at the right time, and on a regular basis*. But in the All Blacks we saw it slightly differently: *we did the right things at the right time, to the right standard, and then we did them again*. (*And again. And again . . .*) That standard was expected of every player in black because structure without discipline was known to be ineffective, and it caused the best laid frameworks to crumble under pressure. Of course, in the world of high performance, *discipline* isn't exactly a buzzy term, like *creativity, resilience,* or *next-level thinking*, but I'd argue that it is the kick in our cocktail. Discipline sharpens a person's focus. And it drives their processes and facilitates consistency.

For example, it's no good an All Black simply turning up to a training session on time and in the correct kit. They must give 100 per cent to the moment, every moment. Equally, it's no good someone arriving at a team presentation in the designated office at the designated hour and expecting everything to run smoothly. They must consistently deliver their part with skill, confidence and authority. I know from years of experience that an All Blacks team without discipline can turn hot-headed. They play without control. They stray offside. They're penalised for high tackles. However, when operating with structure and discipline they become cold-blooded and clinical. They perform with a ruthless efficiency. They operate like assassins.

This happens because structure, when aligned to discipline, acts as a game-changing weapon in the psychological war between emotion and thought – the conflict that arises during moments of high pressure. If a person knows exactly what to do, and when, even if their fight or flight response is kicking in (which it does in moments of high stress), they only need follow the designated structure to succeed, no matter the stresses involved. *Go there. Do that. Communicate this.* The information acts as a compass, and the brain can then locate a route forward. After that, any fears, doubts or past traumas will seem insignificant, or at least manageable.

The 24-Hour Challenge: Feel the pain (and power) of discipline by committing to it relentlessly for the next 24 hours. Be on time for everything. Execute every task to the best of your ability (even when flossing your teeth or packing your bag for work). And when you're in the car, stick to the speed limit and pause/stop at every junction before moving ahead. Note how this experience feels in your journal.

Throughout his career, Dan Carter has adjusted his horizons to negotiate episodes of high pressure. He explains how the process helped him during a particularly turbulent moment:

I didn't really use Bert's skills one-on-one during my first few years as an All Black. My attitude: Everything's all right. Then in 2005, while playing in Wales, I broke an All Blacks curfew and let the team down in a big way. It got into the media, and I felt like I let the fans down, my teammates and coaches, and my family too. The next game was six days away and I wasn't in a fit state to play. I wanted to hide in my hotel room for a whole week.

'I can't pretend I'm OK,' I said to myself. 'I need help.'

That's when I knocked on Bert's door.

'I can't stop focusing on the people that I've let down,' I said. 'It's consuming my energy and my thoughts. I keep thinking about the mistake, the future, what's going to happen this weekend, and what people think about me . . .'

Bert told me I had to focus on the present and bring my horizon forward. To do so, I only had to focus on the minutes and hours ahead of me, and we broke down the day into 24, hour-long blocks. Then we gave every block a job.

Wake up at six am.

Have breakfast at seven.

Physio at eight.

Team meeting at nine . . .

And so on.

With Bert's structure, I was able to focus on the here and now. If ever I wondered about the future, or my mistake, I looked at the day planner and switched my attention to the next task. Then, at the end of every day, I'd review the 24 hours, looking at what I could have done better and how I might improve it. Before long, I'd calmed my mind, and I went on to play an incredible game against the Welsh in the Millennium Stadium, where everything I did came off. I was on fire, scoring 26 points, a haul which included two tries.

'Shit!' I thought afterwards. 'If Bert has done this for me in a week, what can he do if I see him more regularly?'

It was the start of a powerful friendship that helped me to thrive in moments of extreme pressure.

Structure, Discipline and the 2011 Rugby World Cup

In the build-up to the 2011 tournament, the All Blacks devised a series of structures to help us in environments where the emotional demands placed upon the team would be high, or the expectation from outside forces, such as the media, fans, even ourselves, might feel overwhelming. These were designed for two distinct timescales.

1) The Macrostructure: The big picture stuff. This included the way in which we approached the overall campaign, our travel and training schedules, a timetable of commercial obligations, along with methods for dealing with decompression, team bonding, the media, and so on.
2) The Microstructure: The smaller details, such as team and individual pre-performance routines, pressure management, techniques for controlling momentum within a match, and in-game strategies for a variety of scenarios, including the way we protected a lead, or what to do if a player had been sent off.

MACROSTRUCTURES: The Rugby World Cup was *all* pressure; the intensity was unavoidable, and the team that went home with the trophy was usually the one that best negotiated its unique challenges. This understanding was hardly groundbreaking to anyone preparing for such an event, and the big picture details were often handled well by most people. For example, the matches would draw big crowds, so the players were readied for the increased noise during play. But it was one thing to define the physical parameters, such as size and sound, and another to manage the psychological turbulence that accompanied those changes.

During my career, I'd learned that whenever teams broke down, in any context, it was often because the people involved hadn't worked to a psychological framework with discipline. Bearing that in mind, any big-picture stuff involving the All Blacks during the 2011 Rugby World Cup was planned to the nth degree, including our overall campaign, travel itinerary, hotel locations, style of play, training methods and tactics. We had shied away from pressure in 2007. Four years later, we faced it head-on by planning thoroughly, and our big-picture planning was guided by several key understandings, which we wrote out for the players:

1. We need to process the demons of 2007. *Let's confront them and discuss.*
2. Alignment between the coaches and the Leadership Group is paramount. *The most connected team will prevail – especially under pressure.*
3. The environment will drive the standards. *Create it and maintain it.*
4. Self-motivation will be key. *Players that drive personal improvement across specific domains, such as strength and conditioning, technical skills and mental performance, will underpin our success.*
5. Selection is paramount. In a Rugby World Cup, it's important to pick the people who can handle it. *If you can't trust them, don't pick them.*

We even installed a series of support structures that assisted the players' partners and their wider families. Our aim was to help them manage what would be an emotional rollercoaster for everyone and this work began before the first match:

- A designated support team was made responsible for dealing with all family-related issues, including travel, accommodation, ticketing, hosting, and home support.
- Education sessions prepared the families for pressure. It was pointed out that the All Blacks, in many ways, were going into a war and the players might become quiet or

withdrawn at times. It was helpful for families to recognise the symptoms of stress.
- In between games, we allowed some members of the squad to return home for short spells, so they could reconnect with their loved ones.
- My door was always open for conversations, which I encouraged. Although anyone visiting often had to fight past a barricade of flipcharts, whiteboards and files to get inside. Like everyone else, I was in a unique headspace during tournaments and dedicated to winning the competition.

To assist decompression, we instigated structured activities and events inside our environment. It was important that the Rugby World Cup felt like *fun*. We had a regular *club rugby night* (where everyone wore the jerseys of their original club team). There was also a weekly rest day where our physio, Pete Gallagher, arranged a 'tour' – an optional, half-day activity that took place away from the team hotel. These trips were always well attended. Pete was the perfect host and talking shop was banned. But that's because we wanted the players to have a safe space in which to relax and tune out, especially as we'd deliberately located the team inside the heart of the action, in hotels near the stadiums. Rather than hiding away on the edges of a city, as we had done in 2007, we were determined to use our supporters and their passion as a valuable source of energy. We tapped into them when appropriate.

MICROSTRUCTURES: A series of specific microstructures can often define a campaign or contest, such as a Rugby World Cup. (Or, in a non-sporting setting, a product or company launch, a personal endeavour such as a fitness or nutrition programme, or an educational course of some kind.) In 2011, they helped us to navigate a range of tournament scenarios, including *The Big Pressure Occasion*, our prep for a knockout game, set piece strategies and their execution, and any moments in which success or defeat was determined by what happened, such as those times when every refereeing decision seemed to go against us. These were developed by the coaches and leaders to prepare us for every possible scenario.

One of these microstructures was *The Foxy* – a play for when the team needed a drop kick to win a game or change momentum. Its specific requirements were designed in detail before the players were briefed on when and how to use it. *The Foxy* and its patterns of play were then repeated over and over in training until its execution became second nature. Finally, a summary, with a series of bullet-point-style cues – like a military-style Standard Operating Procedure – was pinned to a board in the shed. The players only had to glance at it to be reminded of how *The Foxy* should be applied.

The Foxy

WHY DO IT? When we want to get three points – to win a game or change momentum.

MINDSET: Be deliberate. Patient, but not obvious. Direct the ball into the drop kick zone.

STRUCTURE: To be done from a set piece. Get to the drop kick zones – two squares either side of the goalposts and between 25 and 10 metres from the try line – and then execute *The Foxy*.

OUTCOME: Three points.

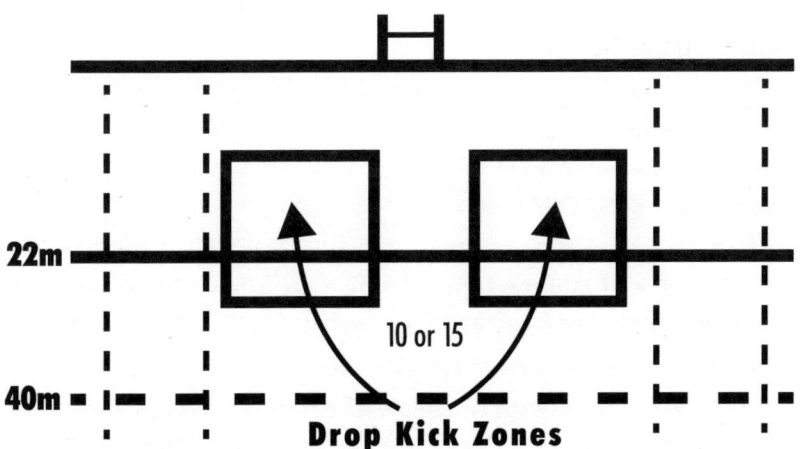

Power Play

We also introduced a *Power Play* microstructure for whenever our game required a change in tempo. This action was triggered by the skipper and initiated a two-minute *call to action* where everybody upped their energy levels to arrest or shift momentum in our favour. We got off the ground quicker, ran the first two metres faster and stronger than our opponents, and looked to be a split second earlier to everything. In using the *Power Play* we became adept at managing the tempo of a game and this tactic became huge for us during 2011. We utilised power plays in every knockout game, though they were never overused. Instead, we applied them a couple of times inside a fixture, usually when we needed to hold onto possession or to arrest the ascendency of an opponent. On many occasions they were our ticket out of trouble.

Elsewhere, we managed the temperaments of one or two players by giving them a calming microstructure for flashpoint situations. (That psychological war between emotions and thought I mentioned earlier.) This was particularly useful for when a decision went against us during a match, or when an opponent was playing on the line and engaging in the dark arts, and our tempers frayed. To set this work in motion, I asked one or two of our fierier characters to describe their mindset when a referee called a decision against them, using a scale of one to ten. (One representing calm; ten turning nuclear.)

'Well, I usually want to punch them in the head,' said one player. 'So . . . *an eleven.*'

When I then explained that a simple structure could be applied to bring calm, he didn't believe me.

'Bert, that's bullshit,' he said.

Undeterred, I presented him with a microstructure to use in the next game, for when a call went against us.

Step #1: Walk away from the official.

Step #2: Connect with the nearest teammate and ask a question: *What are you seeing?*

THE LETHAL COCKTAIL

Step #3: Assess the situation, draw breath and move onto the next task.

The player agreed to give it a go. And after the next match, I asked him how this process had worked and he explained there had been one or two heated moments but having stepped away and connected with a teammate, his emotional levels were brought down from a dangerous eleven to a manageable six or seven. While not exactly perfect, this progress offered evidence that a decent structure, when executed with discipline, could shift his mindset in a high-pressure situation.

*

There's no doubt in my mind that *The Lethal Cocktail* helped us to navigate the 2011 Rugby World Cup and all its obstacles. Every aspect of our operation, both playing and non-playing, was given a clearly defined macro- or microstructure, and to succeed we only had to commit to them with discipline. Our in-game communication had structure. Our pre-match preparation had structure. Our post-match discussions had structure. Even Pete's Tours had a structure. And over the course of the tournament, we realised there wasn't a situation or challenge that couldn't be tackled with *The Lethal Cocktail* – not even the loss of our world beating Number 10, a debilitating injury to team captain Richie McCaw, or the reintroduction of a player that, 12 months previously, had been cold-shouldered by our fans and selectors. They say adventure is dangerous, try routine . . . it's lethal.

The tournament was incredible, but several occasions along the way remain firmly in my mind. Beating France 37–17 in the pool stages helped to exorcise the demons of 2007. Then, ahead of a tricky quarter-final with Argentina, the former chairman of New Zealand Rugby Union, Jock Hobbs – an All Blacks legend in the early 1980s – presented powerfully to the group, even though he was very ill with leukaemia. (Jock would sadly pass away the following year.) His message was pertinent and sincere.

'I never considered myself one of the great All Blacks,' said Jock. 'But what I do know is that when I put that black jersey on, I always gave the very best that I could.

'So that's what you've got to do. Get out there and be the best in the world.'

The boys left the room feeling ten feet tall. It was as if the entire All Blacks legacy had spoken, and we moved past Argentina in the quarter-finals and then our old rivals Australia in the semis, setting up a final with the French.

On 23 October, we ran out winners at Eden Park in Auckland, Stephen Donald's 46th minute penalty dragging us over the line in an incredibly tense match. A huge weight was lifted from our shoulders. The nation seemed to stand as one, which made me very proud. I've always loved how sport can unify people in a way that politics and politicians can't. As we sat in the shed afterwards, the realisation of what the All Blacks had achieved sank in. There was joy, but the most predominant emotion was relief – it wasn't spoken, *but I could feel it.* In the four years following our defeat to France, every game had mattered, but only one thing counted: winning the Webb Ellis trophy at home. And in getting across the line, we had broken our reputation of being World Cup chokers.

The celebrations went on for days. The cup had been handed over to us with a set of white presentation gloves, with the expectation that anyone wanting to hold it should wear them to prevent any smudging or damage. Nobody took the instructions seriously; the gloves never came out of the box. Instead, we filled the cup with beer and gave her a good old Kiwi christening. In the weeks that followed, the trophy went on a tour around the country, where every player and staff member was allowed to keep it for a day or two. This was an important gesture, because it was the people's cup, not ours alone, and to be able to share it with our friends, families and communities was a privilege.

Not that I dwelled on our successes for too long. It wasn't in my nature to go overboard and within a week, I'd already moved on. No team had won two Rugby World Cups, back-to-back. The All Blacks, meanwhile, had only ever won the trophy on home soil. In 2015, we would be travelling to England as reigning champions, but my aim wasn't for us to defend our title. *It was to reclaim it.*

And *The Lethal Cocktail* was going to get us there.

Te Puna o te Kī: A Tale of Two Haka

If ever there was an image that summed up our lack of structure and discipline during the 2007 Rugby World Cup quarter-finals, it was a photograph that had been captured as we performed the haka in front of a defiant French team. Our boys looked crazed. The veins in their necks seemed to be popping, and their eyeballs looked set to burst with aggression. Nothing about our approach was controlled. The French, meanwhile, stayed resolute. Dressed in the white and blue of their national flag, they linked arms and faced us down, and when Byron Kelleher squared up to Sébastien Chabal, the Frenchman didn't even flinch. Nor did his teammates.

My antennae had been going off during the build-up to the match. The French were very quiet in the media, which always unnerved me because I rarely feared the loud opponent, but the quiet ones made me nervous. There had been no baiting in the media, no trash talking or mind games. France were quietly going about their business and seemed confident in their plan and their ability to execute it. When the coin toss was performed ahead of the fixture, to determine who could choose the jersey colours for the game, France called correctly and opted to wear a darker shade of blue. That meant we'd have to wear a different coloured jersey as our famous black kit would clash.

This was their first psychological blow. The French believed that our intimidating jersey gave us an advantage, that it instilled fear in its opponents, which was true. Meanwhile, our grey second strip placed significantly less psychological pressure on our opponents. This was also true. We held our own for most of the match, but as the momentum swung towards the French, cracks began to appear in our game. We were exposed tactically and mentally. We'd failed to create a structure that would defend us in the worst case scenario – for when the unexpected occurred and we couldn't change momentum. We were found wanting on many fronts and paid the ultimate price. The shed was like a morgue afterwards, but we made a powerful promise to ourselves: *no more surprises.*

Fast forward to the Rugby World Cup Final against France in 2011, and everything was different. We had structures locked in place for every possible scenario. (Because it was better to have them and not need them, than to need them and not have them.) These structures helped us to reshape our identity – we knew who we were and what we represented. When twinned with discipline we had *The Lethal Cocktail*. And once the haka was underway, it was our job to hold the line, connect with our brothers on either side of us, and in doing so we delivered a symbolic representation of our strength, commitment and unity. We were disciplined, we were connected, we were composed, and we were calm. Having worked on the mental side of our game, we didn't fear the pressure anymore, we embraced it, and that made us cold-blooded. Like an assassin preparing to make a kill.

The Wero: Serving The Lethal Cocktail – Your Way

The concept of microstructures isn't sexy, I know. However, when applied properly they can be transformative, helping to change all aspects of an individual's life, from the way in which we approach a meeting or business deal, to the management of any potentially derailing mindset challenges. For example, I've always loved running, and before I was given two artificial hips, I'd often spend most mornings jogging with Nala, the family dog. But even though it was an activity I enjoyed, getting up early in the morning often felt challenging. When my alarm went off at 6am, I sometimes hesitated and the act of getting out of bed became considerably more difficult. On bad days, I'd hit the snooze button, roll over and go back to sleep.

Sound familiar?

To overcome this, I set up a *Lethal Cocktail* for myself. Every night, I'd lay out my running kit at the end of the bed. The second my alarm went off, I'd get up straightaway and dress, not allowing any thoughts to come into my mind. It was *do, do, do*, until I'd opened the front door and collected Nala. Off I went, leaving the demons of indecision and procrastination on the pillow behind me and I soon found that the combination of structure and discipline enabled me to shut down any distracting thoughts, while powering a healthy exercise habit that both my current and future self is very thankful for.

You can do the same . . .

The Library of Learnings

- *The Lethal Cocktail is a recipe comprising only two ingredients, structure and discipline.* As unsexy as it sounds, structure is a leadership and performance superpower. Without it, even the most talented individual will fail to live up to their potential. However, if a person can bring it to their everyday activities, and with discipline, they will become a force to be reckoned with.
- *Every structure must be tended to with the highest possible standards.* In other words, it's no good turning up to a business meeting in a suit and tie and expecting things to happen. Everyone must arrive having done the right amount of preparation and be ready to give 100 per cent to the moment, *every* moment.
- Disciplined action is where it all comes to life. It's also the defining factor in *The Lethal Cocktail* and each component part must be delivered with precision. There are two ways of doing things: 1) The right way. 2) The right way, again. (And again.)
- Structures can be both macro and micro. The macro is big-picture stuff – blueprints for success, business strategies, gameplans and so on. Microstructures deal with the smaller details, such as individual pre-performance routines, tactical details and mindset challenges.

CHAPTER 5

Leadership Accelerators

I knew we were going to be a tough nut to crack from the opening seconds of the 2015 Rugby World Cup Final. By the looks of it, our opponents Australia knew it too. The venue was the famous Twickenham Stadium in England; the date was Halloween, and as the ball soared skywards from the first whistle, all sorts of horrors were dropped on the Aussies. We returned a kick deep into their half before gaining ground, smashing their players down like skittles. Every tackle drew a percussive roar from the crowd.

Boom! Their fullback, Israel Folau, was thrown into the air by Owen Franks.

Boom! Conrad Smith stopped Michael Hooper in his tracks.

Boom! Brodie Retallick charged down Will Genia's clearing kick.

The All Blacks approached the opening salvos of the game like warriors. We ran hard at the weak shoulders and attacked the ball carriers in the tackle. Our energy levels were upped so that we were stronger, quicker and more decisive than anyone in a gold jersey. And all of this was a result of an aggressive mindset that had been triggered upon our arrival in the UK. In an early meeting, Richie McCaw had looked every player in the eye and made two simple demands:

1) Commit to every action, 100 per cent, on and off the field.
2) Don't think about what you're doing after the 2015 World Cup until our business is finished here.

Everything came together at Twickenham. The Aussies, who had been so cocky in the build-up to the game,* seemed to wilt in front of our eyes.

I turned to George Duncan who was sitting next to me on the bench. 'They won't be able to live with us today, mate,' I said.

I wasn't wrong. We smashed Australia 34–17 in a ruthless display that left very little doubt about our status as the sport's generationally dominant team. At the heart of the action was a fully fit Dan Carter, who delivered a career-defining performance, scoring two conversions, one drop goal, and four penalty kicks from four attempts. His game wasn't just about points, though. Dan played like a maestro. A general with the Midas Touch. The orchestra *and* the conductor. He really was God's gift to rugby, and by the time we'd won the trophy, slurping New Zealand's finest ale from the famous cup yet again, everyone wanted to acknowledge his greatness.

How we came to put in such a dominant display, winning two back-to-back Rugby World Cups in the process, was a tale of leadership and leadership accelerators. The squad was already packed with players compelled to motivate and inspire. Many of them had become well-practised in the art, like Dan and Richie, plus the likes of Keven Mealamu and Conrad Smith. But the squad was also made up of personalities that were eager to innovate and grow. As far as the All Blacks were concerned, staying still was the fastest way to fall behind, and we accelerated the confidence and authority of our players behind the scenes using three powerful processes:

---

* Australia's players and coaches couldn't help but run their mouths off in the press. Drew Mitchell had boldly stated: 'We're going to take care of those All Blacks and become Number One.' In the *Sydney Morning Herald*, Michael Hooper said: 'The great tradition of the All Blacks is to have an appointment with disappointment at Rugby World Cups. The only exception was when they played at home, and this time they ain't.' These cheap shots gave us all the motivation we needed. We blew up their words into huge posters and stuck them around the team room, sheds and the quiet places, where the players would see them in their moments of reflection. (So, thanks.)

1) *Probes:* An exploratory process whereby a leader and their team's current position was established, and their ideal future self (their goals, targets and ambitions) identified.
2) *Bridging the gap:* The distance was measured between a player's performances (their current reality) and a challenging next level. A strategy was devised to bridge the gap.
3) *Breaking the frame:* We explored any unhelpful preconceived ideas, or *frames*, that a player might have had about themselves, our opponents and the team in general. We then looked to *break* them.

The work was four years in the making, but it pushed the All Blacks to build upon their greatness. I'll now explain how to apply the same techniques to any situation.

Probes: How The All Blacks Defined Their 2015 Reality

Every leader needs to understand their team's present reality if they're to progress. Prior to the 2011 Rugby World Cup, our mantra was clear: we wanted to go from being good to *great*, and the only way to do that was to win the tournament. Having done so, we reset our mantra: we wanted to go from being great to *even greater*, and, of course, the only way to do *that* was to win it again in 2015. But improving as champions in a fast-moving sport with highly motivated opponents is tough and so we conducted a preparatory phase where our present position in the world game was scrutinised. Our ambitions were assessed and challenged, as were any strengths and blind spots. All of this was done through *probes* – an investigative technique whereby the All Blacks' overall health was analysed in much the same way that a doctor checks their patients with a stethoscope or heart monitor.

In a business setting, the commonly used probe is a SWOT

analysis. An acronym for (S)trengths, (W)eaknesses, (O)pportunities and (T)hreats, this four-part check, while an undoubtedly useful barometer no matter the context, is pretty limited, especially if repeated excessively. For example, after running one or two SWOTs, the collected data can feel overly familiar. It's also unlikely to reveal any revelatory information – once a leader knows their team's strengths or weaknesses, repeating a SWOT analysis tends to reveal the same truths. Instead, we employed a variety of different probes (all of which are available online) to keep our conversations fresh and invigorating, while revealing new information. Among them:

1) Keep/Stop/Start: What are you doing well and want to keep? What are you doing not so well and want to stop? Where are you vulnerable and how can you improve?
2) MIA: What are we (M)issing? What are we (I)gnoring? What are we (A)ssuming/avoiding?
3) WSBD: A comparative process that asks a group to consider their main rival or competitor and identify where they are (W)orse, the (S)ame, (B)etter and (D)ifferent. This works especially well when the comparison is set against a market leader or world beater.
4) MEDIC: What do we need to (M)aintain? What do we need to (E)liminate? What do we want to (D)ecrease? What do we want to (I)ncrease? And what do we want to (C)reate?

In using these probes, the All Blacks discovered fresh and exciting insights that allowed us to set powerful goals, at both the individual and team level. Importantly, there were a couple of guidelines for every session.

- The chosen probes and their frequency were determined by the Leadership Group.
- The players and staff were given preparatory work. This allowed them to consider their answers in advance.

- Once a probe had been completed, a follow-up action or task list was set for the player, coach, management member, or team. For example, after one probing activity it was decided the All Blacks should adopt a 'crow's nest' approach to tactical analysis. This required us to scan the rugby *horizon* and anticipate how the game was changing around the world, and how we might meet those changes and get there first.

On a larger scale, we found a sharper perspective on our current reality, and where we wanted to go, while highlighting several inconvenient truths about the challenges ahead. (These were facts that we needed to address, no matter how uncomfortable or daunting they might have seemed.) This work allowed us to clarify the truth about the All Blacks, post the 2011 Rugby World Cup, and the obstacles ahead of us. Our results were then presented to the squad:

> **Current Reality v Inconvenient Truth**
>
> - We're the Rugby World Cup holders v No team has ever won back-to-back Rugby World Cups.
> - We won the Rugby World Cup at home v No All Blacks team has won a World Cup offshore.
> - England is hosting the 2015 Rugby World Cup v No All Blacks team has been in a World Cup Final in Europe.
> - We've won two Rugby World Cups (1987, 2011) v No team has won three Rugby World Cups.

An analysis of this kind can bring fresh insight to your practices, no matter the environment. (You don't necessarily have to be in a position of leadership either. Probes work equally well in all areas of self-development.) For example, a team leader in an online retail store might use a MEDIC check to assess the parts of their operation that need (M)aintaining, (E)liminating, (D)ecreasing, (I)ncreasing or

(C)reating. The manager of a health store franchise can compare their business to other successful franchises within the industry using a WSBD probe. A writer, photographer or filmmaker would benefit from using an MIA probe to assess any emerging opportunities in their sector, or check for new threats to their business, such as Artificial Intelligence. My advice would be to run through a variety of probes – perhaps create some of your own – to get under the hood of your team, business or organisation. Because the more you explore, the more you'll learn.

> **The 'What's Missing?' check**: Identify an area in your life – work, sport, personal – that would benefit from a probe. Apply the MIA questions and reflect on what's revealed.

Bridging the Gap: Going from Good to Great . . . *to Even Greater*

Every All Black must have a next level. *No exceptions.*

This was an unwritten rule that existed within the squad because making self-improvement an everyday action was the fastest path to success – not just in rugby, but *everything.* As a result, the emphasis on personal growth was huge. But we didn't just tell our players to get stronger or smarter, we helped them to get there by identifying *how* they could grow and develop. Meanwhile, the same expectation was applied to the coaches and wider management team, because without self-challenge, the leadership of a group grows lazy and stagnates. Every All Black player, coach and management team member needed a next level for themselves, no matter their track record, achievements or status.

Even Richie McCaw, *the G.O.A.T.,* was faced with this test in 2011, during the mid to late stages of his career. After all, what does an individual do once they've reached the pinnacle of their profession? In Richie's case, he strived to go even higher by redefining what it meant to be a G.O.A.T. He decided that winning one Rugby World Cup as captain wasn't enough; he wanted another while helping the All Blacks to become the most dominant team in the history of world rugby. Richie had figured out that the best could get better, and no one got to be the finished product. His hard work and self-sacrifice were an inspiration to everyone around him.

When a next level is determined, like the one set by Richie in 2011, an individual or team creates a gap between their present self and a future one, and it can arrive in two forms: 1) A Performance Gap: where a person strives to improve their personal results, whether they're an athlete, business owner or team leader. And 2) A Possibility Gap: where a person or group strives to improve in the way they play, work or achieve success. This can be done through new tactics, methods of training or the introduction of different tools or technology. Once established, the actions required to make the leap should be identified, but in both cases, the gap must feel significant and intimidating. This discomfort then creates a sense of urgency, which becomes a fuel. It's my view that comfort ages a person, but challenge keeps us feeling alive.

To identify a next level for ourselves we only have to follow a simple three-step structure . . .

PHASE ONE: *Role definition*. In the All Blacks we first asked the individual a series of questions about their role.

- *What do you do?* I'm an All Black and a member of the Leadership Group.
- *Can you describe where your role is at today?* I'm committed to helping the players around me improve as we try to win the next Rugby World Cup. I want to accelerate my skills in this area.
- *What does your next level of performance look like?* To lead by example, on and off the field. To identify the key behaviours that will help drive the team forwards as we become the first

All Blacks team to reach a World Cup Final abroad. To win a third Rugby World Cup for New Zealand and take two back-to-back tournaments.

These questions can be applied to pretty much any role. For example, an aspiring manager in a retail store might respond in the following way.

- *What do you do?* I'm part of a sales team in a popular high street chain.
- *Can you describe where your role is at today?* To maximise the profitability of the store by improving my performance levels. I want to be more consistent in offering support and driving standards that I know will help each member of my staff.
- *What does your next level of performance look like?* To learn the skills that will help me to become a team leader, whether that be inside my current role or in a different company. I want to assist and motivate my teammates to fulfil their potential because it will increase their performance levels at the store and enhance my leadership abilities.

PHASE TWO: *Create discomfort.* An identified next level of performance should feel daunting, challenging, even unnerving because those emotions tend to create desire. When a person becomes concerned about a future event, they will – more often than not – take actions to prevent anything from going wrong. *They learn, practise and prepare.* In doing so, they make the necessary steps to bridging the gap they've set for themselves, even in the short term. I remember working with the New South Wales Blues during the 2024 State of Origin series, when Madge Maguire created a significant atmosphere of discomfort for our players ahead of what was a decisive game at Suncorp Stadium in Brisbane.

'To win the State of Origin decider at Suncorp I need you to put in the best defensive performance in the history of Origin.'

Talk about raising the bar. The next steps required the Blues to work their socks off in training, and having done so, they reduced Queensland to just two penalties, and defeated them 14–4. Thanks to Madge's work, a next level of performance had been identified and a gap was bridged.

It's my belief that this framework can work for every leader, whether they're the captain of a professional sports team, the director of a major corporation, or a small business owner. Defining a distance between the present and an inspiring next level for an individual or team – and doing whatever's necessary to cross it – is a potent accelerant that powers up performance.

PHASE THREE: *Involve the critical friend.* Often, we're blinded to our greatest strengths and weaknesses, so it's advisable to call upon an outside perspective for advice – a critical friend or a respected colleague. During the run-in to the 2011 World Cup, every leader in the All Blacks was asked to identify someone that could assess their results or behaviours. In one such example, Mils Muliaina and Isaia Toeava began calling each other at weekends to discuss one another's performances in the Super Rugby competition. Both players were competing for the same fullback position in the All Blacks. Both were eager to nail down the starting spot. Yet they put aside their rivalry, acting as critical friends and exchanging ideas on how the other person could improve, knowing it would benefit the team in the long run.

When bridging the gap, this three-phase structure can work in a variety of situations – not just for a leader looking to accelerate their performance levels.

- The small business owner looking to improve their profit margins.
- A student planning their educational journey through school and into college and/or university.
- A couple assessing their financial position and goals.
- A family wanting to spend more quality time together.

In all four examples, a current reality and the challenging next level can be identified by answering the three questions. (What do you do?

Can you describe where your role is at today? What does your next level of performance look like?) Once the answers have revealed an energising but uncomfortable gap, a small list of necessary steps can be taken to bridge it. Finally, a critical friend can be brought in for an honest outside perspective.

> Having a specialist available for the key aspects of your life can be beneficial, so draw up a dream team of potential critical friends. Just three in this instance will be fine. For example, consider the friend who knows a lot about finances, or someone that's knowledgeable about health and fitness and so on. Approach them for help when the time is right.

Breaking the Frame

Too many of us live with fixed mindsets, or *frames* – beliefs about ourselves, the individuals around us, and the way we think certain things should be done, or how people should behave. Often, we hold onto these ideas so tightly that they set like concrete, rooting us to the spot. This is a major problem for a leader, *for anyone,* because as the All Blacks understood, standing still was risky. A good example of this was presented to me by a friend recently when they showed me a photograph from the 1919 Tour de France. In it, the lead cyclists, riding side by side, could be seen sparking up cigarettes ahead of a gruelling hill climb. At the time it was believed that nicotine's quickening effect on a person's heart rate was helpful when tackling a steep incline. Fast forward a century, and the frame has moved on; the idea sounds preposterous.

On a personal note, I once held the belief that the longer a person did a job, or role, the easier it became. On one hand that was true.

Experience is a fantastic resource. However, familiarity also leads to complacency and an entrenched person might not push themselves to create a next level. By default, they won't seek the help and assistance that might provide a new perspective, theory or skill, whereas someone starting out in the same position will. Throughout my career, I found it useful to have several mentors and critical friends to lean upon for advice, guidance and inspiration. I'd check in with one of them from time to time for a different perspective on my methods or ideas, and in early 2015, the person I was talking to asked how long I'd been working with the All Blacks. I mentioned it had been 15 years, and in that time we'd won the 2011 Rugby World Cup, and an impressive haul of Bledisloe Cups and Tri-Nations/Rugby Championships. Without knowing it, I'd given myself a hearty backslap of self-congratulation.

My mentor looked at me and smiled. 'Nice start,' she said.

Immediately my perspective changed. *She had broken my frame.* Up until that moment, I'd considered myself to be experienced, but that attitude had become a self-made prison, one that increased the chances I might drift through my role in the upcoming season. If that were to happen, I wouldn't be serving the All Blacks jersey in the way I needed to. Given this was a World Cup year, I'd put myself at risk – 2015 had to be my best-ever campaign and a springboard to greater successes. That conversation challenged any preconceptions I might have held about myself and the team's progress. Rather than seeing those accrued trophies as a status symbol, I had to view them as the first rung on a very tall ladder and keep climbing.

The frames facing the All Blacks ahead of 2015 – those inconvenient truths I mentioned earlier – were also potentially debilitating. (Remember: no team had won two back-to-back Rugby World Cups, and reaching a World Cup Final on foreign soil had eluded us so far.) These frames were strengthened further by our status as champions. In 2011, we'd had nothing to lose, but by 2015, everything felt as if it was on the line, and we were being weighed down by expectation. To overcome the negative psychology that could subconsciously exist in an individual or team – especially when leading into a big event – we broke the frame in two ways, firstly by reworking the language used when discussing our aims, and secondly through an experiential activity that shifted our mindset. Rather than adopting a burden mentality – which was fear-based and focused on past and future thinking – we stepped into the headspace of a warrior:

- We talked about the honour that comes with recapture.
- Adversity was a gift and a privilege. We had to move towards it.
- We had to be dedicated to the moment.
- Our sacrifice would cause discomfort, but we embraced the discomfort and pushed through it because the prize on the other side was huge.

To further assist us with breaking the frame, we leant into the work conducted by our friends from the New Zealand Special Forces by taking the players to their base in Auckland. From a viewing point, we watched as they performed what was called a door-kicking raid on a staged compound, sweeping through rooms and capturing mock 'prisoners'. The players then put on military gear and conducted a similar operation for themselves. The thinking behind this exercise was clear. When it comes to breaking the frame, information doesn't necessarily lead to transformation – but experience does. By conducting a Special Forces-style mission, we wanted the All Blacks to learn from the experience of taking something they wanted by force, in an extreme environment, so they could face the Rugby World Cup without trepidation. Our hope was that in doing so, they would embrace a braver outlook, identify the attributes that delivered success in high-stress moments and then transfer them onto the field at the upcoming Rugby World Cup. At the centre of this was the understanding that to get the job done, a person – whether they were a highly trained military operator or a pro rugby player – needed to be fluid and free on the field, rather than tentative and tight. It was the mindset that would transform the All Blacks from a great team to an even greater one, while making us a tough nut to crack.

Te Puna o te Kī: The Parents' Charter

In 1999, my friend Phil Duns was coaching the East Shirley Under-12s cricket team. I often helped him while he was training the kids or setting them up for a match, but whenever I watched them compete, I was often struck by the conversations taking place on the sidelines. They were horrific. The parents bitched and moaned about what was happening on the field of play, criticising the kids as if they were international cricketers. On some occasions, the language was borderline abusive, and while I'm sure some of the instructions being dished out were well intended, the players' confidence was being dented. This negatively impacted their performances, which then led to more criticism. And so, the negative spiral continued. If left unchecked, I knew that some players would soon opt out of the game altogether.

The only answer was to break the frame. The truth about parenting is that a lot of mums and dads see their offspring as being full of potential, especially in sport where they're viewed as The Next Big Thing, a future All Black, or an Olympian-in-waiting. They want the best for their babies. But in pushing them to run faster, tackle harder, or bowl more aggressively, they sometimes lose sight of the most important detail about children's sport: it's supposed to be fun, *not suffocating*. The frame that had been built around the team at East Shirley was that the highly critical language from the sidelines was educational or inspiring. In reality, it was instilling fear and causing the kids to shrink into themselves.

Rather than moaning at the parents or banning them from offering any comments as spectators, we asked them to reconsider the preconceived conceptions on what it took to be a supportive parent. At the start of the following season, we approached the players' families and presented them with *The Parents' Charter* – a document containing a list of suggested behaviours that would help make the matchday experience an enjoyable one for everybody: the kids, the mums and dads, the coaches and the umpire. Among the guidelines were suggestions for what to do during a game, so that a child and his/her teammates would feel encouraged and supported. Elsewhere we presented a series of helpful behaviours to be implemented before training, while playing in the backyard at home, or when driving home after a match. Our hope was that the kids would feel comfortable when making mistakes, knowing they could learn from them rather than face unhelpful criticism.

PARENTS' CHARTER 1999
EAST SHIRLEY CRICKET TEAM, UNDER-12s

Things we will do as parents/caregivers to ensure that children's cricket is a positive experience for everybody.

In the backyard

- Avoid giving excessive instruction – we want the time we have together out the back to be *fun-filled* not *instruction-filled*.
- The wrinkles that form on our faces should come more from *grins* than *frowns* and there should be more *nodding* than *shaking of the head sideways*.
- Respond to questions asked with care and simplicity!
- Ask questions to get answers – listen and affirm the responses.
- If several people are playing, encourage them to settle disputes within their playgroup in a fair and equal manner.
- Ensure the experience is a positive one.

In the car on the way to practice

- Avoid saying, 'You must do this', or 'You must do that'.
- Instead, try the following: Have fun. Work hard. Support each other. Take turns. Do your bit. Say, 'Thank you'.

During the game

- Affirm effort. We want to be rewarders of good effort – we value 'trying' as a most special behaviour.
- Encourage our children: look for situations to say, 'Well done', or 'Good effort'.
- Applaud supportive behaviour: when our children do things that show they are supporting their teammates we want to really highlight it.
- Ignore the mistakes that our children will inevitably make. Trust your coaches to pick the time to work on these.
- Negative comments are not welcome on our bench. If you feel like saying it, then remove yourself so that it is not said to or in front of our troops.
- Acknowledge that our body language sends clear messages, so keep it positive.
- Attempt to ensure that our children include everyone in activities they may embark in on the sideline.
- We all need to be monitors of good language.

After the game

- Avoid asking, 'How many runs did you get?' Or 'How many wickets did you get?' Instead ask the following:
'Did you play well?'
'What things did you do well today?'
'What things did other people in your team do well that you thought were great?'
'Is there something that you would like to do better if you could do it over again?'
'If so, how can I help you achieve that?'
'Shall we set some time aside to do that?'
- Ensure that everyone does their bit to help the coach clean up.

If you've managed to do half of this then you should have had a neat time. Here's to ensuring that we **GROW TOGETHER!**

The Parents' Charter was transformative. The mood around East Shirley's fixtures lifted as a more positive environment grew around the kids. A lot of the parents in attendance hadn't realised their actions had been negative or destructive – especially when their comments were being made in earshot of another player's family, one that might not have been performing very well, or was one of the less talented members of the group. People don't experience your intentions; they feel the impact of your actions. Having broken the frame on what was considered encouraging behaviour, the dialogue around the players changed too. Prior to *The Parents' Charter,* whenever a kid was collected after a match, the first question was usually results-based. (*Did you win?*) This sent out the message that the result was the most important thing, and nothing else mattered. However, if that same child was asked how they'd improved that day, what they'd learned, or if they'd supported their teammates, the experience became a more nourishing and enriching one for everyone involved.

The Wero: Find Your Next Level

Regardless of whether you're in a leadership position, looking to develop leadership skills, or hoping to grow in some way, I suggest you spend some time identifying your gap and then determine how it might be bridged. You can start this process by completing the following steps:

ONE: Get clear on what your current reality is by asking these three questions:

- What do you do or what is the role you wish to change?
- Can you describe where your role is at today?
- What does your next level of performance look like for you in this role?

TWO: Check the level of discomfort. Set the challenge high. Your next level should feel energising and inspiring . . . *but a bit scary.* Pick a target that makes you feel slightly unsettled and remember: if an established leader like Richie McCaw can pick a next level target, you can too.

THREE: Identify one or two people that can give you feedback – critical friends, peers or mentors. Ask them to appraise your performance levels and to challenge you where appropriate.

FOUR: Assess the feedback, then adjust and build a plan that can help you achieve your next level. This process is all about imagining future possibilities and then pulling the present forward to meet them.

The Library of Learnings

- To accelerate their growth, a leader should engage in a series of *probes* – an exploratory process whereby a leader and their team's current position is examined. Make sure to take note of any inconvenient truths.
- Do you have a gap? If not, set a target, or a next level that creates discomfort. Then identify what you need to bridge it.
- All of us have frames – preconceived notions about ourselves, the individuals around us, and the way we think certain things should be done or how people must behave. But these beliefs, once entrenched, can stunt a leader's growth. We should take time to challenge these ideas, *to break the frame*, whenever possible.

PART II

Culture

INTRODUCTION

Better People Make Better All Blacks

Reshaping the way the All Blacks thought about leadership wasn't the only change that occurred after my arrival with the team. We also embarked on a cultural revolution, and a small section of the management group and the team captain got together for a period of intense soul searching, introspection and analysis. Together we started overhauling the team's standards, and the values and goals that would drive our actions, setting us on a path towards success. In doing so, we explored the All Blacks' identity, the traits that made us such a unique force, and the rituals and traditions that had been embraced by the legendary teams from our history. This work enabled us to create a powerful set of behaviours that would make us one of the greatest sports teams of all time.

Changes came thick and fast. A sense of entitlement had infected the group and some of the players believed, wrongly, that they were entitled to special treatment because of their standing and status as an All Black. The symptoms of this issue were manifested in episodes of sloppy behaviour and bad habits, one of which was a general indifference to team housekeeping. After most games, the sheds were left in a mess, which was a nightmare for the people who came in to clean up after we'd left, and it created the impression that we were a group of untidy and disrespectful individuals. (Which we were.) To correct the issue, Brian Lochore, then an All Blacks selector, established the phrase 'Better people make better All Blacks'.

Several years later, Steve Hansen introduced the practice of sweeping the sheds, an idea rooted in the principle that respect needed to be shown everywhere, even in the dark places, away from the public and the media. This wasn't just about correcting an era of bad behaviour either. Sweeping the sheds reinforced everything the new All Blacks represented, and it became a route map for who we wanted to be going forward. As we contributed to a cause much bigger than ourselves through self-sacrifice, the group experienced an amplified sense of belonging. Whenever we *swept the sheds,* it was done with a level of application that matched our diligence in training and playing.

It wasn't all plain sailing in the early years of this transition though, and our cultural redesign would hit one or two psychological speed bumps – the 2007 World Cup was evidence of that. But wherever we went, the sheds were left spotless. Most tellingly, the first people to pick up the brooms were usually the leaders, and their work was always done quietly, away from prying eyes, and without any fuss or fanfare. That's because no All Black was considered bigger than the team, regardless of their talent or experience. Our view: *never above you, never below you, always beside you.* Interestingly, this act was also translatable to all walks of life and was known to create a feeling of belonging in any environment. See also: the team leader who stays late to help their department meet a deadline. The staff member who makes coffees for their work colleagues, unasked. And the parent who volunteers for a school event so that the kids and their families can have an enhanced experience.

The All Blacks jersey required humility. It demanded respect. The standard of sweeping the sheds reconnected the players with these notions and it quickly became a representation of who we wanted to be and what we stood for. Elsewhere, we redesigned the cultural cornerstones of the team such as the haka and the group's vision and values. In doing so we identified the power of ritual, which when applied correctly brings a huge competitive advantage. That's because *culture is kingdom*: it's like the fortified walls of a castle, and it brings strength to a collective of differing personalities, beliefs, ethnicities and religions.

I've learned that if everyone buys into the culture of a team and nourishes it by committing to the standards and behaviours required to succeed, that team becomes an unstoppable force. The people within it feel belonging. They give everything to their teammates. And they find new ways to win. This is true across all contexts and environments, and is applicable not only to sport, but to business, personal challenge, and even relationships. Having said that, we're not dealing with a menu-driven approach here and creating a success-minded culture requires patience, effort and continual application. Over the following chapters I'll give you the tools to get you there.

CHAPTER 6

Set Your Standards

When Steve Hansen stepped up as All Blacks coach in 2012, he set the tone for his leadership with an incredibly bold statement.

'I have a vision for this team,' he said, during one of his early meetings with the squad. 'While I'm sitting in this chair, I want us to be the most dominant team in the history of world rugby.'

As the words left his mouth, I felt the atmosphere shift. At the time, the room was packed with world-class players. An uncomfortable silence settled in the room. Everyone looked at one another nervously as we began considering the implications of Steve's announcement: *Bloody hell, what about the generations of All Blacks that have gone before us?* I realised we were being placed into a position of discomfort, but Steve didn't care. In fact, he loved it. *He thrived under stress and so would we.*

Coming on the heels of the 2011 World Cup victory, this mindset felt like a much-needed breath of fresh air. Starting again after such a huge success can be tough sometimes. In such circumstances, complacency creeps in, bad habits too, and what the players and coaching staff needed was a powerful reset. Redefining our culture – the ways and whys of doing things – felt like the best place to start because it would provide a set of guidelines for every action going forward. My job was to help everyone as we outlined these principles. To achieve this end, a three-part framework was established, one we believed would create a powerful team ethic:

- Identity. *Who are we?*
- Vision. *Where are we going?*
- Standards. *How do we get there?*

In answering each question, we revolutionised our culture and transformed Steve's vision into reality.

Identity (Who Are We?)

Shortly after making his bold statement, Steve invited the Leadership Group to a meeting at the Clearwater Golf Club in Christchurch. As we discussed how we were going to bind the All Blacks' culture to his bold ambition, he asked another pertinent question.

Who are we?

As with before, the room stirred uneasily. Nobody had an answer, and despite working together for several years, it was clear that a solid team identity had yet to be defined. This was a failure on our part. It's well known that a group without an understanding of who they are can feel rudderless. They lack motivation, particularly when working under pressure. Whereas a group that feels connected to a sense of self will be driven to give everything to the cause. It becomes a secret power they can tap into.

Steve looked around the room. 'Well, clearly we have some work to do,' he said.

Having spotted the vacuum, we pushed hard to fill it. Shortly afterwards it was decided that the best way to understand our identity was to look to our past and pick apart the All Blacks' DNA. By exploring our incredible history, the future could be nourished and strengthened with inspirational achievements, legends and behaviours, and to get to that point, we asked the Leadership Group a series of questions, including: *Who are we? And what does it mean to be a New Zealander and an All Black?* When the results came in, they echoed the content of an old document called *The All Blacks Story* that had been sitting around for a while but hadn't really been thought about. Instantly, the All Blacks' identity, which had previously been a hazy picture, came into focus.

THE ALL BLACKS STORY

New Zealand is a small country on the edge of the earth that has produced the greatest rugby legend the world has ever known.

Rugby is New Zealand's game.

The people, cultures and rugby teams of New Zealand have woven many threads into a black jersey.

The jersey personifies a nation.

It symbolises excellence and respect.

The team towers above the individual.

Those who play in the black jersey carry the people's hopes and dreams.

To each generation is passed the guardianship of the legend.

That was our identity.

When this document was later handed over to the players, it gave them an understanding of who we were and what we represented. They then used it as fuel for everything we did – during Tests, at training, and as they represented the All Blacks off the field. Conrad Smith, who played 94 times for his country between 2004 and 2015, and won back-to-back Rugby World Cups in 2011 and 2015, later told me he loved the idea of having such a clear identity because he felt as if he was playing for a cause much bigger than himself.

'The All Blacks are flagships for a multicultural nation,' he said. 'We punch way above our weight and have done so for over 100 years. Anything that tapped into our history, our stories, and our multicultural aspects was a massive driver for me and it made me do things that I didn't think I was capable of.'

Of course, defining an identity was a relatively straightforward process for an international rugby team, given we had over a century of history to lean into – there was plenty of source material to play with. The challenge for a lot of teams, businesses or collectives, no matter the field, is locating a starting point. Some groups forget or lose their identity over time. Others don't bother to establish one in the first place. But I've learned that every entity has a central core – AKA, *the reason they started in the first place* – whether they know it or not, and in order to bring it to the surface it helps to ask several probing questions. Among them: *Where did our Big Idea come from? What problem are we solving? How do we make money?* Once these questions have been answered, an identity can be built.

Imagine a health and beauty business that uses seaweed and plant-based materials to make its products. Everything is sourced from their location on the coast and their packaging is 100 per cent recyclable and environmentally friendly. In answering the right questions (*Where did our Big Idea come from? What problem are we solving? How do we make money?*), the company's identity tells a story whereby everything is sourced from the sea and is returned responsibly to the environment. Yes, they're a health and beauty brand, but their *unique selling point*, or USP, is making products that are natural, devoid of chemicals and unpleasant additives, and everything that goes into the product, from the creative process to the packaging, is either recyclable, reusable or returnable.

That is their identity.

Vision (Where Are We Going?)

The vision is an outcome and/or challenge. It is a target to achieve or a hurdle to overcome and it tells a team with an identity where they're going and what they're striving for. In the All Blacks' case it was to become the most dominant team in the history of world rugby. For a business it might be to become a market leader in innovation, or to have one of their products in every household in the country. For the individual it might be to buy a house, start a family, or reach financial freedom. However, when it comes to vision building, it's not enough to throw out a grand statement in the hope it might stick with the group. The words must resonate, and to achieve this, a vision must be both future-facing and inspirational.

Steve's target was all those things. Its announcement caused a ripple of discomfort to wash through the team as we contemplated the power of what had been put in front of us. Internally, there must have been questions. *What about the other teams? What about the people from our past? How do we surpass the legends?* But this response was understandable and encouraging. A vision, by its very nature, is supposed to be unsettling. If a team doesn't experience discomfort when planning, it's unlikely they'll leave their comfort zones, and as a result they'll fail to grow. A challenge as big as the one set by Steve was important because it required bravery. The very idea of it took everyone's breath away.

What was also important was that Steve's vision, while daunting, didn't feel like a burden. The concept wasn't so huge that it caused everyone to wilt under pressure. Instead, it motivated us to work even harder, and that's because a basic facet of psychology states that a target should pull a group forward, not drag them down. It must also generate so much excitement that the people involved will do anything to ensure its success, even if they don't believe in it fully – the point is to strive for it. One or two All Blacks later told me that they'd not been convinced that Steve's plan was achievable at first, but it hadn't mattered because they'd believed in the *idea of it*, and that was enough. The effects were instantaneous, they became fired up, and a year later, the All Blacks went unbeaten through 2013. Suddenly the plan to become the most dominant team in the history of world rugby felt more realistic.

Visions are just as applicable to the individual, and to work they only need to track the same principles as a team objective. I remember Samuel Whitelock, an All Black with 153 caps, used to write the numerals 3, 7, and 1, in the steamed-up screen of his shower every day after training. Sam was a deep and very clear thinker and the #3 was there because a third Rugby World Cup winner's medal had become his obsession, after winning it in 2011 and 2015. (He was scarred by the 2019 Rugby World Cup in Japan, where we'd been knocked out in the semis.) The #7 represented his desire to win seven Super titles in a row. And the #1 represented a number of targeted *firsts*. Among them, becoming the first player in history to win three World Cups, winning his first player of the match award as an All Black and becoming the first player to earn 150 tests for New Zealand.

3. 7. 1.

In reaching for these aims, Sam eventually won his first Man of the Match award in his 145th Test as an All Black. He claimed his seventh Super title in 2023, though the team fell short in the 2023 Rugby World Cup, losing in the final to South Africa by one point. However, in working to his personal vision, Sam became the most capped All Black of all time. He earned the Player of the Year award at the 2017 New Zealand Rugby Awards and became the fastest-ever All Black to reach 100 appearances. That was some record, but more important was the fact that his drive had made him a player his teammates could rely upon, on and off the field. Interestingly, 371 was also the address of his farm back in Hawke's Bay – a place he and his family would return to and settle in after his esteemed rugby career.

Email to Your Future Self: Write a short letter to yourself to read in six months, explaining what you've learned from this concept and how you plan to create a vision. Set a reminder to open it when the time arrives.

Standards (How Do We Get There?)

Standards are clearly defined behaviours that drive a person or team towards success, especially when fed into an overall vision, which in Steve Hansen's case, was for the All Blacks to become the most dominant team in the history of world rugby. When done correctly they build a sense of unity and help everybody to become mentally and physically stronger, and a hell of a lot more productive. However, the challenge for any team – especially one with as much talent and power as the All Blacks – was to define a set of standards in the first place.

To get the ball rolling, a form was sent to every member of the squad and the wider management team. Only two questions were printed on it:

- Which three players in the history of the All Blacks have enhanced our legacy the most?
- What were the personal qualities that these players had in common?

This was a fascinating exercise. Firstly, because it encouraged all 60 participants to consider the team's entire history. And secondly because it helped us to identify a series of positive traits exhibited by some of the All Blacks' greatest-ever players, in the hope that we might spot a series of common standards.

Meanwhile, several rules were applied to the process:

1) The feedback was 100 per cent confidential.
2) No numbers or rankings were required. The brief was to list three players, and what they stood for, rather than to place them in any order.
3) Words trumped players. (The actions of the chosen All Blacks would speak more loudly than their achievements.)

Once the papers were collated and the data was processed (with the help of Doctor Ceri Evans, a forensic psychiatrist we'd brought in as an external consultant to assist us with the methodology), a list of names was drawn up. The chosen players were then grouped into four categories:

1) THE STANDOUTS: Richie McCaw. Keven Mealamu. Jonah Lomu.

2) SIGNIFICANT IMPACT: Tana Umaga. Brian Lochore. Dan Carter. Sean Fitzpatrick. Colin Meads.
3) HISTORICAL CONNECTIONS: Dave Gallaher. Jock Hobbs. Michael Jones. Buck Shelford.
4) THE THINKERS: Wayne Smith. Brad Thorn. Conrad Smith.

The Standouts spoke for themselves, they were the G.O.A.T.s, and of the 60 responses, Richie, Keven and Jonah dominated the data. (It was incredible to see the confidence boost in Richie and Keven, two players from the current squad, knowing their peers had bracketed them so highly.) But it was easy to understand why: all three had put the team first throughout their careers; they were inspiring and courageous; and they'd become known for their drive and mental strength. They were also demanding and innovative and carried an unquenchable thirst for self-improvement. Elsewhere, the *Significant Impact* players were those All Blacks that had positively affected the sport in one way or another. The players in the *Historical Connections* category had made a cultural mark during their careers (for example, Michael Jones was a Christian and had famously made a stand about not playing on Sundays), while *The Thinkers* were those players known for seeing the sport a little differently. Every single All Black on the list had played an important role in the legacy of the team.

Anchor Words

With our players identified, we then studied the personal qualities displayed by each one. This was done by working through the answers to question #2 and looking out for any regularly repeated phrases. The responses were clustered into what we called *anchor words*.

DRIVEN: The players on the list were driven to be the best, to pioneer, and to redefine the All Blacks' history. Their actions encouraged everyone to be better than they were the day before.

INSPIRING: They showed the way; they put the jersey first; they added to the legacy. This attitude showed through on any occasion, regardless of the circumstances.

GRATEFUL: They were grounded, caring and humble, and their behaviour showed everyone that they recognised and appreciated the opportunities being afforded to them as an All Black.

FIERCE: On the field they were intimidating. They left their mark and felt the hurt. They believed it was important to show ferocity in the battle.

COURAGE: The best All Blacks never ever gave in. They took risks and broke limits, no matter how scary or painful the challenge. Or, as one player put it: *They put their head into the spokes of the wheel.*

When amalgamated, these anchor words formed the acronym *DIG FC*. They were used as cues to create a powerful set of standards.

DRIVEN

What it means: To be the best. Loyalty trumps all things – to the legacy, the team and yourself. Put the team first, always. To be on time, always. To display behaviours in the environment that enhance the legacy. Show good judgement in terms of what you do and don't do. Lead by actions. Know what structures work for you and implement these consistently. Focus on the role and deliver what's required every time. Don't compromise. Persist and persevere when others meet their limit. Push through setbacks. Have a hunger that others can feel.

What it doesn't mean: Taking shortcuts. Going missing in action – on and off the field. 'Talking it' but not doing it! Undermining others. Compromising on the small things. Losing balance. Personal standards are inconsistent. Living a culture of secrecy. Showing a blatant disregard for team protocols, for example: women, alcohol, drugs, supplements. Complaining in private. De-energising through your body language and spoken language.

SET YOUR STANDARDS

INSPIRING

What it means: Show the way – on and off the field. Pull others upwards with your personal actions. Be a living example of how off-field behaviours translate to on-field excellence. Actively contribute to the team's benefit. Perform at a high level regardless of occasion. Leave your mark – on and off the field. Break limits. Be a towering influence. Motivate through speech and actions. Be the first to rise to a challenge when others hesitate. Be decisive when others go quiet. Lift others through your passion. Stand for something bigger than yourself. Bring people together for the cause.

What it doesn't mean: Saying one thing but doing another. Pulling others down to your level. Being afraid of big decisions. Punching below your weight. Playing within your limits. Leading within your limits. Waiting for others. Flinching under pressure.

GRATEFUL

What it means: Be an All Black, 24/7. Treat relevant sacrifices and opportunities as a privilege. Be grounded. Value different perspectives. Be a good person. Have a 'YES' attitude. Put the team before individual accolades. Know where we come from. Serve others. Make unseen contributions. Be non-judgemental. Don't compromise with anything that weakens the culture. Put others first if it helps the team. Help others.

What it doesn't mean: Taking more than giving. Doing the right things sometimes, but not always. Complaining to others. Gossiping. Making sacrifices a burden. Being disrespectful. Taking the rewards but not contributing to the culture. Sulking for more than one minute off the field. Sulking for more than three seconds on the field.

FIERCE

What it means: Remain composed and clear under pressure. Be uncompromising with unseen behaviours. Have your mate's back. Show utter domination through preparing and executing ruthlessly. Be fearless in the heat of battle. Intimidate. Against all odds. Love the hurt. Never ever give in. Punish the opposition 'moment to moment'. Embrace the big occasion. Respect everyone, but fear no one. Come alive under pressure. Stand up when adversity appears. Keep it simple so that you're single-minded.

What it doesn't mean: Making excuses. Taking mental breaks. Getting 'over the top' and losing self-discipline on the field by giving away penalties and suchlike. Being hot-headed and losing clarity. Letting the opposition divert you and needle you. Getting caught in two minds and losing intensity. Being one metre behind on the field. Being one minute behind off the field.

COURAGEOUS

What it means: Speak up. Don't be afraid to say what you think is right. Talk straight – at the right time, and face to face. Respect boundaries and confidentiality. Ask probing questions – in meetings, on the field, and off the field. No mountain is too high. Work through anxiety to get movement. Punch above your weight.

What it doesn't mean: Saying nothing when you see something that's not right for the team. Being passive. Walking past an unacceptable standard. Only giving opinions and not asking questions. Stewing on things. Walking on eggshells. Following the herd. Letting anxiety close you down.

In everything we did, an All Black had to be driven and inspiring. We had to be grateful. We had to show ferocity and courage. These standards were then displayed in the team's meeting room, and we referred to them constantly. If the squad was heading into the local area for a community event, the word *grateful* was acknowledged, and everyone reminded themselves to be humble, grounded and caring. And while these gestures might seem small when compared to the challenges experienced by an international rugby team, combined they fed into a bigger picture where team strength and incredibly high standards led the way. With Steve's identity and a vision, the All Blacks were transformed as we won and advanced our claim as the most dominant team in rugby history.

Living the Standards

Writing out a set of standards is one thing, but living them is an altogether different experience. During incredibly high-pressure situations, it takes a lot of guts to display drive or gratitude, and I remember on the eve of our 2015 World Cup semi-final against South Africa at Twickenham, an 8:30am meeting was called by the management team. But as the players and staff waited patiently, there was a notable absence. *Steve Hansen had yet to arrive.* When he eventually walked in, a minute late, one of the players from the Leadership Group stood up and pointed.

'Coach: don't be late,' he said. 'Is that clear?'

Steve nodded and accepted the criticism. He understood that for the All Blacks to succeed everyone had to commit to DIG FC – even him, with all his media commitments and logistical responsibilities. Steve then commended the player for calling out his drop in standards, which had taken extreme courage. That's because our designated standards were applicable in every corner of the All Blacks' environment, and no one was immune. If someone left their coffee cup on a table, they were reminded that messiness was not acceptable. If a player wore an unsanctioned clothing brand to a media event, they were called out. The group even became known for cleaning away the dirty plates and cutlery after lunch and dinner, taking them to the kitchens as the service staff shook their heads in disbelief.

We knew that if a team like the All Blacks were to stay true to our identity and reach Steve's vision, it was important that the values of the group were lived by everybody. A rule was quickly established whereby the standards that a person walked past, or ignored, were the standards they were prepared to accept for the team. For example, if one of us walked past a messy training shed it sent a message: *This is a standard everyone is happy with.* But that wasn't the case at all. As a result, the players called out the messes of others and highlighted the negligence, or a slack attitude, even if it meant challenging a leader or a member of the management team. This rule soon raised everyone's bar and prevented a decline in attitude that would inevitably lead to a slip in performance levels.

In making these behaviours central to our way of being, the All Blacks learned a vital lesson about the way we communicated. As with all team environments, where a diverse blend of personalities come together for a shared cause, there was a disparity in responses. Some players were quick to call out a slip in behaviour and did so aggressively, often in front of the group. This sometimes led to the recipient feeling shamed, humiliated or rejected, and their *mana* was crushed, which we knew was detrimental to the team. Other players went the other way and delivered their observations in a very casual way. Their words then carried very little weight, and nothing was done to influence the situation. Having spotted this, we encouraged the group to be themselves . . . *but with skill.* We wanted them to adapt to the people they were challenging, and the situations in which they were raising their concerns. For example, if someone had made a mistake during a match, and their error was due to be highlighted in a team meeting, the coaches often warned them in advance. This stopped the player from being blindsided.

Self-policing in this way, done with skill, allows for the group to practise restraint and understanding. There's a belief in elite sport, as well as business and other high-performance environments, that humans don't need rules – that they only require a powerful purpose, and this alone will drive behaviour. However, it's also important to live in the real world where people have personal issues that can impact their performance. A relationship breakdown, or a family bereavement can lead to a temporary drop in standards, and this should be factored in. Having said that, if a person's poor behaviour becomes habitual, or an incident is so serious, it's important to act decisively.

This happened in 2023 when we were forced to drop a key player from the team before our Rugby World Cup quarter-final against Ireland. He had breached protocol by breaking a designated curfew. Given it was a minor misdemeanour, and the individual was important to the team, nobody outside of the All Blacks would have been too bothered had we overlooked his slip-up. But breaking curfew didn't sit with the Standards of DIG FC, especially in a World Cup when there were self-evident punishments for not respecting team rules and everyone had to be an All Black, 24/7. In this case, the player was made unavailable for selection, and he accepted his omission without grumbling. Meanwhile, the rest of the group also accepted the decision. Everybody knew that in an event as huge as a Rugby World Cup, the margins for error were fine. And walking past an unacceptable standard would trigger a domino effect that might ultimately crush the team.

> **The Silent Leadership Test:** For one full day, focus on leading through actions, not words. Observe how people respond to your behaviours. Make some notes in your journal: *Where did you inspire? Where did you fall short?*

Te Puna o te Kī: Dominate the Decade

Sometimes, when working to a grand vision, like the one outlined by Steve, it helps to refresh a team's goal or goals after a while. That way everybody can feel re-energised and experience a sense of renewal. (It also helps to prevent complacency from creeping in.) After three years of working to the aspiration of becoming the most dominant team in the history of world rugby, the All Blacks won the World Cup in 2015. We were unbeaten throughout 2013 and won the Laureus Award for Team of the Year in 2016. Across 2015 and 2016 we broke the tier one Test nation record with 18 consecutive wins. In 2017, with only two years of the 2010s remaining, it was decided to bring our horizons forward. A new, more immediate challenge was set for the group: To become the most dominant team of the decade – *across all sports.*

The reasons for doing something like this were clear. Becoming the most dominant team in rugby history was a subjective goal, and not fully in our control. When the debate about our position among the sport's greats eventually began, some people would agree with the statement, others would probably dissent. However, to put ourselves into the conversation, we had to extend our aspirations beyond rugby and become regarded as the best sports team in at least one decade. Given the years between 2010 and 2019 were very nearly done (and we were by far the strongest international rugby team during that stretch), dominating the decade felt very much within our control. It was also an inspiring vision; one that fed into our greater goal, and a target the players and support staff were very much up for. Before long the group had zeroed in on the concept of '10', or *DTD* as it had been nicknamed.

There were other equally empowering reasons for adapting our vision in this way. For starters, the target was inclusive. Every All Black from the past and present, and those joining us in the future, would feel inspired by the idea of DTD. As before, we were connecting to a purpose much bigger than ourselves, and those players that had left us earlier would still have a link to our success. To bring everybody into the vision, we gathered the squad together and asked the leaders to nominate their favourite examples of sporting dominance throughout history, with an explanation of why they had been chosen. Some players picked LeBron James. Others went for Usain Bolt. Both Brodie Retallick and Beauden Barrett nominated Tiger Woods.

'Tiger was not content with being great,' said Beauden when explaining his selection. 'He wanted to be the *All Time Great*. And he reworked his shot and technique even after winning his first major.'

Other notable entries included the athletes Daley Thompson and Sir Roger Bannister, the first man to run the sub-four-minute mile. These individuals, along with the DTD concept, became the 'pull' that would lead the All Blacks towards their target and the photos of each nominee were later arranged in such a way that they resembled a jigsaw puzzle, with a missing piece at its heart. This was a space reserved for the All Blacks team, and for good reason too, because we were on our way to becoming the top-ranking team in international rugby for every month for a decade (this ran from November 2009 through to October 2019 – 118 consecutive months). Our only disappointment came in the 2019 Rugby World Cup when we lost in the semi-final to England, though in three World Cups during the decade we were only defeated in one match. Overall, though, we made true to our vision by dominating the decade, and in doing so, put forward our case as the most powerful team in rugby history.

The Wero: Build a Standards List

When building a standards list, start by applying the processes used by the All Blacks in 2012.

PHASE ONE: Draw up a list of people you admire. They could be individuals from your field, or great leaders, innovators or thinkers. Then explore the characteristics that make them so inspirational.

PHASE TWO: When exploring these characteristics, write down the descriptors that show up the most. For example, you might find your list has been dominated by the words 'fearless', 'dedicated', 'honest', 'empathetic' and 'selfless'. These are your anchor words.

PHASE THREE: Establish characteristics for each of your anchor words. These are clarifying terms that define what it takes to be fearless, dedicated, honest, empathetic and selfless. For example, SELFLESS: Put your teammate first; check in with your brothers and sisters; adopt a *hand up* rather than *hand out* mentality.

PHASE FOUR: Write a list of behaviours that will nourish each of the anchor words. *Make a round of coffees for the team. Tidy the communal area at the end of the day. Check the printer is topped up with ink.* These are your standards. Breathe life into them. And as with the All Blacks and our commitment to housework, these actions are most effective when done quietly and unprompted.

The Library of Learnings

- Standards are clearly defined acts that drive a person or team towards success, especially if they feed into the overall aim or goal.
- When building a set of standards, first define your identity and vision. Your standards will show you how to get there.
- Standards must be policed and any failure to live up to them should be called out. Remember: *the standard a person walks past is the standard they're happy to accept.*
- When assessing whether an individual is living up to the group's standards their personal issues should be taken into account. However, if poor behaviour becomes habitual, or the incident is very serious, deal with it decisively.

CHAPTER 7

Preserve the Core, Disrupt the Edges

The All Blacks had a unique relationship with the expectations we placed upon ourselves and those the world placed upon us. During my time as their Mental Performance and Leadership coach, the media scrutiny was always intense, the public interest stratospheric, and as a result, every one of us was acutely aware of our legacy: the results, the trophies and the players that had come before, and those that were going to follow. Having embraced the concept of leaving the jersey in a better place than when we found it, we also had an expectation to uphold the team's standards and contribute to its ongoing success. We were driven to make the exceptional *normal*.

As you can imagine, these factors combined to create a hell of a lot of pressure, but at no point did we see these expectations as burdens. Instead, they were regarded as motivating factors, and we used them to ensure the All Blacks were in a constant state of forward movement. For example, we knew our behaviours could influence rugby's future generations, for good and for bad, so whenever a kid asked one of our players for a selfie, it was always given without a grumble, even in the middle of a terrible day. We were All Blacks. It was our duty to usher in rugby's next wave.

The discipline required to manage these expectations was underlined when I sat on a panel with Richie McCaw. He was asked whether there was a sense of relief at walking through the front door because he could finally be himself. Richie laughed.

'Not really,' he said. 'Because when I get through the front door, I'm no different to the Richie McCaw you see outside.'

Richie had been taught that his behaviour, public and private, reflected who he was and what he stood for – even when no one was looking.

The All Blacks weren't alone in this way of thinking, and our mindset was recognised as being a key indicator of long-term success in 2018 when the Centre for High Performance, a research collaboration between several British universities that aimed to 'become the leading authority on how to create and sustain success', wrote a paper entitled *Radically Traditional: How to Outperform Your Peers for 100 Years*. In it, the group stated that 76 per cent of the UK FTSE 100 companies had disappeared during the previous 30 years, while the average lifespan of a US S&P 500 Company had fallen from 67 years to 15, which marked a decline of 80 per cent over 80 years. Despite this, several groups were bucking the trend and lasting for longer periods, among them the Royal Academy of Music, the Royal Academy of Art, NASA, Eton College, the Royal Shakespeare Company, British Cycling, and, of course, the All Blacks.

In analysing these groups, nicknamed 'The Centennials', the Centre for High Performance learned that each collective generally adopted two approaches that, when applied simultaneously, ensured their longevity. The first was that they embraced stability in key areas, among them *Stable Openness*, a situation in which a team accepted their position on the world stage and understood that their reputation/image attracted intense scrutiny. (Hence the All Blacks' stance on taking selfies with fans.) The second was that they encouraged disruptive thinking. These mindsets delivered long-term results and contained several important features.

Stability

- A stable core: The group understood 1) who they were, 2) what they did, and 3) what they stood for.
- A stable purpose: The Centennials worked for a cause they considered to be higher than themselves. For example, the Royal College of Art aimed to shape the world through the artistic endeavours of their alumni.
- Stable stewardship: The listed institutions all believed in steady leadership. Their top dogs stayed in place for at least ten years, not only at the most senior level, but also in the two or three tiers below. Continuity was considered a strength.

Disruption

- Disruptive experts: The Centennials considered part-time knowledge to be an asset. Rather than stuffing their team with full-time experts, they hired specialists and revolutionary thinkers for short periods of time, usually for one-off events such as rocket launches, or prestigious campaigns (World Cups or Olympic Games). Meanwhile, their in-house staff were encouraged to learn different skills elsewhere.
- Disruptive nervousness: These groups didn't crave growth – they wanted to be the best, not the biggest – and they leant into smaller, positive changes to sustain success. The Centre for High Performance noted that the All Blacks tended to lose immediately after landmark victories, which was true. But having recognised the issue, we tweaked the smaller details to bring positive change.
- Disruptive accidents: The Centennials believed their teams should work closely together, almost like a family. People operated in small groups and moved between departments where they learned new techniques and shared different ideas.

The All Blacks had long worked to the concepts of stability and disruption. We understood the components of our core – who we were, what we did, and what we stood for – and the traits and processes that made us unique. In continually striving to elevate New Zealand's reputation worldwide, we served a cause much bigger than ourselves. We believed in stable stewardship and hated chopping and changing our head coaches. And we accepted stable openness, and the pressures associated with our institution: we operated to an incredibly high standard because it was our job to bring honour to the legacy and to make the people of New Zealand proud. For this reason, the internal expectations set by the All Blacks were very high.

Equally, in maintaining our position as the best in the business, it was important to embrace disruptive change. Our aim was to stay ahead of the pack, and in that context, we absorbed knowledge from outside forces and continuously challenged our thinking by implementing brave and innovative working practices. We were unrelenting in the pursuit of improvement. We had to preserve our core and disrupt the edges – or, as the Centre for High Performance might say, we wanted to be *radically traditional* – and this was done by a) fiercely protecting the All Blacks' legacy and anything connected to it, and b) tweaking the practices and processes that underpinned our drive for continual success.

The best part was that these strategies, used so effectively by the All Blacks and the other Centennials, weren't the exclusive right of elite institutions and highly specialised brands. They could also be implemented by any collective or individual, as I'll now explain.

> **The Connection Challenge:** Engage in a 20-minute, uninterrupted conversation while walking outdoors with a friend or colleague. Switch off your phone. Reflect on the power of stability and disruption in your life and journal your conclusions.

Preserving the Core

When developing a culture, either as an individual or while working in a team, the most important step is to define your core. In many ways, this process expands on the work done when outlining an identity (see the previous chapter). Having developed an understanding of *who you are*, it's also important to consider *what you do*, and *what you stand for*, because the answers will align you to a philosophy or modus operandi, which then serves as a filter through which every decision or action can pass. In the All Blacks' case, this ran as follows:

- *Why do we exist?* As I explained in the previous chapter, New Zealand is a small country on the edge of the earth that has produced the greatest rugby legend the world has ever known. Rugby is New Zealand's game. The people, cultures and rugby teams of New Zealand have woven many threads into a black jersey. This jersey personifies a nation. It symbolises excellence and respect. The team towers above the individual.
- *What do we stand for?* The jersey. But it's not just a jersey. It's a portal through which men pass. It's not made from material, it's a fabric that binds us together. It is not a souvenir. It is a reminder of who we are. It gives us a sense of belonging, allowing us to dig deep and achieve things we may never have believed possible previously.
- *How are we unique?* We are a team with a 100-year-plus history. We embed rituals and traditions. We are a field of dreams for the chosen few. The arena is high stakes, uncertainty, small margins, pain and discomfort.

I appreciate that the idea of starting this process from scratch can feel overwhelming, especially for someone working alone, and it takes some people years, or even decades to answer these questions. (A lot of people never manage it and feel unfulfilled as a result.) This challenge can be even harder in the corporate or entrepreneurial world where a lot of businesses have a vague idea of their core, but they feel unsure of how to put it into practice, or they lose sight of it over time. However, when helping these groups to resolve such a problem, it helps to ask the same three simple questions used by the All Blacks:

- *Why do we exist?* Are we making a positive difference in the world or solving a problem?
- *What do we stand for?* What beliefs do we have that guide behaviour and decision-making?
- *How are we unique?* What are the strengths, skills or approaches that set us apart from others in the same business?

This process works equally well for the individual.

- *Why do I exist?* How am I making a positive difference in the world or solving a problem?
- *What do I stand for?* What beliefs do I have that guide my behaviour and decision-making?
- *How am I unique?* What are my strengths, skills or approaches that set me apart from others?

The crossover found in these answers is usually a good starting point for a core.

With the All Blacks, our core was very easy to identify because it had been passed down from generation to generation. That said, it still fell by the wayside from time to time. There were periods when the idea of honouring the jersey and inspiring the people of New Zealand laid dormant and the leaders failed to honour it. In my time, these situations were rare, but when they did happen, they mostly involved off-field misbehaviour and alcohol. During the early phases of my career, when transgressions took place, it annoyed me considerably, as if I'd been let down personally. I later learned that I was working with young men (and women in the case of the netball teams) and that they were on a journey towards becoming experienced adults.

When the core was used effectively with the All Blacks, however, it became a pathfinder for every team decision, on and off the field. Whenever there were doubts or discussions on what to do or how to proceed, we referenced our core with a simple three-word mantra: *enhance the jersey* (ETJ). At every crossroads we asked the question: *How does this enhance the jersey?* The concept was short, simple and stable and it sent out a powerful message to the team:

We want the actions and power of the All Blacks to reverberate through the eons. To be heard by the legends of the past and held up as an example to those in the future. We want to inspire the next generation, and the generation after that.

Kapa O Pango

To add further power to this concept, a metaphorical building was created called *The House of Black*. An illustration featuring a Māori house, its design was later rendered as a huge mural and it represented the All Blacks' core – who we were, what we did, and what we stood for.

Reproduced with permission © Dave Burke

As a metaphor, the House of Black (or *Kapa O Pango*) was important because it was situated on a communal space called a *marae*, which in Māori culture is regarded as the most important area in the community and a powerful statement of identity – it is where the biggest decisions are made and a location for any ceremonies involving guests and local people. When used in the context of the All Blacks, *Kapa O Pango* was more than an illustration, and its fittings and fixtures made for a carefully scripted story. Anyone walking past it was connected to our core, either knowingly or not. And whenever a new player was inducted into the group, the leaders explained the deeper meanings of every architectural note. This experience was immersive and emotional and it ignited the All Blacks' spirit. In my experience, no player was ever the same after hearing the many stories of *Kapa O Pango*.

1) THE TANIWHA: The carved figure that sat atop the House of Black's gable, a taniwha was believed to be a supernatural creature that lived in New Zealand's deepest pools, rivers and caves, as well as the ocean. Some taniwha are highly respected *kaitiaki* – protective guardians of people, places and traditions, and symbols of ferociousness, strength and power. When the All Blacks performed the haka, it was our aim to bring our taniwha to life.

2) THE RAFTERS: Here the ribs of our ancestors were represented as the outstretched arms and hands of the taniwha. For a new All Black, they were in place to deliver a welcoming embrace. For our enemies they served as a reminder that the taniwha, and all its ferocity, guarded the House of Black. Weaved into the design was a curved motif representing the hammerhead shark, a fish considered by Māori to possess strength, determination and an unwillingness to give in, no matter the challenge. It was said that when a hammerhead was caught and filleted in the old days, its body still quivered; when the head was cut off, its eyes would still look at you.

3) THE RIDGE POLE: Standing upright in the centre of the house, the ridge pole represented our ancestors' backbone. The figure at the bottom symbolised the first New Zealand representative team to be commonly referred to as the All Blacks – the Originals of 1905 – and the ball in its hands was a mark of guardianship.
4) THE LEGS: Two pillars – or *pou* as they're known in Māori culture – stood at either side of the house, and the fearsome looking figures in front celebrated the World Cup-winning All Black teams of 1987 and 2011. (When we won the World Cup again in 2015, another *pou* was placed inside the house celebrating the event.) By positioning them here, the House of Black paid tribute to the achievements of the amazing sides that had come before us.
5) THE DECORATIVE PIECES: Across the House of Black were artistic reminders of the team's legacy. Over the doorway and the words *Kapa O Pango* was the silver fern, the unifying logo that sat across the heart of every player donning the famous black jersey. Elsewhere, the building was covered in a *poutama* pattern – a chevron-style design that symbolised the growth of humanity and its desire to strive ever upwards. The intricate patterns in the window panels, door frames and across the base of the house, denoted the teeth of the taniwha.
6) THE 15 FIGURES: This was the XV taking to the field. The central character represented both the team captain, and the leadership required to uphold the honour and the legacy of the All Blacks. Behind each figure was a silver fern, a sign of respect for the mark we wore on our chest.

Any group can build a monument of this kind – a totem of their core – and it doesn't have to be something as complicated or as lavish as the *Kapa O Pango* mural. What's important is that the chosen representation is both authentic and able to generate emotion within the working group. When deciding what image to use, a good starting point would be to answer those three questions I mentioned earlier: *Why do we exist? What do we stand for? How are we unique?* From there it's possible to land on an idea that symbolises the core. For example, it might be that a cancer charity answers those questions in the following way:

- *Why do we exist?* To increase public awareness on the symptoms of cancer and the type of care available to people suffering from the disease.
- *What do we stand for?* A better life for everyone!
- *How are we unique?* We're able to mobilise local and national support through creative ad campaigns, public events and community events.

In this case, an excellent visual might be for the team to design a logo for themselves (perhaps a line drawing of a pair of holding hands to suggest comfort, togetherness and support). The image should be positioned so that every person in the group can see it and take inspiration as they work. Like the House of Black, it will influence their every move, whether they know it or not. (In some extreme cases, these logos can be worn as a tattoo.) In political spheres, leaders have dressed a certain way to convey an image they feel will inspire the people around them. Former US president Barack Obama was known for giving talks with his sleeves rolled up to suggest he was mucking in for a worthwhile cause. Throughout the Ukraine–Russia conflict, President Zelensky has worn a military green sweatshirt to present the idea he was a man of action. Such totemic gestures can go a long way in defining a team's core.

Disrupting the Edges

No matter the core, growing is your game – it's how you get to be great and how you stay great. And as The Centennials have shown, forward momentum is vital when looking to guarantee long-term success. To achieve this aim, it's important to reject any outdated ways and stale paradigms and instead embrace disruption through the introduction of new ideas, methods and techniques. This was the approach taken by NASA, the Royal Academy of Music, and the All Blacks. And while it might sound like an intimidating process, it doesn't require any radical, wholesale change, or a ripping up of the core. All the magic happens when disrupting at the edges of what you stand for.

The management of the All Blacks jersey, and its design over time, stood as an example of this theory in action. In modern sport, commercial intrusion is a fact of life. It is naïve to think that a team could withstand all forms of advertising, especially as sponsorship money, if spent on the right things, generally enhanced the way in which the players prepared, trained and performed. However, the All Blacks understood that safeguarding the jersey was very important because it physically represented who we were, what we did, and what we stood for. The blackness defined us; the fern united us; and we did everything to ensure that these two things remained uncontaminated by excessive branding and stylistic changes. Yes, there were one or two alterations, such as a minor change to the collar. We also adjusted the jersey for a sponsorship logo, but every disruption was conducted at the edges. The core look remained, the blackness never changed, and the silver fern – though there were one or two iterations over time – never ventured too far away from its original design. When the team was requested to make a tweak, they were done on our terms. For example, the insurance group AIG were allowed to have their name placed on the jersey, but only if the box around their logo was removed and the font was reduced in size.

Elsewhere, we continually experimented and altered our processes with incremental adjustments, especially when it came to the matters of training, planning, playing and even decompressing. Disruptive experts were brought in to lend their knowledge to the group. We embraced disruptive nervousness by applying training techniques that might have seemed abstract or downright weird at first glance, but which then helped the team to learn new skills and deliver a competitive edge. And we continually bounced ideas off one another to gain an advantage over our rivals. These were strategies the Centre for High Performance had identified as being used by the other Centennial institutions on their list, and they helped us during our relentless pursuit of excellence.

No idea was dismissed as being too out there. No suggestion was considered too difficult to implement. In my 23 years of working with the All Blacks, our disruptions tended to fluctuate between the good, the bad, and the occasionally infuriating. Among the weirder experiments was the unsuccessful introduction of saliva testing – an ahead-of-its-time concept conducted during the 2007 Rugby World Cup in France. The theory behind this practical application had been sound and it was hoped the analysis might measure the cortisol levels – a key indicator of stress – in the players and management team. This would help us to assist the most anxious members within the group. Every morning, the players spat into their test tubes and packaged up their samples, but there were issues. The tests weren't 'real time'. A processing delay of several days meant the results arrived 'after the event' and therefore weren't actionable in the moment. Despite this, there was some value in the exercise: retrospective data sometimes validated what our gut instinct had been telling us (in this case, which players were feeling the strain). But in hindsight it was a clunky chore and the players quickly grew tired of it.

Nevertheless, we took these events with a heavy dollop of positivity. The act of introducing something potentially revolutionary, and learning about its flaws as we went, was a healthy sign that we were operating with a growth mindset. Throughout the All Blacks set-up, our *thing* was to challenge the norm, especially if there was a chance it might enhance the jersey. Ticking that box meant we were in the zone, boots and all, though seeing some of these experiments play out in practice might have been confusing for the casual observer. One afternoon at training, I watched the players working on their scrum drills with coach Mike 'Crono' Cron. Suddenly, the heavy guitar riff of Deep Purple's hit single 'Smoke on the Water' rumbled across the field. When I looked more closely, Mike was using the music as a trigger point for the players as they engaged in the scrum.

I later asked Crono what he'd been thinking when implementing this style of training and he told me the idea had come from a famous basketball coach called Boniface N'Dong, who had trained his players to dribble at a tempo that matched the rhythm of a guitar being played on the sidelines. Some younger players had even been filmed bouncing the ball along to the famous drumbeat of Queen's 'We Will Rock You'. In a brainwave, Crono wondered what would happen if our players engaged in the scrum in much the same way, increasing the pressure as they drove forwards in time with 'Smoke on the Water' and its recognisable ascending riff.

'I wanted the players to hit in the scrum and then push up in intensity according to the song's three note tempo,' he said. 'At first, we tried it on our scrum machine. When the music played over a set of loudspeakers, it worked perfectly. I thought: *This is it!* The feedback from the players was positive too, so we attempted it during games and stuck to the tempo for a couple of years. During that time, as the team got ready and put their boots on, I played "Smoke on the Water" over a speaker on repeat, to get the song in their heads. It might have been a load of shit, but the boys loaded in the scrum much better than before.'

With the All Blacks, the thinking behind our ongoing experimentation was very clear: innovation was everything and at the end of each campaign – whether we'd been competing in a World Cup or a Tri-Nations Series – the coaching staff embarked on a period of discovery. Every department within the group was encouraged to spend 10 per cent of their overall budget on research and development and we were expected to travel the world to seek out new techniques, philosophies and technological advancements. The hope was that we'd send waves of disruption to all parts of the All Blacks machine, and this work, unsurprisingly, resulted in some weird and wonderful experiments.

When it comes to introducing disruption to your environment, it's important to remember that every team is unique, and no two entities think the same. Everyone has different hopes, values and working practices, so there's little point in my prescribing a series of disruptive research programmes for you to embark upon. What I can say is that you should disrupt without limits. Take classes that might not carry any direct relevance to your latest project or challenge, but that could help you in a roundabout way. Bring in influential figures to talk to your group, characters that have lived interesting or highly productive lives. (Or, as an individual, attend conferences, lectures and discussions that will open your mind.) Finally, encourage experimentation without fear and embrace mistakes and false dawns. Because it's on the edges of discomfort that the greatest advancements are made.

Te Puna o te Kī: Disrupting the Haka

In 2004, an intense discussion took place. Up for debate were our leadership structures (as outlined in Part One), individual behaviours and the All Blacks culture in general. The team's traditions, rituals and all things relating to our way of being came under scrutiny too. Nothing was spared, everything was analysed – even the haka, which, despite its iconography, was causing some issues among the players. Whenever it was performed, there was a feeling that the TV cameras brought too much unwanted attention. Some players felt weighed down by it. Others believed it was being overly commercialised. Then there was also the general confusion as to why we did it in the first place, and what it meant. This was understandable given our haka was a Māori haka, and only 25 per cent of the group identified with the culture. To this day a lot of people don't realise how close we came to scrapping it altogether during those meetings.

We eventually realised that losing the haka was not the answer because we'd be messing with our core. The ritual was very much a part of our identity, but its meaning and importance had been lost, so a reconnection was put in place because the players needed to understand the truths about its origins and applications – the way the haka fired us up, and ignited us, and its potential as a game-changer. But they also had to tap into what it meant to be an All Black and a New

Zealander. Yes, we were a bicultural nation, but we lived as a multicultural society. This was reflected in several key truths:

- Whenever the jersey was pulled on, an All Black was connected to *Aotearoa* – our home and the land of the long white cloud.
- Regardless of whether a player was Māori, Samoan, Fijian, Asian or European, their bloodlines were mixed with the earth. During the haka each culture brought their own *whakapapa* – the connection to their heritage, identity and belonging.
- In doing so, they added to their own *mana*, or authority, power and respect.

If we were to stand as one, a new haka reflecting these elements had to be created and to achieve this aim we invited Sir Derek Lardelli to guide us through a journey of rediscovery and understanding. Derek was a university friend of mine from Ngāti Porou on New Zealand's North Island and regarded as one of the great Māori orators. For a year we explored the building of a new haka with everyone contributing, from the Leadership Group to the players, and we took thoughts on what it meant to be an All Black and what went through the players' minds as they prepared for battle. Through this work, we disrupted the edges of an old ritual. Derek recalled motifs from haka of old as well as creating several new expressions that connected with the modern players. By the end, a new haka was born, one we believed would mould a group of ethnically diverse New Zealanders into a proud, passionate and highly motivated team.

The process took a year, and the new haka, named *Kapa O Pango* – which sat alongside its predecessor, *Ka Mate* – was first performed in Carisbrook Stadium, Dunedin, before a match against South Africa in 2005. During the build-up, the mood in the shed was immense. Every player acknowledged the occasion and its special nature. All of us felt privileged to be adding to the All Blacks' legacy while presenting something new (and unafraid) to the nation, and the world. The media had been forewarned of what was going to happen so that they wouldn't be blindsided during their coverage, but to everyone else it was a surprise. Once we'd started, New Zealand stood still, as one. It was an amazing moment for the All Blacks' legacy, the country, and the players who reconnected with the team's traditions.

In the stadium, the crowd picked up on it straightaway. Tana Umaga, a player of Samoan descent, led the charge and his contribution was later celebrated by all the tribes across *Aotearoa*. From my position in the stands, the hairs on the back of my neck stood up. (Even now, I pinch myself when reflecting on the moment.) Most dramatic of all was a mimed throat-slit gesture that had been incorporated into *Kapa O Pango*'s design. Originally, this had been a concept drawn from some of the meetings with senior players when Derek had asked them about their feelings as they ran onto the field at the start of a Test match.

'We just want to rip the other team's heads off,' said one.

That was all the inspiration Derek needed. The gesture was vicious. It warned the opposition that our dominance was inevitable, though it was later decided that the mime carried an inflammatory tone, and a modification – whereby the slashing gesture was made across the chest – ensured we didn't cause a controversy beyond the game. Still, whenever there's a big match against an old foe, some of the players will make a call-back to the more violent original. Such is life for a driven All Black.

The team went on to win that day, 31–27, and having created a new haka, we worked hard to preserve its core. That's because *Kapa O Pango* was for sole use of the All Blacks, and nobody else. It was our sacred event, and ours alone. We even formed a guardianship group to ensure it wasn't used for anything beyond the group's control. This was an important boundary because the new haka defined *who we were, what we did,* and *what we stood for*. It represented our core. And nobody outside of our ranks was going to mess with it.

We can all change the traditions and activities in our life that might have previously felt sacred or untouchable. There's nothing wrong with tweaking the ceremonies that aren't working for us anymore or even abandoning them altogether. For example, a lot of working teams hold regular Monday morning meetings where the communication can feel disconnected or uninspiring. In such scenarios, it's possible to bring a little novelty to the occasion by asking a different person to drive the discussion every week, or conducting a quick poll, or asking a *Question of the Day* at the beginning. (Example: what was the highlight of your previous working week?) There are couples who make a conscious decision not to download the negative aspects of the day as soon as they walk through the front door after work. Instead, they agree to connect and talk about the good things that have happened. This ritual then sets a positive tone for the rest of the evening.

Keven Mealamu, an All Black who views the haka with great passion, explains how disrupting tradition brought new energy to the group:

> *I led the haka 31 times, with both the* Ka Mate *and* Kapa O Pango *versions, which was an honour because the haka was an important source of power for the All Blacks' culture. The haka was a tradition where we could convey to the world who we were. Whether we were trying to win a Rugby World Cup, a Bledisloe Cup or even a Lions' Tour, it was vital to feel inspired by something bigger than the sport – and ourselves. Sure, we gave our everything to win tournaments. But we also drew a huge amount of energy from the idea that we were pioneers for a country we all loved and part of a legacy that stretched back decades. The people of New Zealand and our native tongue was woven into our every action. And when the team connected to where we came from, we felt unstoppable. Even today I tell myself: My skin might be 45 years old, but my bloodline is 5,000.*
>
> *I always felt a pressure when leading the haka because I didn't want to stuff it up for the team. It was our chance to show the world who we were and what we represented, and before games, my aim was for everyone to feel prepared. To do so, it was important the haka's timing was on point, and we were connected. The players*

and the fans looking on had to feel our energy and passion, and to create that environment we had to show that we possessed the right tempo, that we were clinical – a surging mass of black moving as one, unified by the black of our jersey, and the fern on our chest. Once a haka had been finished it was a bit like turning off a boiling kettle. To start the game well I had to come back down to room temperature, to be calm and calculated, though the fire was still blazing inside me.

In the All Blacks we constantly worked on our culture. While on tour, we weren't just filling our buckets with training, preparation and nutrition, but also with the things that created a connection with the legacy. We honoured it every day, because we'd grown up watching our predecessors in black. I always felt excited to represent my country, and it was my aim to leave the jersey in a better place than when I'd first received it. As a small boy I'd watched Sir Michael Jones, The Iceman. He was of Samoan heritage like me, but he also looked different to the other players in his position – Sir Michael was more dynamic than most. He was fast and explosive too. I spent most of my childhood attempting to score tries like him, and when I played for the All Blacks, I felt proud to be following his footsteps.

The Wero: Writing a 'To Be' List

A person who knows themselves and stays true to their values has a highway to their core. I know this feeling all too well. As I've detailed elsewhere in the book, my upbringing was challenging. Behavioural consistency came later for me because it took me longer than most to grow into myself and define who I was. I then came to understand my core through sport, and I discovered who I needed to be when performing well and what I needed to do to earn the respect of my teammates. I understood that I was old fashioned in my values and my word was my honour. To preserve this spirit, I learned to practise three simple principles. *Know me. Be me. Stay me.* Sticking to them created a route map for *who* and *how* I wanted to be.

- Know me: The ways in which I wanted to act as a leader, or when working on a project with great value. For example, I believed that no one person was more important than anybody else and I sealed deals with a handshake.
- Be me: These were simple, observable behaviours that kept me anchored to my core. Among them: no shortcuts and no corner cutting, even when nobody was watching.
- Stay me: Reminders that ensured I stayed true to my identity and to the *me* I wanted to be at the time. I often met with critical friends to discuss myself and my world, and when seeking feedback, I realised that caution was advisable if I was only hearing what I wanted to hear.

The key to success when employing a mantra, or a code of conduct of this kind, is to develop a series of structures and routines throughout the day that will help us to maintain consistency. One excellent way of doing this is to devise a list that focuses on who you want 'To be' rather than what you want 'To do'. Remember: we are human *beings*, not human *doings* and nailing how we'd like to behave often acts as a subconscious drive that pulls us towards the completion of our designated 'To do' list.

There are times when we all cruise through our day-to-day with an understanding of who we want to be. On other occasions, when life is more chaotic, it's easy to lose sight of our core. But the simple act of writing down a couple of daily cues of how we'd like to behave brings a sense of order and purposefulness to our activities and endeavours. It delivers an awareness of the outside forces that influence us negatively, which then allows us to stand rigid in the face of a situation or person that might otherwise break or bend us. It also helps a person to manage their thoughts and predict their reactions.

For example, it might be that my day has been stuffed with Zoom meetings and phone calls, in which case I'll write down the words 'Be Present' (I want to show up for everyone equally) and 'Be Patient' (because the day will be draining, especially later). On other occasions, an emphasis on being 'Empathetic' and 'Genuine' might be more applicable. Flexibility is important when creating a 'To be' list, because how I want to behave can change from day to day, and even hour to hour. But by regularly writing one, I've been able to remain true to who I am. It's my hope that by using this technique, you'll achieve the same end.

The Library of Learnings

- When building a culture, successful institutions lean into a stable core and encourage radical thought.
- A stable core is an understanding of who the group are, what they do, and what they stand for. For the All Blacks, our core was all about enhancing the jersey (ETJ). For an investigative journalist, a stable core might be the desire to reach the truth of a story, or to right injustice. For a grandparent, it could be to support their kids as they raise a young family.
- Once you've established a stable core, make small, radical changes around the edges. These are experiments that will enhance your day-to-day operations without unsettling your purpose, or long-term goals. This is how you achieve dominance in your field.

CHAPTER 8

We Trumps Me

During my time as a volleyball player, we created a saying that reminded everyone of the team's culture and our desired behaviours. *Don't take the sausage.* This, on the face of it, might have sounded like a jokey, throwaway phrase, but at its heart was a unifying sentiment. Whenever we were together for meals, there was often a queue as we lined up for service. On busy days, the person at the back of the line often got a raw deal and by the time their turn came around all the good stuff, including the sausages, had usually been taken. As a means of ensuring a fair shake for everyone, we took on a selfless attitude whereby everyone showed restraint when filling up their plates, meaning nobody missed out. To *not take the sausage* was to put the needs of the team before any personal wants.

The knock-on effect of this small, but important gesture was undeniable. Subconsciously, it stated three things. The first was that no person was more important than anyone else. The second, that a player who was great for the collective was more valuable than a great player. And finally, there was no title or rank within the squad. This attitude became ingrained and soon impacted every part of our environment. As a result, a powerful camaraderie developed within the teams I played for, such as Pioneer, and I can even remember one or two players fighting over a spot in the backseat of a car, rather than the front, so that their teammate could ride 'shotgun'. (Which most people considered to be the better option.) The concept of *not taking the sausage* was so effective I took it into the Canterbury Crusaders in 1997, where it was embraced by Wayne Smith.

At the Crusaders, this idea was extended into training and matches, usually through thankless 'sacrificial acts' that were critical to the performance of the team. A lot of the time these selfless behaviours went unseen but when they were executed consistently, we generally competed more effectively. At training, everyone performed necessary housekeeping tasks, such as tidiness, without prompting or grumbling. On the field, these sacrificial acts involved a player putting their body on the line for their teammate, or individuals running a series of decoy lines so effectively that our opponents were confused. Then there were the leaders who encouraged and cajoled one another after mistakes. In those moments the Crusaders came together as brothers. No one was left alone, no player was ever isolated, and the shared belief in play was that *we trumps me*.

This concept has since become a cornerstone of every team I've ever worked with, and for good reason. When a feeling of unity takes hold within a group environment, the chances of success increase greatly, especially when sacrificial acts are delivered with authenticity. That's because cultures carrying such an attitude are bonded by respect and love. This then creates a strong familial vibe that's very hard to leave because it feels so supportive. The attractive gravitational force also pulls other talented people to the team, and at the Crusaders we found that a lot of great players wanted to join us after hearing about the culture we had created, on and off the field. The same thing happened in the All Blacks set-up once we'd embraced the spirit of *not taking the sausage*. It's no secret that a lot of New Zealand's best players could easily turn their back on international rugby to make a larger salary overseas. But our boys stayed because the attitude of *we trumps me* had created a connection that money couldn't replace.

Scientifically, there is some evidence to back up the effectiveness of this spirit. In the 1990s, the evolutionary biologist William Muir conducted an experiment where he studied the productivity of chickens. He chose to test his theories with hens because the metrics for success were straightforward – Muir only had to count the number of eggs being laid as a barometer of how well a group was performing. He bred his birds for several generations, after which time his flock was separated into two distinct groups:

1) The average flock: the chickens that laid an OK number of eggs but weren't the stars of the show. They weren't the worst performers; they just weren't the best.
2) The super-flock: the big hitters who produced the largest number of eggs. These 'super-chickens' were the rock stars of the community.

Muir then bred these two groups separately for another six generations where he discovered, weirdly, that the collective sources solely from the average flock was by far the most productive. Every chicken was plump and fully feathered, and their egg production had increased dramatically. Meanwhile, among the super-flock, only three chickens had survived. The rest were dead. It seemed as if the rock stars had only achieved their success during the initial testing phases through physical superiority where they were allowed to thrive. In such an environment, the average chickens hadn't put up much of a fight and everyone cohabited comfortably. But in a group made up only of super-chickens, the flock had pecked one another to pieces until only a few were left standing.

A human super-flock is just as dysfunctional and disruptive. That's because certain people become caught up in their own egos – they want recognition, status and special treatment. As a result, the big hitters won't commit to a shared cause. Sometimes they'll even go out of their way to actively interfere with it, to further their own interests. When the going gets tough, these characters hide or slack off, rather than help their teammates. This creates a series of negative knock-on effects, among them an erosion in trust, loyalty and team culture. As we know, when the culture in a group dies, the connection dies with it. The team then falls apart. That said, it's not impossible to win with a super-flock, but the success is often short-lived because any unity is unsustainable over time.

When I first joined the Canterbury Crusaders, they were a super-flock. So too were the All Blacks. That's because the pervading thought in sport at the time stated that success was best achieved by picking the superstars – the strongest men or women in the room – and giving them all the resources and power. But the results in both cases were no different to the conclusions drawn from William Muir's chicken experiment. Both the early versions of Crusaders and All Blacks I'd worked with were brought down by internal aggression, disruption and waste. And like Muir, it became my view that there was no room for super-flock characters, and instead, a successful team needed everyone if it was to perform to its optimum. This truth was equally applicable to the contexts of business, public services and creative projects. In fact, there's a chance you might even recognise some of the characteristics of a super-flock in your working group. (I'll talk through the telltale signs shortly.)

This idea had previously been recognised by the world's greatest heavyweight boxer, Muhammad Ali, when he delivered the shortest-ever poem to Harvard University in 1975. Entitled *Me, We,* his prose was deliberately left open to interpretation, but one recorded meaning was that the concept loosely echoed the idea of *not taking the sausage.* The 'me' was said to be a reference to the individual and their sense of ownership, personal responsibility and self-awareness. The 'we' acknowledged teamwork, camaraderie and a shared work ethic. Ali had an ego. However, he also understood that so much more was achievable when a team came together for a shared cause. He, like Muir, had recognised the dangers of working in a super-flock.

The *Me, We* concept was later adopted by Wayne Smith and myself as we reworked the foundations of the Crusaders dynasty back in 1997. In doing so, we identified three symptoms of a super-flock environment.

- The trait of silence: People sat quietly without contributing anything of value in meetings or discussions. When they did speak, it was usually to spread negativity in the shadows. Beware the silent one.

- The trait of secrecy: Some individuals were known to scheme away from the group, forming alliances with other negative personalities. Together they made plans, formed cliques and disrupted the harmony of the team. Beware the whisperers.
- The trait of self: When a person was only focused on themselves and personal gain their attitude yelled: *What do I get?* Instead, they should have been asking: *What can I do?* Beware the individual who sticks their hand *out* rather than putting their hand *up*.

I remember witnessing some of this behaviour during my early days with the Canterbury Crusaders. At one point a player became so frustrated at being dropped from the starting XV, he refused to leave the team bus. Rather than joining with the pre-match preparation and supporting his brothers, he remained in his seat and sulked. (This player was coming to the end of his career, and after we'd spoken to him, he modified his behaviour slightly. He still sulked. He just sulked away from the others.) During my early years with the All Blacks, where the individual trumped the group, I often noticed a cluster of players huddling together after matches. At first, I thought they were debriefing the performance, but I later learned they were planning their *court session* for the night – those boozy get-togethers in which the senior players acted as judges (hence the name). These super-flock types created rules for the others to follow in a series of hardcore drinking games where punishments were dished out to anyone who failed. This ritual created an atmosphere of fear, and in what was a survival of the fittest, cliques formed, and one or two individuals were treated more harshly than others.

If a rot of this kind is to be treated, the traits of silence, secrecy and self must be tackled. At that point in the All Blacks story, Wayne Smith was the coach, having joined from the Crusaders in 2000, and he immediately recognised the issues in play as being symptomatic of a super-flock. He then worked to tear down the three barriers and set about righting the wrongs in several ways. Meanwhile, I helped him to remind the players of their history and we introduced a series of techniques, tools and strategies that I'd previously used elsewhere in my career to create a positive team culture around the truth that *we trumps me*. These were:

- Co-opetition.
- Whinge up, but don't whinge down.
- Values cards.
- Who's in the frame?
- The treasure chest. (Better than before.)

We engaged with these activities every day. They nourished the team and created a camaraderie that was incredibly powerful, especially when transferred to the field. I'll explain them in detail now, but it's important to recognise that they're effective in all contexts. Rugby, like life, is a rough and unpredictable business. From time to time, a team will need to dig deep, especially if their backs have been pinned to a wall. And in such circumstances, if the demands of the individual take priority over the unity of the group, failure is inevitable. However, if that collective can remember that *we trumps me*, and the people within it love and support one another, they'll become a resilient opponent.

> **The Courageous Conversation:** *Are the symptoms of super-flock present anywhere in your life?* Think of someone you may need to have a meaningful conversation with regarding this topic. Whether it's to praise or address something difficult, plan the moment and commit to doing it within the next 72 hours.

Co-opetition

In some team environments there's a high level of internal competition, which is healthy and to be encouraged. In sport it tends to happen when two or three players vie for a certain position within the starting line-up. In business, it might be that a handful of people are pushing for promotion to an open role within the company. In these situations, the individuals involved can either compete against one another, or they can co-operate. When competing, they run the risk of putting their own needs before those of the team, which can result in the traits of silence, secrecy and self. In co-operating, they might allow their rivals to steal an edge. When I first arrived at the All Blacks and the super-flock was alive and well, there was a fierce level of competition for places in each position, but it was unhealthy. The incumbents blocked their rivals, and self-preservation became a priority. At times, the super-flock characters spent too much time belittling their challengers in front of others rather than working to improve the team.

The positive approach to such a scenario is *co-opetition*. As the name suggests, this is a process that combines 'competition' with 'co-operation' as several battling individuals agree to shrug aside their egos and personal ambitions to fight for the greater cause. Rather than focusing on point scoring or one-upmanship, any rivalries are used as fuel to improve the overall strength of the group. For example, imagine that three hookers are vying for a starting position in the All Blacks. Each one works hard during the week to earn their spot. But rather than undermining or belittling one another, the players co-opt skill drills and offer up helpful tactical observations and comments to one another. When the starting line-up is announced, the sidelined players are given 24 hours to self-reflect and accept the decision. It's then their job to help the selected hooker prepare for game day, and they must commit to it genuinely and unselfishly. Meanwhile, the selected hooker should show compassion to his rivals and encourage them to push him every day. In doing so, everyone enhances the culture of the team and the power of their performances.

Whinge Up, But Don't Whinge Down

There's a well-known character in a super-flock that must be dealt with at all costs. Known as *The Grey Person,* this character is easily spotted because they tend to display two very distinct characteristics. When placed in an environment where team contributions are valued, they generally say nothing and offer very little to the group. However, once away from a figure of authority, The Grey Person becomes the expert on everything. They know better than the leaders and are highly critical of their peers. While this behaviour isn't overtly disruptive at first, it can be insidious, acting like a cancer.

To handle The Grey Person, they must be manoeuvred into a position where they'll feel compelled to give but not take. This starts by bringing them into the team's culture. Familiarise them with the group's identity, vision and standards because often, in many situations like this, difference isn't the key issue, disconnection is. If this is still an issue, then remind them that they joined the team, the team didn't join them. Finally, install a system whereby everyone is allowed to complain, but only if their issues are communicated vertically, and directly, towards the group's leaders, rather than across the hierarchy to peers, or below, which is the favoured technique of The Grey Person. This ensures that any constructive criticisms are heard and are actionable, without undermining the team's effort. (Which is what happens when complaints are made horizontally.) As Steve Hansen used to say: *the moaner must moan to the moanee.* This is important because, as stated in Chapter Six, the standards we walk past are the standards we're willing to accept and it's upon the group to police this behaviour. If a person sees their peers whinging across or below, it's their duty to call them out.

Value Cards

A few years ago, I attended a Hall of Fame event for the Canterbury Crusaders. A lot of the players I'd worked with were in attendance, and halfway through the dinner, one of the inductees, Justin Marshall, stood up and waved his wallet about.

'Who's still got one of these?' he shouted, pulling out a red credit-card-sized piece of laminated paper.

When I looked closely, I realised Justin was holding the values card. They had been given to the players and management in 1998 and featured a series of cues reminding the holder of who the Crusaders were, what we did, and what we stood for. At the time, the cards were held dear by the team. So much so that some of the old boys in attendance still carried them around 25 years later.

On the front was a list of values created by the team's members. Some were performance related; others were personal disciplines:

- Attitude – there is always a way.
- Honesty – to yourself and each other.
- Pride – in everything we do.
- Ruthless – take, don't wait.
- Relentless – never give in.
- Kaizen – small improvements every day.
- Enjoyment – contribute to this.
- B, S and G – blood, sweat and guts.

Meanwhile in the middle, along the fold, was a signed pledge:

I, **NAME***, a fearless Crusader will honour this pledge:*
We few, we lucky few,
For he today that sheds his blood with me shall be my brother,
All things are ready if our minds be so,
Brother to brother – yours through good times and bad.

These cards played an invaluable role in amplifying the message throughout the team that *we trumps me*, though they weren't given out to every player or management team member, not immediately anyway. Instead, every member of the Canterbury Crusaders had to earn their right to carry one, and they did so by displaying the values[*] mentioned on the card. (They were originally listed in a tour folder so

---

[*] Values are different to standards. When differentiating the two, it helps to think of them accordingly: Values are the way a team goes about their business. Standards are rooted in what the group stands for.

everyone in the team knew about them.) Meanwhile, the Crusaders had several designated *custodians*, and it was their job to distribute the cards to those people they believed worthy. Over time, everybody received one, but under a very strict rule: if a player, or a member of management believed that they'd not upheld the values of the team, or they'd acted selfishly or put themselves before the group, they had to hand back their card. In essence, they became the guardian of their own values and this process created a wonderful level of trust because nobody wanted anyone looking over their shoulders, or to feel as if they were being judged.

The honesty within this self-policing system was impressive too. On any given day, I'd go back to my hotel room to see that two or three cards had been pushed under my door. Usually, it was for a small misdemeanour, an action the individual felt had put them below the expected team or personal standards. But some of the reasons for handing them in seemed ridiculous to me and I often asked people to change their minds. They rarely did. The Crusaders believed so vehemently in the concept of *we* over *me,* that not to stick to the values on the card meant a player had failed the group, and they always worked doubly hard to earn theirs back. (Also, if a player failed to self-police any misdemeanours, their behaviour was pounced upon by the others, because to mess with the values was to mess with the soul of the team.) Seeing this process first hand was very special. I realised it was one of the few occasions in a group environment where it was possible to observe the beating heart of a team's culture, and as I moved forward into other sporting environments, I made sure to introduce the values card system to each one.

Sometimes a collective, or certain elements within it, will refuse to get behind a shared set of values. When that happens, it's important the team leaders look back at their actions because there's a good chance they haven't communicated the determined identity and vision properly. Under those circumstances, the Leadership Group within the team – such as the captains or department heads – should be reintroduced to the concept, so they can become advocates for it. It also helps to redefine the values from time to time because the process tends to re-educate the whole group on *what they mean* and *why they're there*. During these sessions any doubters should be asked for their opinions on certain things. This will help to bring them in line, because once a person has been given ownership of a process, they're more likely to work for it.

Who's in the Frame?

Whenever the All Blacks squad reviewed a match together, we always watched the footage on a large video screen, pausing the action every now and then to play a game called, 'Who's in the Frame?' This usually happened when a transitional moment was being studied – attack turning into defence, defence turning into attack, and so on – events where the players were expected to react instantly, switching momentum and mindset. One example would be an opposition player turning over the ball and racing towards our goal line. In such a moment, an All Black's job was to give everything by chasing their opponent down. And having frozen the recorded footage, the coach, or whoever was conducting the review, would then ask a simple question.

Who's in the frame?

With the image held fast, the players that were visible on the screen – those that were doing everything in their power to gain ground – were counted. If there were five or six All Blacks in view, this was taken as a good indication that *we* was trumping *me*. If only one or two players were giving chase and the rest were walking back, or somewhere off camera, there was a problem.

These turnovers, and the sacrificial acts that come with them, are important, because a) they give everybody the chance to make a difference in the moment, and b) they help a team to work to their maximum. In a non-sporting scenario, a comparable example would be the leader that cleans up the communal breakout area as they're about to head home, so that everyone can walk into a welcoming space the following morning. It's the receptionist who smiles at everyone walking through the door, even when they're having a crappy day themselves. It's the department store manager who mucks in with the stocktake. These are the plays that turn *me* into *we*. But we can only harness their power if we pause the action and ask the question: *Who's in the frame?*

That's because recognising these sacrificial acts is a motivator. What you measure, you move, and if people are aware that they're being acknowledged for their efforts in some way, they're more than likely to execute them. Whenever I've worked with a team, awards have been presented to a player or group whenever they've excelled in their sacrificial acts. That's because a person striving to be number one in the thankless tasks helps the group to operate as an effective unit. In doing so they give themselves the greatest chance of realising their talents, and the talents of everyone around them.

Case Study: Building the Kingdom

The best kind of leadership comes from the quiet person, the player who leads by example. Characters of this kind are generally humble, but not weak, and their personalities are powerful enough to build kingdoms and forge cultures. Keven 'Kevy' Mealamu was one such individual, and he came into the All Blacks as a quiet, softly spoken, humble young man, but he soon grew into a powerful and influential figure inside the group. Kevy had a radiant aura, he exuded presence, and I never witnessed a more respected person in my time within the All Blacks.

One story sums up his unifying personality. I remember walking down the back of the bus on our way back from training. I was looking for Kevy because he led the team's standards off the field and drove all things 'culture' within the group. At the time we were in the middle of a Bledisloe Cup series – a trophy we'd held for a while – and the silverware needed a little TLC.

'Kevy, the Bledisloe is looking shabby,' I said, sitting down next to him. 'It's all smudged and dirty, and I get the feeling the boys are taking the fact we hold it for granted. Can you get a couple of the younger boys to clean it for us?'

There was a long pause. Then Kevy looked at me and said, 'Sure, Bertie. And I'll do it with them.'

That night, I went up to the team room to get some water. In the middle of the floor was Kevy with three or four of the young boys. They were sitting cross-legged, surrounded by cleaning cloths, polishing the Bledisloe Cup. As they did so, Kevy spoke to them about past All Black campaigns, the successful and not-so successful, and the stories associated with them. When it came to feeding the culture and building the kingdom, there was no better player.

These are some of his thoughts on the process.

Having an understanding of the All Blacks culture helped to keep me grounded in difficult times, as it did for a lot of the players. This was important because a person can become out of touch when they don't work 40, 50 or 60 hours a week and it would have been easy for any of us in the All Blacks to take our position as international rugby players for granted. Learning about the history of the jersey and the sacrifices that went into the All Blacks story kept our feet on the ground. We worked our hardest on the field and paid our respects off it. That attitude helped us to build a kingdom around ourselves and to become better players. And a better team. I knew that when I'd had a hard day, it was really a good day, because that's what the role of being an All Black demanded.

Life was very different when I first started playing international rugby in 2002. Back then, there were one or two older players in the squad who had cut their teeth in the amateur era, and they looked at their roles very differently to the new guys. They were more relaxed and carefree, and not as demanding on themselves during training. The younger generation were different: we ensured we were on top of our game every day, and I remember many of the new All Blacks stretched in the hallways after training and went to bed at a time that ensured we could be at our best the next day. Those things hadn't been a given in the past and I was proud to be a part of that change. As far as I was concerned, I was an All Black 24/7; I spent long periods away from home and missed important birthdays, weddings and other special occasions to play for the team. I was driven to do everything possible to improve on and off the field, and to never have an off day.

And I constantly asked myself these questions:

How am I going to fill the jersey this week?

How do I want to be remembered?

How do I want my teammates to remember me?

These challenges fuelled my desire and passion to give to this great legacy. I always felt honoured to be able to contribute to the All Blacks culture.

The Treasure Chest (Better than Before)

In 1999, while working with the New Zealand cricket team, we attempted to drive home the concept that, no matter what had taken place in the team's past, they could be BTB – or *better than before*. During this phase, we created a list of things the Black Caps could improve upon both at the macro and micro level. On the macro, they had never beaten England at Lord's, the home of cricket, and had never won more than one Test match in a series while playing in England. On the micro, specific personal and team goals were targeted relating to the squad's improvement in bowling, batting and fielding. By accepting this aspiration, the individuals inside the team were inspired to work together and to support one another. We monitored these areas, acknowledging and celebrating any successes that might have happened by compiling an ongoing list of BTB achievements on an honours board.

Finally, a treasure chest was introduced, an old toolbox I'd picked up from a $2 store. *But it represented so much more.* Watch any pirate film and you'll see a dusty wooden crate, brimming with gold and diamonds. The toolbox was something similar, and while it didn't look like something you might find on the boat of Captain Jack Sparrow, we created a fictional narrative that stated it had been 'rescued' from a metaphorical galleon named the *BTB Endeavour*, aptly named by John Graham, the former All Black and New Zealand Cricket Manager. Once opened, every member of the team and management staff was then encouraged to put an item of importance inside the treasure chest. The hope was that its contents would remind the Black Caps of their unity, spirit and the effort required to hit their macro and micro targets.

Day by day, the treasure chest filled up with interesting trinkets, keepsakes and literal cues. Someone entered their values card as a reminder of how we wanted to live. Another player added a packet of chewing gum to encourage his teammates to stick with it. The list went on . . . A candle so the team could burn brightly; a box of matches to light our fire, even when we were burnt out; and a Tootsie Roll to warn the group not to bite off more than they could chew. The treasure chest became an ever-present fixture in the changing sheds, and the players rummaged through it and drew inspiration from the contents.

A concept like this can work brilliantly for a business team or group looking to build camaraderie during an important project, or for a period of intense effort. In such a situation, each item initially acts as a humorous, emotive or inspirational trigger when placed inside the treasure chest. But the psychological impact of building such a collection runs much deeper than a laugh for dark moments or a mental boost in tough times. The simple fact that every team member has contributed to its contents should work as an indicator of the collaboration and care running through the team. This then generates a deeper connection among its participants. Unity is created in the giving. The results that flow afterwards are a happy by-product.

Te Puna o te Kī: The Power of the Cube

Whenever I'm working with a team, I like to introduce them to the concept of The Cube – a small, three-dimensional wooden box with six equal square faces. From a distance it looked like a variant of the Rubik's Cube, though its psychological purpose was very different.

BECOME UNSTOPPABLE

Each face was designed so that the owner could stick several images or inspirational messages to the outside, transforming The Cube into a portable visual tool. When used correctly, these additions reminded the Crusader, Black Cap or All Black of their values, BTBs, inspirational figures from the past, and the team's history. (The All Blacks version had ETJ, or *Enhance the Jersey*, printed in every corner.) One side had a whiteboard-style surface so the individual's 'To be' list for the day could be written down. Another was mirrored, to encourage the holder to pause and reflect. (Some mirrors had the words, 'If not me, who . . . ? If not now, when?' printed on the top and bottom.) When the cube was opened a space was revealed for more images, notes or messages. These elements, when combined, told the owner that *we trumps me*.

When these cubes were given to a Crusader, Black Cap or All Black, every recipient was presented with a brief guide for how it should be used: *The Cube acts as a visual representation of the challenges we accept as we embark on our tours of duty. With each twist and turn of The Cube, images appear that are reflective, thought provoking and emotionally charged.*

The document then detailed several guidelines for how to make the most of The Cube's inspirational power:

- It is a very individual thing. You can put up a certain image for a given day that means something to you.
- Your captain may ask you to bring it to a meeting.
- The Leadership Group may ask you to apply a certain image for a certain day.
- It would be good if you kept The Cube in a prominent location in your room where you will catch the images you selected for the day . . . often.
- When used appropriately it will provide a powerful force that will irresistibly propel you and the team to our goal.
- We keep The Cube's presence within our circle.

Whenever these cubes were handed out, the players became very creative with their additions. Some All Blacks affixed a picture of the jersey to one side, as a reminder that it was the blood in our veins and the air that we breathed. *It powered up the All Blackness.* Others used a picture of a mongrel dog as a representation of the spirit required to be an All Black: *When your body says, 'No' and your head says, 'Maybe not', it's the mongrel dog heart that keeps you going.* One or two players even selected a picture of the NBA legend Michael Jordan because he'd believed the greatest achievement of any team was the ability to connect both physically and mentally every time they stepped onto a court. When combined, The Cube's imagery inspired the players to put their bodies on the line, individually and collectively.

The cubes were then left in a prominent place at the players' homes, or in their rooms on tour, so they could see them every day. They put them in their lockers before Tests and carried them around in their gear bags. Sometimes, during a team meeting, one of the leaders would hand out 35 copies of the same image, such as an inspirational player from our past with a message for the moment, and the squad was asked to stick it to one side of their cube. This joint exercise created an invisible umbilical cord between the group while strengthening the brotherhood that was already in place. Whenever we played games, I was usually the last person out of the shed. I often looked around the locker room and saw a cube at the seat of every player, all of them with different inspirational images or messages. That told me the group was determined to strengthen their *we* by powering up their *me*.

The Wero: Enter the Cube

When making a cube of your own (and I recommend you do) it's not a requirement to spend a chunk of money on a specially designed wooden box. A cardboard one will do the trick, if it's robust enough. What's important is how the cube is used and what's applied to it. But I would recommend following these cues to maximise its impact.

1) Encourage everyone in your team to create a cube of their own, and make it a part of the discussion. While this is an individual device, it should also be used to connect the group. (Don't worry: it's just as powerful if you want to make one solely for yourself.)
2) Use inspirational imagery that connects you to your past, present and future.
3) Apply messaging that connects you to the collective rather than any personal glory, although some individuality is encouraged.
4) Use a mirrored side to remind yourself that you are accountable for your actions and a 'whiteboard' side for your 'To Be' list.
5) Always leave it in a prominent place.

As a connective device, The Cube might seem like a small object. But when used correctly, its impact can be inspirational, unifying and defining. That said, its power might not resonate with everyone reading it – some people will breeze through this section and dismiss it as being impractical. However, the success of such a project rests in its delivery. The Cube should be set up as a regular part of the connective process. The way in which it's used must feel fresh and invigorating and connecting to the challenges of the moment so it doesn't feel like a one-off, or gimmicky.

One way of doing this is to call a weekly meeting in which The Cube is updated, while encouraging one person from the team to drive the discussion. For example, it might be that the collective is facing a deadline and a week of intense work. In this case, the team leader might bring a replicated photo of a famous inspirational figure and ask each person to stick it to The Cube. Alternatively, they might pose a question: *What person inspires you to do what you do?* An image of that person should then be fixed to The Cube the next day. It also helps to change up the individual driving the discussion each week, to keep everyone involved and connected. Because, as we all know, ownership feeds commitment.

The Library of Learnings

- *We trumps me*: this is a feeling of authentic unity within a team environment. When it takes hold, the chances of success increase greatly.
- *Me* serves *we* and *we* strengthens *me*.
- A group full of hierarchical individuals (known as a super-flock) can be identified by the traits of silence, secrecy and self.
- To foster a *we trumps me* environment, a group should lean into co-opetition, effort plays and values cards.
- Remember: *Don't take the sausage.*

CHAPTER 9

The Belonging Place

Dangling from the doorway in the All Blacks shed was a long line of rope. A regular fixture in the space since 2004, the harvested and intertwined flax, made by the *tangata whenua* (the people of the land), was dyed with three colours: silver, to represent the fern; black to signify the jersey; and red to represent the blood. Everywhere the All Blacks went, the rope* travelled too, because it was a part of our unifying story: no matter a player's birthplace – the Cook Islands, Fiji or Tokelau – the colour pumping through our veins was the same as the person sitting alongside us. Meanwhile, everyone's ancestors were buried in the ground, whether they were Māori or non-Māori. Their blood had been mixed with the soil. The fern pinned to our jerseys had grown in it. *The red told us we all belonged.*

This idea started at a very early age. When a child is born in New Zealand, one of their first gifts is often a rugby ball, or a black, baby-sized replica jersey. As they grow older, our kids and grandkids watch the team performing the haka on TV. But long before they've seen it, or even heard of it, they'll have *felt* it. I know, because I've got a grandson who's barely out of nappies and he currently does the haka instinctively in front of the telly. For a lot of All Blacks, the jersey

---

* The rope also represented our passage through time, and fixed to the line were a series of scalps, each one marking a win over a nation or a victory in a landmark series. Hanging alongside them was the occasional black thread to indicate a defeat, because it was important not to lose sight of the chastening lessons from history.

and its sense of belonging runs deep from the very beginning, long before they've played for the team. The rope and all its stories only add to that vibe, so much so that a lot of players even touched it on their way to the field.

'It wasn't so much seeing the rope that created the power,' said Keven Mealamu. 'It was understanding it. It emerged at the same time we created *Kapa O Pango*. The in-depth learning of what every movement, and what every word meant, and how that connected to us really strengthened that sense of belonging and identity for me. My brothers too. We were all one, playing under the banner of the black jersey. I felt that every day when I touched the rope, and we performed *Kapa O Pango*.'

A sense of belonging is just about the most important thing a collective of talented athletes can possess – or builders, or salespeople, or scientists, or public servants, for that matter. The intense feeling reassures a group that they're working for a cause much bigger or greater than themselves, which is important because unless you can encourage a collective of individuals made up of different backgrounds and personalities to buy into *who you are*, *where you're from* and *what you're doing*, you'll never receive their full commitment. Yes, they might push themselves for a while, but not for long, and they certainly won't give you 100 per cent, all the time. However, if a group has a strong sense of belonging, it's highly likely they'll deliver their best in tough times because they're being powered and sustained by a shared vision or belief. *They are connected.*

For example, elite soldiers are bonded by a sense of honour and the fact they're defending their country; doctors and nurses working in an accident and emergency ward connect over the understanding that they're saving lives; and volunteers in a charity shop know their efforts for a chosen cause are making a difference. Our higher purpose as All Blacks was the jersey and everything it represented, including its history. Our belief was that the individual and the team should leave it in a better state than when they found it and this legacy was far more intimidating than any opponent. It forced us to be better, and we did so together, knowing that a significant achievement was unlikely without a significant connection.

I first discovered the power of belonging at a young age, mainly because I didn't have a lot of it. As I mentioned earlier, during my time in the children's home, I knew that everyone around me was an outcast and none of us felt like we'd belonged to anything or anyone. Instead, we floated through a superficial existence without any real link to a tangible *other* and as a result I experienced an unsteadiness in everything I did. Even though we were well cared for inside the institution – and I'd found a common link with the other kids because we were all what I called 'Unchosen Ones' – there was an emptiness. I often sought reassurance and validation from the children around me, usually by asking direct questions ('Am I doing this right?') or by subtly looking around to gauge the group's response to an event or instruction before acting or expressing my own opinions. I had a sense of trepidation. I criticised myself and framed my contributions in a way that downplayed my real value. All this was a direct response to the belief that I didn't belong.

That feeling followed me around after I'd left the care home, once I'd realised that isolation and a lack of belonging had defined my upbringing. This was amplified further having started out in the world of sports psychology, which was considered taboo in cricket, netball and rugby. In the early 1990s, my work, which today might have been considered trailblazing and cutting edge, was viewed with scepticism. There were times in the early days when I was very alone and gripped by insecurities. It was a painful reminder of my days in the orphanage where everybody felt excluded and worthless.

But this heavy shadow soon became a powerful teacher. It showed me that belonging was an important aspect in the culture of any team, and once I'd become successful with the Canterbury Crusaders in 1998, and my role in their progress was credited, I learned that connection was love. In sport, this feeling was represented by the sense that a person would do anything for their mates* and I tried to build it wherever I went. In teams like the All Blacks or the Black Caps this feeling spoke loudly. It said: *I am here, and I belong. I gain strength from others who stand with me, grow with me, live with me, and fight with me.* I then realised that if a team accessed a strong sense of belonging it became a limitless power source, but only if everyone approached the concept with a genuine sense of commitment. It wasn't enough to pay lip service to the idea. Instead, the players had to accept they were buying into the pursuit of a shared dream – a championship title, a cup or a legacy – rather than focusing solely on some of the parameters that underpinned high performance, like physical strength or tactics.

From 2004, the All Blacks recognised this truth. Wherever we played, the team made sure to create a belonging place, or a *tūrangawaewae*, a word which, when translated, meant *a place to stand.* During my time, this was done by immersing the players in our history, and we travelled with a container filled with important artefacts from our past, such as the rope and team memorabilia. There was also an honours board celebrating the All Blacks legends, and photos from our past trophy wins and tournament victories. These items were shipped ahead of the squad and positioned around the walls of our team room and changing shed. With a little work, the *tūrangawaewae* soon felt like a home away from home – a space filled with photos, memories and stories that tapped into the souls of the people within the group. Everyone was reminded that we belonged to the All Blacks family and were battling for its cause, no matter

---

* In truth, we said that we would die for one another, though I appreciate that for most people, the thought of dying for the person alongside them, while compelling in a setting where physical endeavour and suffering is a major factor – such as sport or military service – probably isn't as applicable in most walks of life. (Whenever the All Blacks left the shed before a match, Wayne Smith used to say the famous sentence, 'It's a great day to die.') In this context, the concept of 'dying' is really a catchall term for 'sacrifice' and it can show up in all sorts of ways. One example of this might be the team leader who sacrifices their day off to help their workmates during periods of high workload.

our age, place of origin, religious beliefs, sexual orientation or political views.

The knock-on effect of this environment was powerful. Before every game, I watched the players as they prepared in the shed. Whatever the occasion, hardly a word was spoken, but a thousand were shared and I noticed the nods that were exchanged between certain individuals. The glances that said: 'We're going into war together today, brother. And, boy, am I glad I've got you beside me.' Given the work we'd done in understanding our identity, vision and standards, everybody knew who the All Blacks were, and what we stood for. When set inside a feeling of belonging, this understanding became a superpower. It encouraged everybody to give everything to the cause.

This sense of belonging was later expanded in 2023, on the eve of the Rugby World Cup in France, when every All Black was gifted with a *pounamu* – a greenstone pendant sourced from the Arahura River on the west coast of the South Island. The stone, which could only be found in that area and was known to be the darkest jade in the world, had been delivered to us as a 35kg boulder before being shaped into 55 individual amulets, one for each player and management team member. In New Zealand, it was believed that every *pounamu* contained a *mauri*, or lifeforce. This was important because without a *mauri*, there could be no *mana* – the power and essence of the people, *or the tribe*. Importantly, it was believed that the actions of the *pounamu* wearer enhanced or diminished the *mauri* contained inside, according to their behaviour, and it worked as a reminder to always act in the right way, even when no one was watching. It was our hope that the stone would remain with the player and his family for generations so that the wearer, and whoever they passed it on to, would feel a powerful connection to the legacy.

To create an even greater sense of belonging among the All Blacks squad, the presentation of these pendants took place deep inside the Arras tunnels in northern France, where New Zealand's troops had played a significant role during World War I. This was a momentous occasion for everyone in the group. Though we were thousands of miles away from New Zealand, everybody felt a deep sense of connection to our homeland. On collecting his *pounamu*, Dane Coles, a hooker with 90 Test match appearances, experienced a real sense of pride. 'There was a responsibility to represent those men after the sacrifices they had made in the war,' he said. 'It made me proud to be a Kiwi. I knew I belonged to a power higher than myself and receiving a *pounamu* reminded me that the best way to honour them was to do the business at the Rugby World Cup.'

This reaction revealed the stone as a valuable source of power. If a person or team can draw on a higher sense of belonging, even when they're physically detached from it, they will feel both inspired and determined. The creative mind will dream and design. The problem-solving brain will crack codes. The All Black will be clinical in their execution. Or as Dane said, they'll *do the business.* All because they want to contribute to a cause much greater than themselves.

How to Create Belonging

I've found that when building a sense of belonging within a group it's important to remember that every individual operates on one of three levels of performance.

LEVEL ONE: This is the individual that plays for themselves. They might be a brilliant rugby player, or brain surgeon, or Wall Street trader, but they're only interested in their own performances, and their own results.

LEVEL TWO: A person who plays for their tribe. They're a team player and highly committed.

LEVEL THREE: The person who's prepared to give everything for the brother or sister alongside them. This is a characteristic found in top level sport and the military elite, such as the Kiwi, UK or US special forces.

Belonging is the well from which these levels are drawn. So, if an athlete doesn't feel a sense of connection to their teammates, they will more than likely find themselves in Level One, whereas an athlete with a strong bond is more likely to be bracketed in Levels Two or

Three. There's no sugar coating the truth, though: belonging can be very difficult to build in a team setting, especially if the concept hasn't previously been practised by a group. Genuine connection takes years to create and sustain. It also requires constant care. And it certainly can't be turned on and off like a tap.

For example, when I first joined with the All Blacks, there was a camaraderie between the players, but not a deeply rooted connection. They got on with one another. They were able to compete and function in their roles. But their belonging was loose, a lot of the players were being driven by ego and personal gain rather than collective success, and in such a superficial situation the team's flimsy connection will always be exposed, especially if the heat comes on. When attempting to create belonging, we learned it was important to ask questions of everyone inside the group. Among them:

- What are you prepared to give for the cause?
- How far will you go to help your brothers and sisters?

This is not a step by step process and it's important to establish whether a group is being dominated by a Level One, Two or Three attribute. When working with a team for the first time, I'll dig into the connections between the individuals working together by drawing a diagram comprising circles and lines. Each circle represents a person, and every line marks their connection to the people around them. The more connections, the more lines join each other. If everyone in the team is familiar with one another, and they work well and connect with each other often, there will be many lines between them. On the other hand, a team of strangers with no working relationships will have very few connecting lines. The ideal scenario in such a diagram is a blackout, where so many links have been established that the spaces between each person are filled in. Such an example would suggest a strong sense of connection within the group: the blacker the spaces between individuals, the more powerful the team.

Improving the number of lines between teammates is the key to

success because connection enhances belonging, which then draws other like-minded people to the cause in a multiplier effect. That's why a lot of high-performing teams have previously looked to belonging as an effective method for achieving sustained success, from the creative minds at a successful tech firm to an all-conquering Premier League-winning team. Their attitude? *Your vibe attracts your tribe.* Weirdly, this concept is often overlooked everywhere else, a fact that's usually confirmed to me when I visit businesses and organisations and present them with a concept I call *The Drivers of Culture* – a list that contains the following elements . . .

- Vision: Where the team see themselves going; their hopes and aspirations.
- Values/standards: The behaviours the team set for themselves to help them succeed.
- Environment: Their place of work.
- Belonging: The sense of connection to each other and the team's cause.

When I then ask the room to pick one of these categories as their foundation for success – a platform from which everything else should be built – they rarely select 'belonging', if ever. But the reality is this: a group without belonging as their foundation will fragment under pressure. That's because when things get tough, everyone within the collective will do their own thing. In a sporting context, a team without a foundation of belonging might compete effectively for a short period of time, but as soon as the pressure cranks up, they tend to become individualistic and things can fall apart. This is the same for a department in a company, a group of friends working together on a project or challenge, and even a family working towards a common goal. However, with a genuine sense of connection, everyone in the team will feel valued, supported and included. The greater the sense of belonging, the bigger the commitment. The bigger the commitment, the stronger the resilience. And a team with resilience will more than likely stay in the fight longer, push harder and overrun their opponents – no matter who they are.

The world's greatest teams have long understood that to live well, mix well and perform well, it's important to have belonging as the foundation, because it taps into a deep-rooted psychological drive. As humans we all have a fundamental need for connection and inclusion. For as long as we've wandered the planet, the idea of being part of a group has been hardwired into our consciousness – instinctively, we understand that by connecting to a tribe, or group, we facilitate our survival. On a basic level, there's safety in numbers, and we are motivated to belong. (And when we do so, our emotional wellbeing improves.) That's why a person with belonging will possess loyalty. They're also more likely to make an emotional investment in the people around them. Yes, a team's vision and values can guide strategy, and a positive environment will foster a productive working culture. But to truly become a resilient force and maintain a healthy organisational culture, it's imperative to cultivate a sense of belonging.

To achieve this end, several simple rules should be followed:

#1 Authenticity Is Everything

Belonging is a by-product of the meaningful interactions that take place between teammates. But those interactions must be genuine. It's not about completing a to-do list, rattling off a series of emails to the right people at the right time, or performing the bare minimum of communication with the person alongside you. A lot of people think that they're doing enough by simply moving through their shift and saying 'Hello' to everybody they encounter, but that's not the case at all. It needs to be much, much deeper than that. Sure, when you next walk into your office, or even your neighbourhood store or coffee shop, say 'Hello' to the people around you. But also look them in the eye or shake their hand. Then check on their wellbeing and ask if there's anything you can do for them that day, if it's appropriate. Genuine engagement, from the heart, is known to kickstart an incredible chain reaction where the result is that everyone gives their all to the tasks in hand. This is the culture we fostered with the All Blacks.

> Think back to your connections from the past few days. Were they genuine? Note down some ways in which you might have been able to connect with the people around you better. Commit to strengthening these bonds moving forward.

#2 Inclusive Connections Must Be Built

The All Blacks were a diverse group with different belief systems and attitudes, but despite this, we were able to cultivate a *team first* philosophy very quickly. This was achieved by first breaking down the cliques that had formed within the group, while putting measures in place that would stop them from forming again. We became deliberate with our rooming lists so that people from different age groups, races, religions and experience levels shared a space during tours. As a result, they learned about the differences between them and found new ways to connect. This structure was repeated with table placings at dinners and group nights out.

Elsewhere, we held social events where one of the different cultural groups within the squad took responsibility for the theme, curating the food, music, dance and any other traditions that were unique to their specific culture. For example, the Pacific Island boys sometimes organised kava sessions, a traditional ceremony based around the Fijian drink of the same name. While not alcoholic, kava had a 'mildly narcotic' and sedative quality to it that helped everyone to relax. (It was nicknamed 'grog' and could sometimes send you on a bit of a journey.) Based on Fijian traditions, the liquid was pulped and served from a communal *tanoa* or bowl, and everyone was invited to drink, not just those players originating from the Pacific Islands.

This wasn't a one-size-fits-all approach though. The experiences and activities we put in place were specific to the team, as yours should be, because different things resonate with different people. I remember being on the bus with the New South Wales State of Origin rugby league team in 2024 when the manager Frank Ponissi walked down the aisle and performed a head count. Having returned to his seat, I suggested he maybe consider the buddy system, a set-up we'd established with the All Blacks where every player was given a partner to check in with, and vice versa.

'So, if one person in the partnership is late for the bus, it's the other bloke's job to warn them about their timekeeping,' I said, before explaining how it had also been a great way of improving the inclusive connections within the team.

Frank smiled patiently and nodded. 'That sounds great, Bert,' he said. 'But I won't get to banter with boys as I walk up and down the bus.'

I learned a very good lesson that day. What works for one group might not work for another, so select your strategies carefully, while remembering that the aim is to deepen the existing (or non-existing) connections. Yes, this process might involve an activity or a cultural event. But it could also be a challenge or work process that requires mini-teams, in which case place together people that wouldn't ordinarily communicate. (And encourage them to ask questions of one another.) In the All Blacks we found that community events, especially those where the emphasis was placed on volunteering, were beneficial to the team's togetherness. That's because any sense of hierarchy is stripped away when the collective is peeling spuds in a homeless shelter or mopping the floors in a hospital – the process is equally valuable to the giver, the receiver and the observer.

#3 The Back of the Bus Drives the Front

There was a saying we used in the All Blacks that stated: *You can't move the front of the bus without moving the back.* Originally, the idea stemmed from a culture of hierarchy within the group that was identifiable by the seats on the team bus, and whenever we travelled, a distinct pecking order was established whereby the most senior members of the All Blacks – the players with the most caps – sat at the very back. The players at the front were the newbies. Everyone else jostled for position in-between.

This hierarchy stayed in place for generations, though certain protocols changed over time. Back in the day, Brian Lochore told me that a player's position on the backseat was challengeable by anyone else in the team, even if they hadn't played a similar number of Test matches. Sometimes a fight broke out, and if a challenger usurped their rival, the seat changed hands. These victories didn't come easily, however. As the backseat boys took on more and more challengers, they established a system whereby several trusted lieutenants worked around them as minders. Positioned in the seats nearest to the final row, it was their job to take down any contenders before they could reach the rear of the bus. Nowadays the seating arrangement is organised according to tenure and respect, and stripped of violence, but one important truth remains. The direction of travel in the All Blacks has always been determined by the leaders. *The back of the bus.*

To create a sense of belonging in any group, it's important to encourage those people with the most seniority to drive the culture and exhibit the correct behaviours. In our case, this was done through the leaders. They set a good example every day. They were the first to sweep the sheds. They were first out to training. They were last to leave a community event. And they were always available for selfies and signatures. This was all part of the process of enhancing the legacy. The back of the bus led the way.

All great cultures have a simple, but effective, strategy for when connecting on a deeper level. Instead of thinking, 'What can I get from it?' they ask, 'What can I give to it?' They then establish traditions or protocols that feed into this mindset (as we'll discuss in the next *Wero*.) Sadly, we live in a world where too many people expect something for nothing. Professional sports stars look at their trophy cabinets and feel a sense of entitlement based on what they've achieved. In companies the world over, leaders – good and bad – check the years on their clock and expect to receive special treatment or benefits according to time served. But no culture can truly connect if that kind of attitude prevails. The All Blacks mindset was one where the leaders were encouraged to put their hands up (to give), rather than to stick their hands out (to receive) and their dedication to enhancing the legacy was the engine that kept the bus on track.

There are all sorts of ways to foster such a mindset, the most common of which is the yearly or quarterly company awards ceremony where people are celebrated for certain achievements, such as the reaching of a sales target. But while these events can be a nice touch, they often miss the opportunity to connect on a deeper level because they value individualism. However, if those awards were to recognise any behaviours and attitudes that strengthen the team's bonds and behaviours (and move the group forward powerfully), they'll stimulate even more connection. For example, a company that places an emphasis on leftfield thinking should acknowledge any revolutionary or bold ideas. Likewise, those people who perform selfless acts, or do the thankless tasks, should be recognised in a collective where giving is important. Not only do these gestures reinforce the connections within a team, but they also encourage its members to stick to the all-important standards and values.

#4 Vulnerability Is Power

It used to be that if an All Black, or someone attached to the group, ever displayed vulnerability, they were viewed as being weak. The attitude: *It wasn't the way an All Black should behave.* That mindset, thankfully, shifted and it later became commonplace for the players to be given free rein to speak their minds during debrief sessions and one-on-one meetings. There were no sacred cows and nothing was off limits, though the players and coaches had to speak to the issue not to the person. We didn't want to engage in a blame game. Because of this work, and the frank conversations that took place, we discovered that some of our men had become averse to pressure during the biggest games. Rather than using expectation as fuel, they'd wanted to escape it. But that discovery only happened because the squad and the coaches had engaged in a series of open and honest discussions on how they'd truly felt. Suddenly, a greater power was realised.

Vulnerability was the new strong.

The All Blacks then entered an entirely new space of operating. After games there was usually one of three scenarios: 1) The team had won well; 2) The team had won (but not won well enough); 3) The team had lost. In all three situations, our initial review structures – the analysis that took place in the aftermath of a result – were the same because the aim was to foster connection and vulnerability. Win or lose, the milestones were celebrated (such as a player reaching a certain number of caps), and any problems were identified, though they weren't to be solved there and then. Meanwhile, if somebody had an issue or was struggling emotionally (for example, having had a poor game), the others always rallied around them in support or they could discuss the issue in private with me at a later date. Afterwards, everyone was encouraged to have a drink with their teammates, so they could connect and just be together. Experience has shown me that being vulnerable is a personal thing and people enter it through many different doorways. Some players share their thoughts openly. Others park them for a while. The most important thing was for everyone to sit with their emotions and to feel their weight until the time came when they were ready to share. This was the All Black way.

Within the group, vulnerability came to be viewed as a way of powering up the team, rather than something that might pull us down. But the process took time. In the early days, some players were resistant to the idea of using my support and methods and there was a fear among one or two of the boys that by seeing me they might be considered as being soft – or worse, that they didn't deserve to wear the jersey. At first, I operated in the shadows; I picked my moments when approaching certain players, and when the time came, I presented my work as an equivalent to the other performance parameters, like cardiovascular or muscular strength. I did this by explaining that performance was like a three-legged stool. One leg represented physical conditioning, another represented your skillset, and the final one represented mental performance. As a professional sportsperson it was important to maintain all three. If one leg was missing or weakened, then the stool would fall over. As the years passed, more and more players came to understand the role of the mental game and I was able to assist many in helping them to hit their performance goals and enhance the All Blacks legacy. Meanwhile, the coaches gave my work *visibility,* by encouraging me to address the whole group with increasing regularity.

This attitude shift was particularly important when introducing newbies to the group. The beginnings in the life of an All Black were fast and furious, and potentially overwhelming. There were media commitments, commercial meetings, and introductions to the legacy and the tribe. It was a lot for someone to take in, but we generally left the fresh faces alone so they could find their feet in their first few days. Then the induction period began. It was here that an All Black began the formal process of *becoming* which underpinned the powerful force of *belonging*. We ran meetings with any new additions to the group, alongside myself, the Business and Operations Manager Darren Shand, and a few of the leaders. Together we explained the opportunities being afforded to the players and what was expected of them. They were told about the jersey and its place inside the legacy. We outlined the rules (You're an All Black 24/7, so own it. Have a 'yes' attitude. You have joined us; we haven't joined you. And so on . . .). And we detailed how their lives had changed forever: from that day on, they were an All Black and everything they did would be viewed from that perspective. For example, if ever they behaved badly, their position within a very elite club would be mentioned in any news headlines.

Arguably the most important stage in creating a sense of connection took place when a scene-setting meeting was called. The newbie All Blacks sat in a circle with the full squad and were encouraged to share some insights about who they were, where they had come from, and what their aspirations were. In doing so, they were invited to show vulnerability through several discussion points. Among them:

- Tell us about your family and where you have come from.
- Tell us about how you felt when you found out you had become an All Black.
- Tell us about what your call up means to those people closest to you.

To establish a sense of trust, one of the leaders would then show vulnerability by talking through their answers to the same questions. I found that this was one of the most special gatherings to be a part of as an All Black – for the players and management. There was lots of emotion, and people often broke down as they talked through their challenges and experiences. But in completing this activity, a bond was created between the new men in black and the rest of the team. They showed an openness to one another and any burdens they might have felt about stepping into such a pressurised environment were replaced with something far more powerful.

Belonging.

It's all very well and good running meetings of this kind in a sports team, where there's a relentless pursuit of self-improvement. It's another to do it in an office environment where cynicism can disrupt the best-laid plans. The workaround in such a situation is to encourage vulnerability on a smaller scale, and this can be done by dividing people into pairs at the start of the working week. In a brief meeting they could be encouraged to discuss three questions:

1) What did you do at the weekend?
2) What's your biggest challenge at the moment?
3) What are you looking forward to?

The participants can be as deep or as shallow as they like with their answers, there are no rules. Notice also, that in the above questions, the second invites vulnerability and it's sandwiched nicely between two safe enquiries that give the recipient an easy entry and safe exit. Vulnerability works both ways and I've found that too few people are willing to vent about their joy. They feel embarrassed or sensitive to the situation of others, and they hold down their happiness or excitement. But this is stifling. If we only talk openly about the things that are going wrong in our lives, we risk missing out on the warmth that's created when sharing the things that are going well. An exercise of this kind helps us to celebrate one another's successes, and provides comfort during life's heavier moments, all while utilising the power of vulnerability.

One player who understood the power of vulnerability was Dan Carter. He explains how he used it to reach his optimum performance levels during the most testing of circumstances . . .

> *As an All Black I'd needed to get vulnerable, because it was the fastest way to problem-solve, accept responsibility and grow as a leader, especially when it was done without judgement. This was the environment the All Blacks were keen to foster. I remember starting a campaign in 2013 where I was feeling demotivated. I was struggling after a rough Super Rugby season, and in my first leadership meeting, as the other*

guys were talking about how they were feeling ahead of the next match, I sensed some of them were on a real high. But I wasn't.

'Man, am I losing my love for the game?' I thought.

I'd been playing with the All Blacks for a decade and something was missing. There was no point in hiding it though, not in a group as open and honest as the one we'd built for ourselves.

'Look, I'm not as energised as you guys,' I said. 'Maybe I've been playing for too long, and I'm just not feeling it. But we're a week out from the first Test match and I'm not as excited as I know I should be.'

Communicating this reality lifted a huge weight from my shoulders. It also helped one or two of the other men in the room, who then admitted to feeling the same. But rather than it being viewed as a problem, or a sign of weakness, this admission became a springboard. Vulnerability was our strength, and Bert then took those players who might have been feeling a little out of sorts, me included, for one-on-one meetings. In my case, the issue was broken down. We looked ahead to the season and reset my goals. Then a structure was put in place that would help me achieve them. Bang! A few days later I was thriving and back to my emotional best, but without that meeting I'd have probably hobbled into the first Test match. Who knows how my season would have panned out? Sometimes as New Zealanders we can be a bit too nice; we like things to feel warm and fluffy. But being in a leadership meeting, where people were encouraged to speak honestly without being judged or criticised – or worse, said things for the sake of it – had allowed us to problem-solve faster.

Te Puna o te Kī: The Belonging that Exists in a Silent Room

After any loss, the mood in the shed was often intense. You could cut the air with a knife. The players were warriors, but if victory had eluded them in a big game, on the big stage, or in the big moments, there was always a feeling of devastation. Such was the expectation of the All Blacks. Some of that hurt was visible for everyone to see, some of it was hidden away. That's because everyone was built differently and so the players experienced it differently. Once the initial review had taken place, the common theme was silence. It was eerie, no words were spoken, but as with those quiet acknowledgements before matches, plenty was being said. Every player sat with their thoughts and acknowledged their individual shortcomings, as we felt the collective weight of each other, of the team, of the jersey, and of the legacy.

Taking things personally was the All Black way. For example, after a defeat, Keven Mealamu often looked in the mirror and asked a simple question: *What could I have done better to ensure the team had won?* He did this regardless of whether he was in the starting XV or not. I did something similar too, but this heavy atmosphere was never about shame or blame. It was a period of shared pain and reflection. This was important because in such a space of vulnerability, a profound sense of belonging usually emerged, as the individual looked inward and asked, 'What more could I have done for the team?' Meanwhile, there was an understanding that nobody in the room was alone. Everyone was in it together and sharing in the deep emotional journey of striving for greatness. Our attitude? *We stand together – always have done and always will.* That's because wearing the jersey was about showing up for one another in every moment, especially the hardest ones.

It's my belief that belonging is about remaining unified, not just in victory, but in moments of despair. That's because as brothers, or sisters, we strengthen our bonds during circumstances of shared pain, even if we're being silent. It's not necessary to fill a room with false optimism or noise. In the immediate aftermath of defeat, a team doesn't have to dissect every mistake. Yes, it's important to feel the sting – it's what gives us the drive to work harder next time and fix any problems. But self-flagellation doesn't help anyone. Instead, it's better to sit with one another and acknowledge the human side of elite sport – the doubt, the fear, the pain, the emotional toll – because we can find a deeper connection in doing so. Only then we can lean into an open and honest debrief session to help correct any issues. (See: #4 Vulnerability Is Power.)

That's because *belonging* transcends results. It's rooted in the silent bonds of trust, mutual respect and shared experience. (Where nothing is spoken but everything is said.) And in all the elite teams I've worked with, belonging was most strongly felt when the pressure was greatest, when the outside world doubted us, and when there was no choice but to call upon our teammates in the trenches for support. In those quiet, raw moments, our sense of belonging was forged, and the strength of our connection was revealed.

The Wero: The Plus One

As I've mentioned earlier, when members of a group feel emotionally connected, their commitment skyrockets. They anticipate one another's needs, take calculated risks together, and protect the vulnerabilities inside the team. In doing so, a powerful synergy is created that exceeds the sum of a team's individual parts. Put simply: a group that's strongly connected will drive both individual and group performances to new heights. It's often the difference between good teams and great teams. And as Richie McCaw once told me: 'Building bonds off the field flow onto the field where you'll do anything to help your mate out – whatever situation you're in.' That is the power of belonging in a nutshell.

One way of strengthening the connections within a group is to introduce the concept of a 'Plus One' to the people around you. This is a process whereby, if a person is required to execute ten tasks to fulfil their role or brief, they should execute them fully – no excuses – and then perform a task for somebody else. This doesn't have to be backbreaking work. It could be something as simple as making a cup of tea, helping somebody with a job they find difficult or unpleasant, or pitching in with suggestions if a colleague or mate is struggling for creative ideas. The most important thing is that the Plus One protocol is performed daily, because when a person regularly gives to the people around them, the unity of the group is strengthened as a result.

The Library of Learnings

- The most important thing to give a group is a sense of belonging. With it, they will deliver their full commitment.
- Belonging is the well from which performance levels are drawn. If a person doesn't feel a sense of belonging, they will more than likely act in a selfish or self-contained way, whereas someone with a keen sense of belonging will give everything to their teammates and the cause.
- There are four rules to follow when building belonging. 1) Authenticity is everything. 2) Inclusive connections must be built. 3) You can't move the front of the bus without moving the back of the bus. 4) Vulnerability is a superpower.
- By presenting vulnerability to the people around you, it's possible to connect on a deeper level. Any burdens someone might have felt about stepping into a pressurised environment can be replaced with genuine support.

PART III

Mental Performance

INTRODUCTION

It's Easy to Sweat

The All Blacks were eager learners. To stand still was to fall behind, and running alongside our Leadership Groups were several self-contained *strategic teams.* Made up of players and coaches, it was their role to research and develop emerging skills, techniques and even technologies that might help the All Blacks in a forthcoming game or tournament. For example, one collective dealt with rugby's attacking processes. Nicknamed *Pouākai*, after the extinct bird of prey, their work kept the team ahead of any tactical trends taking shape around the world. Another group, *Black Plague,* fixed their attention on the defensive game. These groups presented their findings to the squad every week, and in doing so, ensured we were armed with the right tools with which to crush our opponents.

Within this set-up, the Maximising Mental Ability group, or *MMA*, was my baby, and as the title suggested, our work focused on mental performance. (Specifically, MMA was tasked with developing a mindset for the coming week, every week, and I had assistance from Doctor Ceri Evans who acted as an external consultant.) The name of our collective was coined by Anton Lienert-Brown, and came from the ultra-violent, mixed martial arts discipline, which the players loved. We even set up our meetings into an octagon shape, the seating arrangement mirroring the sport's famous eight-sided ring, in a respectful nod to its traditions. As with a fighting arena, there was no place to hide in the All Blacks: if a player wasn't in the right headspace, they were putting themselves and the team at risk.

Under the leadership of head coach Steve Hansen, the MMA group was given a level of influence equal to the other more traditionally focused strategic teams. This was a pioneering move. At that time, around 2015, mental performance was still full of misconceptions, especially when compared to more tangible, result-bearing subjects such as biomechanics, nutrition, or strength and conditioning. A lot of coaches believed that its greatest use was motivation, and the role of its practitioners was to fire up the players, nothing more. However, the truth of our work was very different. Mental performance was about leaning into the high-pressure moments and succeeding. It helped an athlete to be at their very best when their very best was needed. And it gave teams the greatest possible chance of winning the big tournaments, where matches were decided by the finest of margins.

Thankfully, a major transformation has taken place in recent years and athletes now embrace the mental game, knowing it to be the difference between an Olympic gold medal and last place, or a starting spot in a World Cup Final and a seat in the stands. But a similar reality applies to all of us. Given the power of the mind and its undoubted impact on performance levels in business, endeavour and everyday life, why wouldn't a person apply a huge amount of effort to sharpening their mental performances? After all, when it comes to physical training, it's easy to sweat. *Anyone can do it.* But the true champion knows that mind as well as muscle are required to succeed at the highest level. For example, it's all very well knowing how to perform an intricate skill such as heart surgery, or nuclear engineering. But executing those skills under pressure is an entirely different game. This is where mental performance techniques such as visualisation, breathwork, emotional control or pressure management make all the difference.

This work conducted by the MMA group was a game-changer for the All Blacks, and as with every other team I've worked with, the players' *bibles*, or journals, were a key resource in every session. There were tasks to complete too. For example, in one meeting, the squad had to imagine any potential obstacles that might derail their performance during game day. They were then asked to picture a positive reaction to those obstacles, followed by a successful outcome in whatever it was they were doing. (For example, some of the men saw red in the face of provocation. It was their responsibility to prepare healthy emotional responses for these flashpoint events.) The players spent ten minutes noting down their thoughts and priming their minds, before discussing their chosen scenarios with a trusted teammate. If their identified trigger then took place in the game, their buddy could lend support.

Elsewhere, we often trained in the matchday venue, such as Twickenham in England or Suncorp in Australia, ahead of fixtures. Sometimes the physical drills were swapped out for psychological ones, and as I walked across the field, the players could be seen 'visualising' in different parts of the stadium. One or two All Blacks sat in the stands and pictured the match from a fan's perspective – they saw themselves performing to the best of their ability. Others laid flat out on the grass, their eyes closed, as they imagined themselves performing. Others walked or jogged in the areas of the field where they spent the most time and executed actions specific to their position. Some players sidestepped phantom tackles. Others chased down their opposite number. And these routines readied the mind for the action to come, in much the same way that a cardiovascular programme readied the body.

Preparing in this way helped transform the All Blacks into back-to-back Rugby World Cup champions. Our work enabled the players to face adversity in all its forms; they mastered the never-ending duel between thought and emotion; and they came alive in crunch events by tapping into their mental resources. Bench pressing the mind made them an unstoppable force. Following the lessons in the forthcoming chapters will help you to do the same.

Just don't forget your *bible*.

CHAPTER 10

Pressure Is a Lifestyle

Sport at the highest level accentuates pressure. The smallest moments are amplified into Big Events with dramatic consequences for failure, and huge rewards for success, where only the emotionally prepared can manage the strain. In a pressure cooker environment, like an Olympics or a Super Bowl, the best athletes (and coaches) understand that these pockets of emotional intensity are calls to action. Richie McCaw was one such player. He was built for pressure, and nothing seemed to faze him. I remember the All Blacks always conducted a very low impact team practice called a walkthrough before our Rugby World Cup games. It was a way for the players to connect outside of the team hotel and I'd often check in with Richie beforehand. It wasn't a face-to-face catch-up, more a casual impromptu connection. I'd look at him and nod; he would nod back; and in that tiniest of gestures a hell of a lot was spoken: *Everything we've worked for comes down to today.* There was no need for grand statements. Richie knew and I knew that our preparation was done. We were ready.

Pressure, in any context, springs from three combining factors: 1) *expectation*, 2) *scrutiny*, and 3) *consequence*. For the All Blacks in a Rugby World Cup, or tour series, the fans and general public bring an intense level of expectation – they want us to smash the opposition. (There is also the expectation created by ourselves, which is incredibly high.) The media creates a high level of scrutiny through tactical analysis, think pieces by former players and speculation and gossip. And the consequences of failing to win or play to a high standard are obvious – there's criticism, abuse and embarrassment. These circumstances aren't confined to the sporting arena either. A political leader, for example, will face expectation from their electorate, scrutiny from the media, and face the consequence of a lost seat should they fail to deliver on any high profile promises. When performing at the highest level, these three factors are inescapable.

There's a saying that pressure is a privilege, and for the most part, this is true. A life without it can be dull and many people who exist without expectation, scrutiny and consequence tend to feel unfulfilled until they stagnate. While the unhurried existence might feel comfortable at first, there's an intense joy to be found in facing up to pressure and succeeding. That's because being challenged can help a person, or team, to grow in ways they might not have previously imagined. The All Blacks loved this space because it helped us to become pioneers, break new sporting horizons and achieve things that seemed beyond other teams. The players' efforts appeared superhuman at times. In that context, facing pressure was an honour – that's how we viewed it in the All Blacks anyway.* But the important truth about pressure is that nobody's born with the skills to perform under the weight of expectation, scrutiny and consequence. *They learn them.* And once that reality is understood, a different perspective appears.

Pressure is a lifestyle.

That was certainly the case for the typical All Black during my time with the team. Regardless of where a player was, or what they were doing, their status followed them around, and it was important they handled the pressures that came with the role. Questions arrived all day, every day. *Am I fit enough? Am I strong enough? Am I training, resting and sleeping enough?* Then there were the worries about form and selection. *Will I make the squad? Will I make the bench? Will I make the starting XV?* There was no hiding place from this sensation either. A player could go out for a family meal and find themselves bombarded with wisecracks from opposition fans. They might wake up in

---

* Of course, there are the uncomfortable pressures that are forced upon us, such as the stress of a sick loved one, a failing relationship, or a financial or health concern. I'll get to those shortly.

the morning to see an unflattering headline about their recent form on the paper's back page. (Or worse, the front.) Then there were the requirements that came with the position – media commitments, commercial commitments and community commitments. Pressure was a 24/7 event, and the only coping mechanism was to accept it as a lifestyle and lean into it.

Kieran Read on handling this pressure:

I can't remember being as nervous for a game as I was before the 2011 Rugby World Cup Final. Thankfully, Bert had given me the mental performance skills to cope, and I spent the week preparing appropriately with the other players by trying to make everything feel as normal as possible, even though it was anything but.

Once I'd arrived at Eden Park with the squad, I went about my mental processes as usual. I was so focused on getting my routines right, that it's hard to recall what was going on around me at the time. The mood seems distant. What the other players were doing around me now feels like a blur. I suppose it's a testament to how switched on we all were but also because everybody was emotionless at the time. We had a job to do, and we knew we had the talent and the psychological processes to succeed – if anyone had attempted to bring emotions into the shed at that point, it would have been a sign they were struggling. Every action, every thought had one aim in mind: as much as we could, we had to treat the Rugby World Cup Final like any other game. It was business as usual.

Routine helped too. Whenever I went into the shed before a match, I prepared my body and mind for battle in the same way. I'd learned from Bert that the habits I fell in to during the hour or so before a match would prime me for success. Rather than muddling through my pre-match routines, I kept a strict schedule in place, depending on how long I had before the first warm-up. I set my boots right. I readied my kit. I set my mouth guard down in the same spot. Most importantly, I hung my jersey so that the number 8 was visible. These actions sent out the message that I was playing in just another game. I had succeeded before. I would do so again.

> *Those mental performance techniques got us over the line in that match. There was no way we could have relied on our technical abilities and physical attributes alone because we had lost so many of our major weapons during the tournament, such as Dan Carter. (Plus the fact Richie McCaw was playing through a painful injury.) Those missing pieces in the puzzle meant we couldn't play the way we wanted to, so we had to think smarter and rely on behaviours that would help us through. When we eventually won the match, and the tournament, the outpouring of emotions was incredible, especially for a lot of the older guys who had been through the pain of 2007. They understood the importance of our achievements and helped to put it into perspective. It was undoubtedly one of the highlights of my All Blacks career.*

When accepting pressure, the *saying* is much easier than the *doing*. In the All Blacks, we learned that the players who generally succeeded were those who knew that stress arrived from one of two sources.

1) Circumstantial pressure. This arrives with the challenges of everyday life and for the athlete it might show up after a defeat, injury, non-selection or a run of poor form. For someone in an everyday context, these will include work issues, poor health, relationship challenges and financial headaches. *Circumstantial pressure creates discomfort through irritability.*
2) Self-imposed pressure. The combination of expectation, scrutiny and consequence that a person brings upon themselves as they strive for improvement. In the All Blacks, players want to learn new skills, show reliability under pressure and become faster, stronger and more effective. In real life, we all want to improve our general health (better sleep, nutrition, exercise), mental strength (resilience, emotional regulation), personal relationships (communication, vulnerability, acts of service) and adventure and exploration (new experiences, travel). *Self-imposed pressure creates discomfort through opportunity.*

Both channels are equally powerful: irritability pushes a person to improve, while opportunity tends to pull them along. But I've found that most teams or individuals are more effective when working with circumstantial pressure. In the All Blacks we always bounced back strongly after a defeat or a poor game, when our irritability levels had skyrocketed. However, when playing after a great performance or preparing to face a so-called lesser opponent, it was much harder for us to get going. Comfort became an unwelcome curse and unless we identified a new standard to be embraced by the players (and genuinely) we struggled. This was a constant challenge and though some players mastered it, they were more the exception than the norm.

If the pressures of irritability or opportunity are to be accepted as lifestyle choices, then the way in which we tackle them becomes crucial. The strategy for doing so is a simple, three-part process we called, *See It; Accept It; Embrace It*, which runs as follows . . .

SEE IT: The All Blacks were often told: *If you're not working on the mental game, someone else will be – and one day you're going to meet.* Naming our concerns became a standard, and before and during any major events we asked our players and staff to anticipate as many potential pressure points as possible. (For example, home sickness.) Once identified, these issues were shared, and *The Lethal Cocktail* from Chapter Four came into play. (Remember: *Structure + Discipline*. And with high standards.) Plans for each issue were discussed. Then, when the pressure mounted in waves, we had to stick to those plans. The team could bend, we could even buckle, but under no circumstances were they allowed to break them because then we'd become helpless. And that would inevitably lead to disaster.

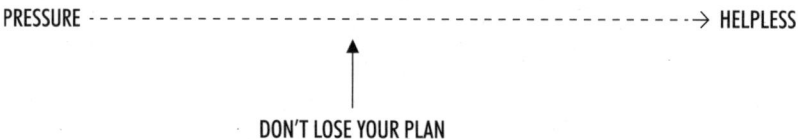

Ultimately, the group was under no illusions that pressure was inevitable, whether we liked it or not, but its associated discomforts could either dominate us or energise the next effort or performance. The choice was ours.

In many ways this work was a happy by-product of the 2007 Rugby World Cup, where the players and coaches had rejected the idea that we would become affected by pressure, when, in fact, the opposite was true. *No one was immune.* Rather than acknowledging that reality and tackling the situation head-on, we ran from it. When it then showed up during our quarter-final with France, there was an overwhelming sense of shock, there was no Lethal Cocktail, and our unstructured approach and poor discipline caused us to become helpless. The rest is history. That situation later weighed heavily on my shoulders because it was inside my brief, I should have seen it coming, but I'd fallen short in my preparation.

Never again.

ACCEPT IT: When pressure arrives, the body reacts in all sorts of ways. We sweat and our heartrate spikes, the simple act of breathing becomes laboured as the panic crashes into us like waves on a beach, and unless we're emotionally prepared with a strategy, we can be dragged out to sea. To avoid such a situation, it helps to see pressure as a launchpad to success. To some people, sweaty palms, racing adrenaline and heavy breathing might feel like a sign of fear. To champions, they're indicators of readiness and a physiological response to threat. When harnessed correctly it can help them to run faster, think sharper and fight harder.

Reframing our view on pressure makes the discomfort easier to accept. It feels like a trade-off, because we're approaching an opportunity pregnant with potential where, if we succeed, an exciting opportunity will follow. When handled correctly, it can even become addictive. Often, when people work in high-pressure jobs, where deals are brokered, or adrenalised activities take place, they complain in the moment that the effort is too heavy or exhausting. But once they retire, they miss the thrill of the chase and find themselves yearning for a return to the pressure cooker. The bottom line is this: pressure means you're operating at a challenging level. If you're not feeling it, you're not in the right place.

EMBRACE IT: Of course, you don't have to experience pressure. You can always walk away. *But then what?* I've found that simply acknowledging that the option to quit exists is enough to help someone embrace the presence of pressure. A good example of this took place when I was coaching the Hillmorton High School volleyball team. We had reached the schools' championship semi-final, which was a big deal, but on the eve of the game all the boys looked stressed. When I faced them during our final training session, I asked if they fancied swerving the event.

'What do you mean, Mr Enoka?' asked one of the boys.

'Well, by the looks of it, you're pretty nervous,' I said. 'Do you not want to play tomorrow? Because if I told you the competition was being cancelled, and all our hard work had been for nothing, how would you feel?'

I'd broken the frame. The thought of not facing the semi-final presented them with a feeling of unfulfillment and there was a mindset shift. Rather than being weighed down by pressure and locked into a burden mindset, they were lifted by the opportunity. They weren't thinking about what might happen were they to lose; they were looking forward to the possibilities ahead of them were they to win. When I repeated my suggestion that they abandon the semi-final the next day, their response was very different.

'Hell, no,' said one boy. 'Let's do this.'

> **Flip the Lens:** Identify a moment in the last week where you've reframed (or could have reframed) a difficult situation in real life. What did you do? What would you do differently next time?

Te Puna o te Kī: Never Walk from the Truth

Reon is my nephew. A most wonderful human being that I love dearly. Reon has an intellectual disability. He also has a unique talent – the gift of personality, which he uses to light up the world and bring joy to everyone he meets. Sometimes Reon can be loud, and he'll burst into the room to hug me shouting, 'G'day, uncle.' Other days, he'll lean gently into me, clasping my hand and resting his head on my shoulder.

'I love you, uncle,' says Reon.

I love you too, nephew. He always makes me happy.

And there are times when he looks into my eyes, says nothing and smiles so widely it pierces my heart with all the wonders of love. I find so much power in these small gestures and quiet moments with Reon. It's connection in its purest sense, and no person is ever the same once they've been touched by it. Reon is the greatest gift our family has ever received.

You're probably wondering why I'm writing all this in a chapter about pressure. Well, Reon has developed the perfect attitude towards the stresses of everyday life. It bounces off him, no matter what's happening. He operates with a mindset of opportunity, and dismisses the circumstances that accompany life's irritabilities. He has an attitude that silences the noise, draws out the best in other people and lifts up everyone he meets. There's not an ounce of jealousy in his makeup and he is the first to applaud the achievements of others. I recently asked his dad, my brother Tony, to explain what we could learn from Reon's life experience and its associated challenges. He put together the following teachings . . .

LIFE: Live each day to the fullest, no matter the pressures. Have fun, laugh and be kind. Let your family and friends know you love them unconditionally. Never hold a grudge. Everyone is a best: a best uncle, a best auntie, a best niece, and a best nephew. Reon is a superhero, and his superpower is Down syndrome. He is a straight shooter. The takeaway: Never walk from the truth. Even if it hurts, you'll always be stronger by confronting the brutal facts and hearing from someone with no agenda.

LEADERSHIP: Reon wants to do what everyone else is doing, *so he does*. When he was born, we were told not to expect much. But wow: he listens and when he understands, he follows instructions. He is a champion golfer and an Olympian. He plays basketball. He's a competent darts player, a good swimmer, and an excellent drawer who sketches *Star Wars* characters with an island twist. He sells his portraits at the market and organises his own business. He follows an authentic path and believes in the following truths: Be patient and be organised. Have determination and tenacity. Get the job done. Be kind and polite. Greet everyone. Be a negotiator. Have compassion. Be motivated, passionate and confident. Believe in yourself and have confidence . . . Even if you sing out of tune.

LOVE: Reon has an unconditional love for all, and he adores his family because they adore him. When you help someone that you consider to be lesser than you, you'll likely discover they're greater. Reon loves his friends, and he loves his dog. In many ways he's a teacher and he's shown me how to forgive, to be patient, to love everybody, and to give people a second chance. *What other 40-year-old would thank you each day for the meal he has just eaten or would tell you that he loves you morning and night?*

These are values that can be taken on by all of us. So, when the pressure comes, remember the belief of my magical nephew: In times of trouble, move on quickly. See the possibilities. And rather than worrying about the things that happened yesterday, put a positive lens on tomorrow. In a world where pressure is a lifestyle, everybody would benefit from thinking like Reon.

The Wero: Control the Noise

In 2022, we lost two games against Ireland. This was followed by an away defeat against South Africa. It was the first time since 1998 that we'd been beaten in three consecutive Test matches and everyone was baying for the blood of our head coach, Ian Foster. The pressure on the team was huge, and we were becoming overwhelmed by *noise* – a word we used to describe the chaotic chatter surrounding the All Blacks. The truth is that a professional sports team, or high-performing group, will always experience noise, it's part and parcel of the elite experience, but it carries two distinct tones – positive and negative. The negative manifests itself in hurtful criticism and public abuse. The positive is the media acclaim that kicks in after a great result. Both forms can be debilitating if left unchecked.

Generally, a person will hear the noise around them and either use it to their advantage or allow the noise to use *them*. For example, an All Black being influenced by critical chatter will become stuck in self-doubt. They'll feel tense and tight and consumed by sensations of loneliness. But if they're able to use that same unpleasant noise to their advantage, the situation can be accepted as a welcome challenge in which they can reset or improve. They'll become energised by the opportunities being presented to them and focus their mind on the tasks ahead. The strongest mental performers know how to connect with the noise, even in the cauldron of a World Cup Final, or a decisive Test match when the planet is watching, and every action is exposed to extreme analysis.

Nobody can silence the noise, or mute their inner critic, not when they're operating in a moment brimming with potential. Think back to those moments when you were under extreme pressure – an exam, job interview, an important presentation or speech – and I can imagine you might have been mulling over a series of negative thoughts. However, it is possible to adjust the intensity levels in just about any circumstances by resetting with the environment around you. To do so, I recommend another Lethal Cocktail, one I suggest you use when feeling overwhelmed by pressure.

- *Catch it.* When acknowledging the presence of noise, I always nod a *yes*, rather than shaking my head *no*, because it sends a positive physiological message to the nervous system rather than a negative or fearful one.
- *Check it.* In such situations, I reconnect by pressing my left big

toe into the ground and then my right. Doing this several times takes my focus, and any associated tension, away from my head and into the feet. (Other people use breathwork, or a mantra for this moment – whatever works for you. Some players will even twang an elastic band looped around their wrist.)

- *Change it*. Re-engage with the moment directly in front of you, by directing your attention onto something external. It's often good to focus specifically on a small micro action inside a bigger task; something you can execute with strong positive intent.

Next time you feel the pressure rising, I challenge you to engage in this process. With a little practice, your state will become less tight and tense in tough situations.

The Library of Learnings

- Pressure, in any context, springs from three combining factors: 1) expectation, 2) scrutiny, and 3) consequence.
- Improvement occurs inside discomfort, which shows up in one of two ways – irritability or opportunity. Your greatest growth will occur when you proactively embrace improvement through these channels.
- To cope with pressure, adopt the strategy of *See It; Accept It; Embrace It*. See the challenge for what it is, accept it's happening to you, then embrace it as a moment of potential. When working through the moment, don't forget The Lethal Cocktail!

CHAPTER 11

The One Guarantee

No matter who we are or what we do, there's one guarantee in life. *Adversity will test us all.*

For the All Blacks, it arrived whenever New Zealand exited a tournament ahead of time. Amid the heartache and embarrassment of defeat, the media often lashed out at us, and no one was left unscathed. The criticism, usually delivered when we were at our most vulnerable, created some heavy scars, and if ever an image summed up this gruelling experience it was of Richie McCaw, head in hands, during his post-game press conference following that disastrous 2007 Rugby World Cup quarter-final against France. Richie looked a broken man. But while the circumstances were both extreme and high profile, his emotional pain would have been familiar to everyone watching: moments of adversity, like unfair criticism or judgement, are inescapable, whether that be in our family, work or social lives. Adversity is an equal opportunity employer and can cause no end of suffering.

I faced a lot of it in my early life, firstly during my time as an orphanage kid in Marton, but also during the opening phases of my career when I was made to feel like the outcast of New Zealand's sports psychology community. As I mentioned earlier, very few people took me, or my methods, seriously. There was criticism from my peers, and later, some jealousy, when I started working successfully with Wayne Smith at the Canterbury Crusaders. After one or two newspaper articles had praised my achievements, the Psychology Association of

New Zealand claimed I shouldn't be described as a working sport psychologist and threatened to take legal action against me. Then there was the roasting I received from the sporting old guard who viewed my work as being 'New Age nonsense'. They believed the players at their clubs were too tough to require any mental support. Psychology was for wimps, they said, and any rugby, netball or cricket players in need of mental assistance needed to 'toughen up'.

My work was then slammed in the papers and on television, and the criticism was particularly brutal if ever one of my teams had failed in some way. When a commentator or pundit was given the opportunity to put a boot into my involvement and processes, they often made sure to use the other boot too. Understandably, these were difficult moments to navigate, both personally and professionally, and the abuse caused me to build an emotional shield around myself. I eventually realised that the individuals in opposition to my methods were figures from a previous generation and they'd become fearful that the teams of their era would be outdone by the teams of the present day. That didn't make my situation any easier to manage; a lot of the criticism was very hurtful to me and my family, but as the famous saying goes, 'If you're going through hell, keep going.' Moving forward was the only way to reach the other side.

So that's exactly what I did.

Push Through the C.R.A.P.

How we manage the emotional discomfort that accompanies challenge, can set the tone for our future performances. Adversity, while painful in the moment, is a great teacher. Nobody learns about themselves by going *around* a mountain or getting a piggyback to the top – the growth comes from the *doing*. Meanwhile, the opposite response, *standing still,* is absolutely the worst thing a person can do in testing times. In my 23 years spent working with the All Blacks, there wasn't a single player I'd met that didn't experience self-doubt or fear during the big moments. These were very human reactions to highly stressful events, but they only become a problem if they trap a person. The challenge for every athlete is to work through them and not get stuck.

When helping a player or an entire team to manage personal adversity, whether that be rugby-related or otherwise, we encouraged them to push past the feelings of C.R.A.P. that generally accompanied moments of misfortune (an acronym introduced by Canadian author, analyst and speaker Richard St John which we adapted for our own purposes).

(C)riticism – For the All Black this might include a period of unfair media scrutiny or scapegoating following a poor game.

(R)ejection – A player in a bad run of form may miss selection, or someone who makes a mistake off the field could find themselves out of favour with their peers or friendship groups.

(A)rseholes – After a defeat, or disappointing performance, abuse was sometimes thrown at an All Black, and their families, in public.

(P)rejudice – The assumptions made about a player regarding their looks, age, race, religion, size, or even attitude or belief system.

These same elements affect us in the everyday world too. A first-time parent caring for their sick child might experience criticism from one or two other mums and dads at the nursery, especially if their methods feel different to theirs. An individual who lets themselves down in some way will occasionally experience rejection from a certain section of their work or friendship groups. Somebody who is grieving can encounter people who are unsympathetic, uncaring or ignorant to their pain – in other words, *arseholes.* And a talented person might be overlooked for a work position because of assumptions based purely on their appearance, character or background.

I pushed through the C.R.A.P. that accompanied my early career as a mental performance coach by batting away all the criticism, rejection, arseholes and prejudice. Don't get me wrong, it still hurt, but after a while I was able to stand on my own two feet, relatively unchallenged. My work and achievements with Wayne and the Crusaders did the talking for me, and whenever the Psychology Association of New Zealand wrote one of their threatening letters, I called them up and talked through the issue. Afterward, I understood what they were broadly trying to do – to protect the integrity of the discipline and to prevent any shady individuals from undermining the wider practice of sport psychology. They also wanted me to toe the party line and to gain the qualifications required of a traditional psychologist, and for a while, I was happy to comply. I completed a Bachelor of Arts degree in Psychology and enrolled in an Industrial and Organisational post graduate degree at Canterbury University.

The first year flew by with honours, which allowed me to go directly to a PhD thesis and I loved the learnings, even though there were many aspects I felt were not in sync with what I was experiencing in the field. At the same time, the Crusaders (whom I was working with) were on their way to winning Super Rugby titles in 1998 and 1999. Suddenly, I had a choice to make: I could complete my Doctoral thesis or continue my path with Wayne who was bound for the All Blacks.

Then one of my university lecturers sealed the deal.

He said, 'You know, Gilbert, you're working to get a qualification. One that will give you an opportunity to get the *very opportunity* you've already been given.'

Forget toeing the party line. From then on, I forged my own path at Crusaders, avoiding unwanted scrutiny by building relationships at the Psychology Association of New Zealand. I worked with their requests when I could, and I pushed back whenever it felt necessary. (And if a reporter requested an interview, I asked that I not be described as a sports psychologist, to save myself from any further grief.) While all of this was undoubtedly progress, the situation fed into my previous experiences with rejection, and the memories of my time in the orphanage, where I'd felt unwanted, came rushing back. The industry I was so passionate about had tried to push me away with bureaucracy and stuffy notions of tradition. Thankfully, several forward-thinking and very successful coaches had seen the benefits of my methods. As far as they were concerned, I was a trailblazer, and it didn't matter that I didn't have any fancy qualifications to my name.

Later, when it came to pushing through the C.R.A.P., whether that was with the All Blacks, or New Zealand's cricketers and netballers, it was the reporters that brought the most angst – as they did for all sports teams operating at the highest levels. I often picked up a newspaper with bated breath, scanning the headlines to check for the latest assault, especially if we'd lost. The same thing happened whenever I turned on one of the sports news channels or a phone-in show was playing on the radio. The negative attention drained me, but as my career progressed, I created a much healthier understanding. I wasn't going to let another person's opinion define me or determine who I was and how I behaved. I told myself: 'Sport is what I *do*. It's not who I *am*.' This perspective helped me a lot.

Every All Black dealt with C.R.A.P. in their own way. Some managed it better than others. The strongest players channelled their anger or hurt into the next performance. In that respect, the media's attention, or any comments from an abusive fan, could be viewed as a positive catalyst for self-improvement. Others ignored it completely: when destructive opinions came from a person they didn't value they chose not to value those opinions. However, my favourite reaction came from Steve Hansen when he was coaching the Welsh national team in the early 2000s. Steve had been experiencing a torrid time back then. His team had lost every match during the 2003 Six Nations tournament, in what would become a ten-match run of defeats, and his popularity tanked.

Around the same time, I was helping Wayne Smith with the English rugby union side Northampton Saints. One day, I picked up a famous tabloid newspaper and while flicking through the pages, I spotted a photo of my old mate, Steve, which had been stuck underneath the headline, *The Most Hated People in Wales*. Somehow, Steve had ended up in second place and was sandwiched between the murderous dictator Saddam Hussein and terrorist leader Osama bin Laden. I chuckled. *'This won't go down well,'* I thought. In my time working with Steve, he'd built a reputation as someone that would happily lash out at a journo whenever an unnecessarily unpleasant piece had been written about himself or one of his players. Steve never wanted an apology. Instead, his aim was to protect the families of those players taking the flak, especially their kids, who often put up with a lot in the school playground.

On this occasion, he wanted to have a little fun.

Having found the number of the editor responsible for putting the list together, Steve called the paper, introduced himself, and asked a simple question.

So, what have I got to do to get to number one?

The editor, I'm sure, wouldn't have said much in response, and I doubt Steve even cared. This was his way of pushing through the C.R.A.P., because, as the British Royal Marines have long stated, showing humour in the face of adversity is an excellent technique for remaining strong in the middle of a long and gruelling battle.

> **The Post-It Reminder**: Write down one insight from this section that you want to carry forward and stick it somewhere visible for the next seven days.

Mind Where Your Mind Goes

Through all of this, I learned that attention was everything when pushing through adversity. For an athlete, optimum performance is all about focus, especially when operating under pressure. In Test matches and training, an All Black needs to direct their attention to the present, not the past or the future, so that they can see what's going on around them in that moment and act accordingly. We need to adopt the same mindset when dealing with adversity. That's because our brains often become distracted by past mistakes and potential worst case scenarios, all of which creates extra unnecessary anxiety, especially if we catastrophise. This is a dangerous time. When our anxiety levels increase, we lose the ability to stay situationally aware and to make the most of any opportunities that might lie ahead.

Instead, we need to comprehend the events going on around us and react to the best of our ability, and one method for staying in the moment, especially in a high-pressure environment with all its challenges, is to shorten our focus, or *bring the horizon forward*. This is the simple organisational technique (touched upon by Dan Carter in Part One) where an overwhelming whole – such as the countdown to an important exam or a meeting that might decide our immediate work future – is broken down into a series of smaller, bite-sized chunks which we can train our attention upon. This roots us into the *now* and helps prevent our mind from wandering to any historical events or future maybes.

I remember applying this technique to the All Blacks in 2022, having embarked on that run of three consecutive defeats. (See Chapter 10.) This was a disastrous scenario for the team, and with a second fixture with the Springboks scheduled a week later, the general rule of thumb was to forget the past performances and focus only on the date of our next game. When this was shared with the players something unforeseen happened – their anxiety skyrocketed. *That present was too far away*. It lent itself to being infected by unwanted distractions, unfocused thinking and the fear of what might happen were the team to lose *four* matches in a row.

Having spotted the emotional turbulence kicking in, head coach Ian Foster, team captain Sam Cane and myself embarked on a plan to anchor the team's attention on the here and now. Rather than setting our horizon to the South Africa match, we shortened it into a series of hourly and daily events. The very next morning we called a leaders'

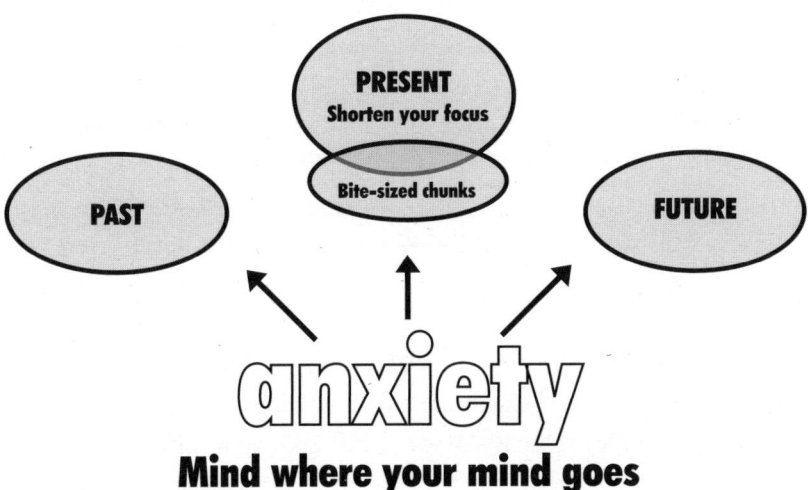

meeting where the players were invited to vent their emotions, before being encouraged to structure their days in such a way that there was very little room for wandering minds or past and/or future thinking. An All Black in the process of bringing their horizons forward was asked to create a day planner that outlined their activities, to the hour, from the moment they got up in the morning to the moment they went to bed. This stopped their brains from anxiously oscillating between the mess of the previous three fixtures and the consequences of another defeat against South Africa.

I've since found that this technique can work for anyone stuck in a moment of adversity or a high-pressure situation, where the simple act of putting one foot in front of the other seems almost impossible. For example, a person that has been given a scary medical diagnosis might want to bring their horizons forward to stop them from considering previous events (*Would I have become ill if I hadn't done X, Y or Z?*) and unknown future ones (*What will happen to my family if the worst case scenario happens?*) as they begin their treatment. The forthcoming weeks might be an overwhelming jumble of doctor's appointments, tests, assessments and consultations. In which case taking things in bite-sized chunks enables them to build a focused timetable for the in-between moments when they might become vulnerable to negative thoughts. Some of these events could be social; others might focus on family discussions; one or two moments of recovery and alone time should be scheduled in too. With each activity written down in a timetable, the person will know exactly what they're supposed to be doing and when. Their attention can then be trained on the present, as they push through an episode of adversity, rather than on events that might never happen, or are in the past and beyond their control.

Te Puna o te Kī: Watch Your Language

Though the players were able to calm their minds ahead of our second game against South Africa, the pressure was still sky high. We were to face the Springboks in the cauldron of Ellis Park in Johannesburg, *their Thunderdome,* and the media, expecting another mauling, were calling for the dismissal of head coach Ian Foster. (More C.R.A.P.) At the same time, our former Rugby World Cup-winning player Brad Thorn, then the oldest player to have appeared in a World Cup Final, and an individual who knew a thing or two about battling through adversity with the All Blacks, was in regular touch with me via text. On the eve of the game, he sent a message that would rally the players and encourage them to embrace the adversity ahead:

> *I'm wishing the Men in Black well, sitting here in Brissy.*
>
> *Let them know that despite all the noise, many are for them, including me.*
>
> *This is what we are about. The expectation, the pressure, the black jersey . . . Lean towards it, embrace the challenge, this is what we do, this is what we've always done.*
>
> *No backward step, everything we've got, how good!*
>
> **Thorny**

I felt uplifted when I read the message; it energised me. Too often in difficult times, people send well-meaning notes that are nothing more than platitudes and word salads. The bereaved are told to *stay strong*. The person going through a break-up is advised to *keep their chin up*. And someone suffering through a nasty illness is encouraged to *hang in there* or to *take care*. I know that some people appreciate that kind of talk in times of adversity, but I'm not a fan. In fact, I hate it, because I feel pitied instead of supported. Really, what's required is a message that chimes with the challenging situation and reminds the person that they have the capacity to endure. It's far better to say: *Embrace the suck. Lean into adversity. And know that support is there for you should you need it.* It also helps if the person is reminded of a time in which they faced an equally testing moment of adversity and came through. Getting the tone right requires a little emotional investigation, so I always take time to understand how the people in my circle of influence like to be communicated with. That way, when one of them inevitably hits the adversity bump, my language can be both reinforcing and helpful.

Brad had understood exactly this. His words lifted everybody. I grabbed a large piece of paper and we wrote down the key points from his message. Then I pinned them to a wall between the drinks station and a New Zealand flag in the team shed.

- *No backward step.*
- *Everything you've got.*
- *How good!*

In Johannesburg, the players rose to Brad's challenge, leaning into the expectation, pressure and the legacy of the black jersey, beating the Springboks 35–23 in what was a game for the ages. The pain of those previous three defeats faded into the distance, and with them the clouds of adversity.

The Wero: Be the Example

When people don't create a structure for managing adversity, life can become one hell of a journey. That said, with a deliberate strategy in place (applied with The Lethal Cocktail) it's possible to manage the most difficult of circumstances. That aforementioned saying about 'going through hell' rings true because the only way to get to the end of any dark tunnel is to walk towards the light at the other end – even if it looks like a non-existent dot in the faraway distance. Grief is a classic example of this. In its early stages, the pain of a lost loved one can feel all-consuming. Sometimes it might even seem dangerously insurmountable. But with time, support and self-care, the hurt becomes manageable, until, eventually, we're able to press ahead with our lives.

Having worked through the processes in this chapter, I'd like you to embrace the concept of leading by example in challenging times. Most of you reading this will have immediate family members, friends and work colleagues. All of them can benefit if you're able to exude a positive spirit when standing up to a gruelling life event. Rather than crumbling under the weight of it, show them that it's possible to tackle hardship with a productive and positive mindset and a defined working structure. Push through the C.R.A.P. Mind where your mind goes. Bring your horizons forward. Elsewhere, broaden your definition of success and take pleasure in the smaller things in life – and then express your happiness for them. Because it's hard to experience gratitude and anxiety at the same time.

Be warned though: adversity doesn't run to a set script. How it affects you could be entirely different to the way in which it impacts your family members, partner, boss or friends. If there is one consistency, it's in the way in which we can approach the challenge. Embrace it. Lean towards the expectation and the pressure. And remember: *No backwards steps.* It's the only way to deal with The One Guarantee.

The Library of Learnings

- Adversity will come for all of us, no matter who we are or what we do in life.
- To manage adversity, you must first wade through the C.R.A.P. – criticism, rejection, arseholes and prejudice.
- Mind where your mind goes by breaking down your day and weeks into manageable, bite-sized events. This will keep your focus on the *now* rather than it drifting to past mistakes or negative future thinking.
- Watch your language: when helping someone through a moment of adversity, avoid platitudes or a pitying sentiment. Empower them with messages of strength and affirmation.

CHAPTER 12

The Four Rules of Engagement for Moments of Uncertainty and Ambiguity

Every team should be relentless in the things that require zero talent. By that I mean they must strive to be their very best in the unskilled tasks – jobs that anyone can do, but so few people do them consistently well. In a sport such as rugby, these activities include: quickly getting up off the ground and back into the game; relentlessly chasing down a player that has made a line break, and not giving up; and carrying out a kick chase with gusto. These tasks require very little skill, only effort, and every All Black is expected to be the very best in the world at them. In a business setting, being relentless in the things that require zero talent might need a team to arrive on time, in an orderly fashion, and be clear and direct in everything they do. However, in any context there will be moments where ambiguity or uncertainty creeps in and even the most basic of standards are hard to stick to. On such occasions, there are four rules that can help a team, or individual, to accelerate dialogue, unity and performance. Talent is not required. But being the very best at them can be a game-changer.

The Four-Minute Rule

A lot of us fail to transition into new situations or environments effectively. We arrive at meetings, admittedly on time, and then waste several minutes messing about with paper, pens, documents and technology, checking a stream of emails and messages as we do so. Or worse, we arrive home from work, slump on the sofa and scroll through social media without engaging with our partner or the people around us. While these events might seem insignificant and inconsequential, they set a negative tone that can prove detrimental to our relationships and to our performance. I learned an interesting practice while watching the famous Doctor Phil in action. Known as the *Four-Minute Rule*, I have adapted it for my purpose and, as the name suggests, this is a reset period in which a person makes a conscious effort to engage authentically with their environment for the first four minutes – whether at home or at work, or in meetings – and the people within it, rather than arriving in a distracted or disinterested manner. In doing so, they create a connection and set a positive intent: *It establishes how the individual wants to be and sends the signal that the people around them are important and valued.*

In the case of the office meeting, show up early. Check your emails, set out the relevant paperwork and technology and be prepared to move forward as soon as everyone else arrives. To create a climate of genuine care, your attention should be directed to people as they enter the meeting space. Likewise, when arriving home from work, keep the phone tucked away, and engage with your family or friends with deliberate intent. In both situations you'll be able to assess the people you are with more clearly and make any adjustments that may be required in terms of assistance in that moment. For example, when returning home, perform the tasks that will help your loved ones. These acts, while small, tend to generate a wave of productivity and encourage powerful communication.

Connections Are a Power Play

The world we live in is busy, volatile and unpredictable, so how can we improve the way in which we engage with others? I've found that some people want to get ahead so badly in work (or play) that they're unable to shift away from the fast track. Their days move at lightning speeds and the rapid changes, small margins and high consequences of whatever it is they're doing seem unshakeable. They want this, they want that, and they want it yesterday – in every aspect of their life. Then, when something doesn't meet their standards, they'll give some clumsy and/or hasty feedback and in doing so, fail to connect genuinely on a human level. This damages their relationships over time.

A lot of us could benefit from bringing a little extra warmth into our connections, especially at work. It's not important that we love everyone in the office, but linking up in the right way can reap huge rewards. For example, messages move quicker, and new ideas take hold more effectively when a team understands itself. On a basic level, connection isn't that hard to do either and there are several techniques for bringing a positive energy to any environment: *Shake hands. Look the other person in the eye. Use their name. Don't overpower or overwhelm them by speaking too fast or too strongly. Ask questions and take an interest in their life outside of their work.* These small actions bring genuine connection to any moment, and when applied effectively can be used as an emotional power play, in much the same way that the All Blacks would increase the tempo of their performance to regain control of a match. Enhance your connections with each one, but don't overplay them – it will diminish their effectiveness.

George Duncan, the All Blacks' muscle therapist, was a master in this field and spent many an hour with our players on the treatment table. Not only was he amazing at his job, but he also had the talent of being able to connect with just about anybody and the men shared things with George that they wouldn't have divulged to another member of the group. That's because he kept their confidences, listened without talking, and allowed them to vent in potentially overwhelming circumstances. George also spoke in a language they understood, met the players for a beer, and let them know that they mattered. His wise ear settled many a wandering spirit, and cooled countless potential flashpoints, and both the players and the coaches loved him for it. George's work helped to bridge the void between the two groups because he understood the power of connection.

Of course there will always be challenges, such as the cold people that come into our lives from time to time, and who seem unwilling to work with us. These characters often carry baggage with them, infections from past associations and experiences that then create invisible tensions. *How do we connect?* Firstly, it's important we don't let them determine who we are or allow them to control our behaviour or attitude in any given moment – that's being submissive. Secondly, we should try to bond with them quietly and genuinely, because by doing so, we might just help them to unlock a troubling issue. Some suggestions for this could include:

- Apply the four-minute rule every time you meet. This allows you to spend some time emotionally checking in with the other person. While doing this think: *Where are you at today?*
- Be an emotional detective, it pays great dividends. If it's someone you don't know so well, such as a new addition to the team, do your homework before you meet. Check in with others who know them to see if there are any resolvable unexpressed needs, as meeting them can be an effective connector. For example, some debut All Blacks feel unsteady in what can seem a strange and overwhelming environment. In such cases, we link them with a 'buddy' who can reassure them and settle them in as they adjust to their new normal.
- Set parameters ahead of your meetings with a difficult person. Sometimes it helps to structure in a little connection time at the beginning. I often start these sessions by raising three discussion points: 1) *Tell me about something that you've been very proud of lately.* 2) *Name someone in your life that you feel very grateful for, and why.* 3) *Talk about an upcoming challenge*

that excites you. These enquiries invite vulnerability and create a safe start to what can often be a challenging conversation. (I view this process in the same way a rugby or volleyball player might view their warm-up drills before a match.)

However, if a person is completely unreceptive, or displays a problematic behaviour such as poor timekeeping, I employ a technique called an *I-Message*, as introduced by Dr Thomas Gordon in his book *Teacher Effectiveness Training*. In it, he describes how to explain your frustration in such a moment in three parts:

1) The behaviour – describe the issue impacting you.
2) The associated emotion – describe the feeling that this behaviour creates inside you.
3) The impact – describe the tangible effect this behaviour has on you.

In doing so, the problem can be communicated in relatable terms, whereas simply stating, 'I'm angry because you're late,' leaves very little wriggle room for problem-solving. (It also puts the onus on the other person when it's you who is experiencing the unwanted feeling.) The I-Message in this situation would run like this:

1) When you are late . . .
2) . . . I get annoyed . . .
3) . . . because it limits the amount of productive time we have together.

I've broken the circuit on many a dispute by using this technique.

One final point on connections. I have two processes, with acronyms, I like to use when a group is working their way through a difficult moment.

1) WIFLS: *What I Feel Like Saying.* In these situations, we are giving someone permission to share succinctly what's on

their mind without criticism or judgement for a set period of time. This is particularly useful when trying to get to the root of a problem, or when someone needs to vent. It's important when using this technique to name it and time it.
2) SUDI: *Shut Up and Do It*. This is an excellent way of communicating information when time is tight, all the talking has been done, and when immediate action is required. Importantly, this method should be delivered with respect, and only once a strong connection has been built with the receiver or across the team. Sometimes issues are best solved by simply working through them. This technique can help you achieve that.

Ask, Don't Assume

Humans are hardwired to assess others. This is a primal instinct built into our subconscious as a way of analysing threat, though how it manifests itself now tends to result in judgements that can prove inaccurate. For example, we sometimes come up with narratives about people according to their behaviour or statements, especially if they stand at odds with how we act or think. It's very easy to make a snap judgement about someone according to how they look, but appearances can be incredibly deceiving. A brain surgeon might have a body covered in tattoos. A NASA technician could have a nose piercing. The priest with neon pink hair. An attitude of judgement never leads to a healthy working culture. Instead, it's more effective to celebrate the differences in the people working alongside us, so that we can function with unity and clear communication.

We live in politically turbulent times. I have one or two friends that have very different beliefs to me when it comes to voting and it's hard not to make assumptions and dismiss them as being bigoted or ill-educated. Rather than falling into those traps, I've recently taken time to pause, reflect and ask about *why* they've come to those political positions rather than challenging them in an unproductive way.

In doing so, I've learned more about their personal experiences and the thought processes that have led them there. That's not to say that I've changed my mind on who to vote for, or I've suddenly agreed with a politician I might previously have considered unsavoury, but it has helped me to find some common ground – to agree to disagree – rather than propelling me into an unpleasant conflict.

This is a difficult step to take because it requires a lot of courage to engage in such discussions. In his book *The Five Dysfunctions of a Team*, Patrick Lencioni identifies things that prevent people from having tough conversations with one another. Among them are:

- A lack of vulnerability-based trust.
- A fear of conflict.
- A lack of commitment.
- Avoidance of accountability.
- Inattention to results.

When approaching a potentially turbulent conversation, Lencioni recommends identifying it as such in advance. That way everyone can understand what it is they are entering into and ready their minds accordingly. In the All Blacks, the phrase we employed when using this technique was *Entering the Danger,* and it became common language in all the high-performing teams I've worked in. When preparing to enter a tricky conversation, the All Black or coach said, 'Hey, if it's OK, I'd like to *enter the danger* with you.' This created a doorway to a difficult discussion and allowed the two parties (or more) to hear one another and hopefully come to a consensus for moving forward. In doing so, the collective became more powerful, regardless of whether they agreed or not, because the egos in play had been put aside.

Asking, and not assuming, is particularly effective in large groups where there will be all sorts of differing lifestyles, cultural identities and beliefs. Difference is never the issue, disconnection is. In these environments, it's vital that everyone invests some time in learning how their teammates are wired by asking considerate questions and making constructive comments, rather than crushing remarks based on biased assumptions. And if the differences can be viewed as assets rather than obstacles, a collective of disparate personalities can save time, apply their energy effectively, and play to their strengths. All of which is a massive benefit to any team.

> **The 24-Hour Rule:** Set an action based on the concept of asking, but not assuming, and commit to doing it in the next 24 hours. Refer to your journal afterwards and note what happened.

Simplicity Is Everything

Whether I'm communicating with athletes or CEOs, my aim is to deliver very complex situations or theories in an easily digestible format, so that a child could understand them. My aim is to be uncomplicated and relatable, but in a lot of high-performance environments such an attitude doesn't exist. People waffle on in corporate speak, or science babble, usually because they want to create an air of superiority by looking knowledgeable, or professorial. But I've always wanted to be spoken to in terms I can understand, especially in times of uncertainty and ambiguity, which is why I try to share my ideas or strategies in the most basic terms. Simple language also tends to carry more power and reaches the most stubborn personalities.

Recently, while attending a camp with the Melbourne Storm rugby league team, I noticed the acronym FAF had been marked as a theme in the team's pre-season training programme. When the strength and conditioning coach ran through the day's activities, he mentioned the letters.

'Remember our goal,' he said. *'It's all about being fit as fuck.'*

The penny dropped. The trainer had taken what could have been a complicated process, with charts, statistics and personal bests, and delivered it in the simplest terms. Similarly, ahead of the 2023 Rugby World Cup, the All Blacks head coach, Ian Foster, along with his staff, discussed how to ready the squad. Rather than overwhelming the group with various team and individual targets, Ian stated that the best team in the world seldom won the Rugby World Cup. *It was the best team on the day*. He then drew an archery-style target on a board. In the middle was a message: *Be the best team on game day*.

No matter what we were doing, our aim was clear. That one instruction enabled us to approach our tasks free of clutter, whether they were technical, tactical or mental. In doing this, Ian reinforced the fact that simplicity was everything.

Te Puna o te Kī: From Stapler to CEO

Not all leadership journeys follow a glamorous path. My brother, Dudley, is the perfect example of this. After spending what he described as three 'average years' at college, he landed his first job at the New Zealand Post Office in 1969 where he held the grand title of *Stapler*. It was his job to pin the toll invoices to telephone accounts and all for an annual salary of $1,235. Over time, this role educated him in the world of business, and he discovered that good leaders knew how to make mundane work feel enjoyable. Dudley spent 35 years at Telecom and as he progressed through the ranks, he experienced 20 restructures and developed a passion for leadership, mental performance and team building.

By 2005, Dudley had developed his own skills to such a degree that he was offered the role of CEO at the business telephone directory Yellow Pages and tasked with preparing the company for sale. This happened because Dudley possessed an ability to connect powerfully with people from all walks of life. He never shied away from the hard questions, or the difficult conversations, and he led in a way that created a powerful group of followers. To this day I meet people who tell me how much they loved working for Dudley. He was a master of the *Four Rules of Engagement for Moments of Uncertainty and Ambiguity,* and he often highlights several leadership learnings that he picked up along the way:

1. You learn little with your feet under the desk, so walk the floor and engage with people at every level. (He deliberately joined the smoking group at Yellow Pages. In doing so, he gathered valuable intelligence on what was really going on in the business.)
2. The best leaders listen to learn and ask rather than tell.
3. People respond to leaders who create a simple vision and regularly share progress on the critical points.
4. Everyone in the business has a family, so strengthen relationships with authentic engagement and personal interactions. (Simple things like sending personalised birthday cards and family Christmas gifts reinforce the human factor.)
5. Feedback is a gift. Dudley discovered it's not what you say but how you say it.

His learnings had some serious upside, and he successfully bonded the team, customers and potential investors to a shared vision. The staff loved their job and talked of having 'yellow blood'. Customers considered the Yellow Pages as the best value outlet for their advertising spend, at a time when Google was a rapidly emerging search engine. And the profitability of the company made it very attractive to investors. When the Yellow Pages was eventually sold in 2007, it was for a then-industry world record sum of $2.2 billion.

Not a bad result for someone who started out stapling toll invoices for a living.

The Wero: Reset the System

Always take a moment to reset yourself before entering a new space. If I've had a full-on day, it can be quite easy for me to walk through the front door like a whirlwind and then spend those vital first four minutes yakking away to a colleague on the phone, rather than connecting with everyone inside the family home. To shift the mood ahead of time, I often sit quietly in my car, which allows me to calm my mind and arrive home in a more attentive mood. Likewise, when arriving at a meeting, I like to reach an emotional state that is both connective and steady.

Not resetting as we move from environment to environment can be problematic, especially if we're busy or stressed. We enter a different room or meeting and rush into things. We want to get to the end of a task or conversation before it's barely started. But this approach can be unsettling to others, especially if the people we're with are in a completely different mindset. In those situations, it helps if we prepare our minds beforehand and then go to work. Sometimes our impatience to win is the reason we lose, so make sure you have a reset system that serves you well ahead of these moments.

The Library of Learnings

- When entering a new environment take four minutes to engage authentically with the people within it, rather than arriving in a distracted or disinterested manner. Put down the phone, look people in the eye, and connect.
- When approaching a difficult discussion, ask the other person if it's OK to *enter the danger.* This allows both parties (or more) to hear one another in a calm and civil manner and hopefully come to an agreed way of moving forward.
- For a team to approach their tasks free of mental clutter, it's important they are communicated to in a clear manner. Don't overwhelm them with word salads or overcomplicated business speak. Present complex ideas as simply as possible.
- Connect before you correct and become skilled at delivering I-Messages. They move people and behaviours.

CHAPTER 13

Managing the Moment Pt 1: Strengthening the Mental Game

Sporting events, as with many things in life, hinge on the big moments. These are the events that happen quickly, sometimes without a player fully comprehending their importance at the time, and they require decisive, instinctive action. In rugby, it could be the fumbled ball that slips from a player's grasp. In a split second, momentum shifts direction, the defensive mindset of one team moves into attack, and they score a try rather than conceding one. Everything changes in a heartbeat. In life it could be a moment when we recognise someone nearby in medical trouble and we step in to help. In business, it's the new person who unexpectedly stands up in a meeting with a bold plan to save the company or project. These moments happen with swift thought, and when they go well, they look effortless, though in reality a lot of preparation has gone into maximising their arrival. That's because when the big moments happen, a successful person has already trained their mind to meet the pressure head-on, knowing it will separate them from second best.

There are several rules to managing the moment, no matter the situation.

1) No person can control their past or predict the future, so only the moment in front of them is controllable.
2) A moment isn't owned until it appears. That's because no one has seen that exact same moment before.

3) Moments are never given to someone – they appear, and the person, or team, must grab them. When they do, *they win*.
4) Not all moments are equal. Some arrive without consequence, like the penalty kick in a one-sided game; others arrive pregnant with opportunity and danger, like Stephen Donald's decisive kick in the 2011 Rugby World Cup Final. (It's possible that, had Stephen known the decisive significance of that one kick at the time, he might have found it considerably trickier to execute.)
5) To make the most of the moment, or moments, a person must keep their eye out for them. Be warned: these openings and opportunities can vanish in a split second.
6) The only way to greatness is managing your way through pressure – and you do that by taking control of one moment at a time.

In rugby, the key to thriving when the moment arrives is to remove fear, uncertainty and doubt beforehand – though every player experiences it from time to time. I can clearly recall an image from 2013 when the All Blacks were playing at Twickenham. Ahead of the game, Dan Carter, Richie McCaw and Kieran Read stood side by side in the players' tunnel, all of them waiting to be called out to the field of play by the referee. For a split second, Dan became diverted. Instinctively, he put his head in his hands, and it was clear that his attention was elsewhere. He had to move on quickly, otherwise his thoughts might derail his performance.

The truth about handling moments in highly pressurised situations is that a person, or team, must work their way through them, taking control of each one in succession, until the day has been won. Dan, despite this brief lapse, understood the importance of not getting stuck in such circumstances. A second later, he'd reconnected with the present and settled himself. Whatever had diverted him in that moment was pushed to one side, and he was ready for the opportunity that was in front of him. I'll now explain how he did so.

The Mind Is a Muscle. *Train It.*

Just as our body is made up of physical muscles, so our brain is a mental one, and like our abductors, biceps and quads, it can be worked in such a way that it's possible to prepare for moments of great importance, such as the one faced by Dan in the tunnel at Twickenham. The All Blacks had structures that supported the strengthening and conditioning of the mind, such as our MMA meetings. Elsewhere, there were training simulations where players worked through drills that replicated the stresses of a pressurised game, or a fixture where momentum had turned against us. These activities were conducted in mini-units either with the coaches or by individuals in their own skill development time. The key being that they were deliberate, planned and reviewed. Because of this work the players were generally able to stay in the present when it mattered, which meant they could maintain a clear mind and play the moment in front of them decisively. Interestingly, the techniques used are translatable to any environment and could be easily applied to your own circumstances, as I'll now explain.

#1 Create a Reset Structure

Our brains regularly drift from the present and into a vortex of past mistakes and imagined disasters that might or might not happen. There's not a lot we can do to prevent that; it's part of being human, and there are all sorts of reasons why someone might become consumed by negative thoughts on the eve of their driving test, or a pitch for a lucrative new business contract. Sometimes these stressors occur out of nowhere. On other occasions we're reminded of a past screw-up by a person, place, or even a song or smell. Suddenly, a floodgate opens, and our thinking is contaminated by all sorts of distractions when we should be laser-focused on the job in hand. In such a situation, becoming skilled at utilising the following three-part reset structure can be super effective at bringing you back to the present moment.

PART ONE: Regain emotional control. Connect to the *now* with a deep breath, a pinch on the arm or clench the fist. (Sometimes if we are prone to unhelpful thoughts, it helps to crack a knuckle or two, or to twang an elastic band looped around the wrist.) This one action can help us to recognise a negative step before it spirals out of control.

PART TWO: Clear the deck. The eyes tell a story, and when someone is looking down at the ground in a moment of pressure, there's every chance they've become locked into an episode of negative thought. Whenever the All Blacks called a huddle, the captain gave a simple command: *eyes on me*. This allowed him to check whether everyone was present and engaged, and to reset anyone who wasn't. Bringing your eyes level with a teammate or friend during a pressurised event will help you (and them) to clear any emotional clutter. You can then direct your attention towards what needs to happen next.

PART THREE: Next action. Having gathered ourselves, it's important to move on from the negative thoughts and meet the forthcoming moment. This is done best by focusing on the next micro-action. For an All Black this might involve a player getting off the ground much faster than his opponent, moving quickly over the first three metres, or connecting with the teammate closest to them. While in the general workplace, it could be the writing of a tricky email or making sure we start a meeting with energy and enthusiasm.

Here's Dan on that moment from 2013:

> *I remember the photo in the Twickenham tunnel very clearly. It was my 100th game for the All Blacks and I had been riddled with injuries that year – there were times I thought I'd never reach the milestone. The week of the game was full of accolades and excitement that I found quite distracting: I knew I needed to go out and perform for my teammates, which was the most important thing. To do that I had to live in the moment and nail each task directly ahead of me. While standing in the tunnel I was focused, and in the moment, but all of a sudden, the occasion and its emotion came over me and I briefly lost*

sight of what I needed to do for the team. I knew instantly that I had to reset and regroup, and to 'go external'. I ran my hands over my face, told myself to take a deep breath and reminded myself to concentrate on the process directly ahead. The rest is history.

#2 Learn Your Watch Words

When preparing to face a series of inevitable moments in, say, an international Test match, or a contract negotiation, it's important to establish a positive psychological state so that we can be ready for whatever's thrown at us. This is tricky because our thoughts shift constantly, either sharpening or blunting our judgement. That's why it's important we always remain in control mentally, and one way of doing this is to draw up a shortlist of *Watch Words* – three or four pointers that can direct our attention to where it needs to go when the moment arrives. In the All Blacks, four words were always front and centre:

- Mindset: This shifts constantly and can lift us up or fog our thinking. Keep it in check. Our mindset establishes the tone for everything.
- Attention: Direct it appropriately so you can focus on the next moment, the next task, the next action.
- Intent: Bring the right levels to the next moment – and your actions, responsibilities and behaviours. Intent creates your intensity.
- Intensity: Our actions, movements and responsibilities must be executed at the right levels of readiness and with the right levels of timing and energy. (Your intensity will be directly related to your intent.)

Whenever the All Blacks came together for a tour or World Cup, these Watch Words became mantras. Our coaches referred to them every day while the players lived their meaning constantly, embedding the concepts of *mindset, attention, intent* and *intensity* into their training regimes and during games.

For example, some players were known for drifting through certain drills in training without the right level of intensity, which then impacted the overall skill execution and decision-making inside the specific game scenario. This was sub-optimal because it was known that if we prepared through the week at a lower intensity then we would play in much the same way. To counteract this, the individuals concerned were called out and reminded (through the Watch Words) about what was required when they executed their role. My advice for you would be to write a similar list. The concepts of mindset, attention, intent and intensity mentioned above are powerful cues for any moment, whether that be in work, rest or play. However, if a different combination feels more applicable to your job, role or project, write them down and reference them as part of your daily routine.

#3 Train Messy

Rugby matches, like offices or households, can be chaotic environments. Nothing goes smoothly, no gameplan runs exactly as imagined, and in an event as pressurised as a Test match, people behave in unexpected ways, and the big moments generally come at a team rapidly and without warning. It's for this reason that the All Blacks rarely trained the perfect game: we knew that chasing the ideal was a mistake. Instead, we liked to bring a ragged, untidy and harassed element to our practices because it was the vibe of every rugby game ever played. As mentioned in Chapter Three, each mini-group in the All Blacks squad (the outside backs, midfield backs, the insides, and so on) had an Independent Operating Unit. These groups trained some of the more specialised skills required of them during a 20-minute block at the end of every session, and *messiness* was encouraged. If we wanted our skills to be reliable under pressure, then we needed to regularly pressure test them, and in doing so we trained everyone to stay composed, smooth and strong inside the chaos that accompanied the defining moments in tight contests. For example, rather than practising our lineouts smoothly, without interference, we created a competitive edge and encouraged the players to disrupt one another either physically, psychologically or verbally, so they could be better prepared for a game-day scenario. (We'll discuss some of these events, known as 'squeeze drills' in a little more detail in the next chapter.)

Importantly, after every training session, or game, a mental review was conducted by the Independent Operating Units. The aim was to improve the next skills block by asking the following questions:

- In what specific moments didn't we perform to the All Blacks standard?
- What specific skills or decisions could we improve in that moment?
- How can our I.O.U. adapt the next skill session to improve execution under pressure?

Importantly, the aim in training sessions was not to get *weird* or *out there*. Instead, we considered the game-day events that generally created the most difficulty or the greatest number of errors. Then we worked out methods for simulating them, while preparing the team in advance. You can do something similar. When learning new techniques (or practising old ones), bring a little raggedness to your process by shortening the deadline, operating without a favourite tool, app, or software programme, or by working with a reduced number of teammates. These challenges will condition you to stay calm in the most chaotic of moments.

> **30-Second Coaching**: Imagine you had to explain the concept of *training messy* to a work colleague, family member or mate in 30 seconds. *How would you phrase it?*

#4 Remember the Power of Zero

When readying ourselves to meet an event packed with moments, it's important we start our preparations at the very beginning, without skipping over any required steps through familiarity or laziness. To identify the importance of this process, the MMA group drew a line chart, marking one end as *zero* – the start point when preparing for an upcoming game – a point in the preparations where we should have experienced a nervous knot in the gut. (Remember: this sensation is there to remind us that a daunting challenge lies ahead and that if we fail to genuinely prepare, or take shortcuts, we'll likely suffer as a result.) The other end of the line was the finishing point – or 100 – a time when our preparations had been concluded, the game was finished and every moment had been met with strength and power and we felt stoked about our performance. The only way to reach 100 was to work from one end of the line to the other, in full. *No shortcuts.*

The problem with winning matches easily is that it creates a sense of complacency once the work, or training, has started again, which means we're not as connected with what's required, or go deep enough in our preparation, as we previously were. (In such situations, I like to describe the connection as being *skin deep*, when it needs to be *bone deep*.) As I've stated earlier, I never really worried about the All Blacks after a defeat. Our mindset was so robust that the players and coaches instinctively understood the power of starting from *zero*, with no shortcuts. It was when we'd won that I became nervous. As humans we all like an easy ride; our brains want to give our bodies some respite from the punishment, especially in tournaments when the games are piled up on top of one another, or in any job where a succession of deadlines can dominate the calendar. Under these conditions, a person, or team, will instinctively reset to 20 or 30, skipping some of the early preparatory phases through laziness, or overconfidence, whereas a recently defeated or less skilful team will begin way before *zero*, starting their work at -20 or -30, as denoted by the X in the diagram. This is why underdogs sometimes land a heavy blow on their more talented rivals. Their weaker technical or reputational position encourages them to work harder and deeper in advance. They have a mindset advantage generated in part because the favourites might have been lulled into a comfortable state by a good victory, media hype, and fan adulation. As a result, they perform a 'soft reset', which is a very dangerous place to live in.

Resetting to zero is not a *sometimes* thing. It needs to occur after every game, each and every day. And after every moment inside a game, big or small. (And no matter the score.) As an All Black, having crossed the try line, you are permitted a moment of celebration. But once that has been completed, the expectation is that everyone resets to zero, or before zero. All conditions, no exceptions. The elephant in the room, of course, is this: *How does the observer know when a team, or person, has started exactly back at zero?* Sadly, science hasn't given us a reliable process to determine this yet, and we tend to rely on gut instinct and observable behaviours as our information source. While it's difficult to know in the moment whether there has been a genuine reset, it does become much clearer after a period of post-game analysis. For the time being, hindsight remains the great teacher.

Be Where Your Feet Are At

Strengthening our mental game in advance of the big moments is one thing; thriving within them, in real time, is an altogether different experience. To succeed, we must learn to switch on and maintain focus, whether we're practising or playing, and this begins by grounding ourselves in the *now*. In Chapter Eleven we discussed the power of shortening our horizons into the next hour as a way of pushing forward in moments of adversity. To magnify that process, it's possible to draw our horizons to an even tighter timeframe – *the now,* or the current second – simply by remembering to *be where our feet are at.* This is an important step, because the key to winning the moment is delivering absolute engagement through both the body and the mind. If this act can be extended to everything we do – in the workplace, at home, in the gym – we can become unstoppable.

Being where our feet are at is a mindset that we drove consistently within the All Blacks environment. Whether we were training and playing; eating and talking; socialising and decompressing – we wanted our people to be present in that moment. Energy flows where your attention goes, so it was important that our players were connected to the moments they were in. This mindset was vital if they were to perform to the required expectations in training and in games, and also to reap the expected benefits from an activity that was designed to fill their emotional recovery tanks. In such circumstances, both feet had to be in every moment – half-hearted never worked.

The haka was a powerful example of this. In those moments, the boys came together and connected to their breath, the *All Blackness*, and to all the faces that had worn the jersey before them. By bonding on a spiritual level, it was believed that we could draw our ancestral spirits from the earth to join us in battle and we saw this union expressed through the eyes and in the facial expressions of the *pūkana*. More was felt in those moments than seen, which was why the pre-game haka represented the most special of moments for any All Black. If a player wasn't where his feet were during this ritual, everything became compromised. At that time, the players had to be thinking of nothing but the haka. If their minds drifted to the game ahead, or their immediate opponent, it compromised the team's ability to connect on a spiritual level.

In the hectic world of business, I see many people not being where their feet are at. A leader with a clear vision will get in front of their people and fail because they are focused only on the future, or some mistake from the past. Of course, forward planning is important, as is self-analysis; however, if their plans and ambitions aren't couched in the *now*, and the company leader is unable to focus their attention on the present, they will lose the people around them. The same thing happens to the smartest kid in the classroom. When given a group project, he or she will race ahead with an idea, expecting their mates to keep pace. When they won't or can't and everyone becomes frustrated, the team often fragments, and the project falls apart. Sometimes a person's desire to finish the moment prevents them from owning it.

For example, I can recall games where we only had to hold onto the ball for 30 seconds to win. In some cases, we'd defended for 25 phases, as every player executed their role patiently, and at the right time. Then, out of nowhere, one of our players became overeager and moved too early, their impatience resulting in a penalty kick against us that caused us to lose the game. But this can happen in business too. A sales rep might be clear on why a prospective buyer should purchase their product, but during the pitch they move too fast and skip over several important details. The buyer, understandably, becomes frustrated and looks for a reason to say, 'Thanks, but no thanks'. And all because the seller got ahead of what was happening in the moment.

Being where our feet are is a constant practice, a bit like meditation, and no one truly masters it. A person can have it one minute and then drift away from it the next. Sometimes it's front and centre in our minds, other times it runs silently in the background like the app on a phone. I've found that the concept of being where our feet are only becomes obvious when we're *not doing it* because we become anxious about a past event or a future consequence. A footballer might have to take a penalty that decides a cup final, while a vet might have to deliver a life-saving procedure to a sick animal. If that event brings fear, uncertainty and doubt, then it's a sign they're not where their feet are at. To bring themselves back into the here and now they should use the reset structure outlined earlier in this chapter.

The true barometer for whether we're fully immersed in the

present is internal, a feeling, and checking for it is a skill we should practise regularly. We only need to ask a few questions of ourselves in our journals:

What takes me out of the present moment?

What are my triggers?

What can I do to ensure I stay connected to the present moment more – at work, at home, at play?

Asking these questions might seem trivial at first. However, by digging into the elicited responses, they can become performance game-changers, and the difference between winning the moment and falling short.

Te Puna o te Kī: Executing the Basics

In 2013, the All Blacks were the first international tier one rugby team to win every game in a calendar year in the professional era. We went a whole year undefeated, a feat unheard of in the modern game. But boy, did we come close to blowing it against Ireland, a team that had never beaten us at the time. We faced them in the Aviva Stadium, Dublin, an intimidating bowl where the fans looked as if they were on top of the field, and for the first part of the game, we couldn't get a foothold. After 18 minutes, Ireland was ahead 19–0. By half-time, we'd managed to claw back some points, but we still trailed 22–7, which was considered a healthy lead back then. The All Blacks were in trouble, and we knew it. Something had to change.

And then the moment arrived.

With two minutes to go, I looked at the scoreboard. *Ireland 22 New Zealand 17.* Despite closing the gap, we were still under the pump, and our situation was to worsen considerably when our opponents were awarded a penalty so close to the goalposts I could have thrown the ball over. But as I watched Johnny Sexton, Ireland's fly-half, step up to take the kick, I sensed some apprehension. This was born from years of experience: I loved watching kickers from the sideline; I'd worked with Dan Carter enough to know a great one when I saw one; and I was familiar with the routines of the world's leading penalty takers. For some reason, Sexton was taking a lot longer than usual. And when he eventually struck the ball, it sailed and wobbled past the wrong side of the post. *He'd missed!* The crowd groaned. The chance to put the game out of reach had passed. The All Blacks still had a chance. A slim chance. But a chance, nevertheless.

To be successful in sport, it's generally accepted that everyone needs to do the basics, to an elite standard. Teams generally don't win big matches, or tournaments, by pulling off a succession of mercurial acts. They consistently execute the standard components of their gameplan to the best of their ability, such as passing, kicking, tackling and movement off the ball. The cumulative effect of this execution puts them in a position to exploit any weaknesses in their opponents and maximise any chances or moments of good fortune that might come their way as play unfolds. Johnny Sexton's miss was undoubtedly a lucky break. But rather than rushing around like headless chickens, the All Blacks regrouped, remained calm, and for the next two minutes coolly retained possession, the ball touching the hands of all 15 players as they patiently worked their way up field. The inevitable opening presented itself and Ryan Crotty scored a try at the death, drawing us level. After a nervy first kick (which had to be retaken when an Irish player charged the kicker too early), Aaron Cruden eventually made the conversion to win us the game, 24–22. The players had grabbed the moment, connected to the here and now, kept both feet in it, and used their patience to succeed in the unlikeliest of circumstances. As a result, history now salutes the 2013 All Blacks, who have aptly been called *The Unbeatables*.

The Wero: The Memo Playlist

Recently, a client came to me with a request.

'Gilbert, could you record a series of voice memos for me, stuff that will help improve my mental performance.'

What a brilliant idea. I set about producing a series of short voice notes, no longer than two minutes each, with messages and cues that would allow him to meet the moment, regardless of what he was doing at the time. There was a voice note to inspire him to be courageous, another to help when his mind started to race, and one that reinforced why I believed he would succeed. Some notes reminded him to bring his horizon forward, others helped him to deal with the inevitable pressures that accompanied his role. I even recorded a short clip that was designed to help him sleep. (He later recorded several of these in his own voice.) There were no rules as to when and where he used the memos, and he set them up like a regular playlist of songs and albums. Apparently, they have been a great help.

All of us can create a library of inspirational, meditative or motivational recordings – we only need to produce some for ourselves or ask a loved one or trusted friend to make some for us. They don't have to be expertly written either, because there is power in using a voice that connects with you and moves you in some way. Getting a much-loved relative to recall a moment when you were brave, empathetic or calm under pressure, can deliver a boost when going through tough times. Equally, someone talking about a time when you came through a moment of adversity, or surprised everyone with your talent, can prove inspirational too. You may also like to find some inspirational quotes from your favourite athletes, politicians or artists, and record them yourself. These audio clips, while short and sweet, can act as a reset, connecting us to the moment, while quietening the trepidation, that can become regular companions during episodes of high-pressure.

The Library of Learnings

- Life is a series of *moments.* These are the events that happen quickly, sometimes without us comprehending their importance at the time, and they require decisive, instinctive action if we're to succeed.

MANAGING THE MOMENT PT I

- To make the most of the moment, or moments, a person must keep their eye out for them. Be warned: these openings and opportunities can vanish in a split second.
- To meet a moment head-on, we must *be where our feet are at*. If we can deliver absolute engagement through both the body and mind in these moments, then we become unstoppable.
- To prevent anxiety in the moment, we must connect to the *now*, because stress is caused by worrying about past mistakes and future consequences. Reset with a deep breath or pinch on the arm to catch anxiety when it is a spark – before it becomes a fire or even worse a wildfire. This one action can help us to recognise negative thinking before it spirals out of control.

CHAPTER 14

Managing the Moment Pt 2: The Duel Within

During World Cups, or Rugby Championships, we often carried out an emotional assessment of our opponents, so the players knew what to look for in the forthcoming fixtures. Rather than confusing everyone with complicated psychological terms, we compared each team to an animal and then listed the characteristics that would likely show up on the field. The Australians, for example, were hyenas and played like scavengers. They were cunning and cocky, hunted in packs, and waited for the opportunity to pounce, usually once their opponents had made a mistake. (They also 'dined out' on victories. If your international team has ever been beaten by Australia, you'll have probably been reminded about it for weeks, even months afterwards.)

The South Africans were elephants, hot-headed and known for playing on passion. This was a powerful resource when it ran in their favour, but if that passion boiled over into anger it became a weakness. At times, they fed off the external factors around them, like the energy of the crowd, or some flicker of vulnerability, hesitancy, or uncertainty in their opponents. In those moments they behaved like bullies, crushing everyone in their path. However, if their emotions ran too hot, and they played without control, the Springboks most resembled a fleet of bulldozers. They telegraphed their thoughts and intentions with words and bluster, and their actions tended to be ill focused, and ill directed, which prevented them from course correcting swiftly.

The All Blacks were very different. When performing to our optimum, the panther became our spirit animal, and not just because of our identical colouring. We both hunted our prey patiently: stalking, waiting silently, before bringing it down with a ruthless efficiency and a sharp cutting edge. But while the big cats were mammals, the All Blacks were cut with a cold-blooded streak and motivated by a deeper drive than simply winning. For example, we placed a huge emphasis on legacy and the respect we showed to the past players and to our present teammates. We fed internally and weren't worried or intimidated by anyone, any place or any occasion. Most importantly, we were unreadable and especially dangerous when an opponent believed that they'd beaten us ahead of time.

Of all the teams competing on the world stage, it was our hope that the All Blacks had the most emotional control. This was important for several reasons:

1) A gameplan is essential, but if the mind doesn't go with it, there will be problems.
2) An individual's skillset won't work if their mindset isn't right.
3) A team/person can only win the moment when their mind is stronger than their emotions.

The last point – the battle of thought over feelings – is arguably the most valuable because it's a duel within that exists in just about every walk of life. The nervous medical student preparing to take their exams. The computer technician executing a complicated skill for the very first time. Or the athlete performing a decisive action in a crunch event, such as a cup final or the Olympic Games. In all three contexts, the psychological processes taking place are identical: a struggle is being waged between mind and emotion, and the results of that conflict will nearly always determine the outcome.

The Red Track vs The Blue Track

Let me explain it this way. Our brain has two distinct *systems*, the Red and the Blue. The Red is unsophisticated; it deals with threats in the here and now, and it works quickly, with intensity, and drives us to react instantly. This isn't always helpful. In Test matches, for example, these threats arrive thick and fast and there are referee decisions to deal with, scoreboard changes to process, and poor decisions and individual mistakes to manage. It's important a player manages their Red System effectively, otherwise they might retaliate, go off plan or become stuck. (See: a player sulking after a decision goes against them in an important game.) The Blue System is more advanced. Goal processing is its main responsibility, and as our mental HQ it works at a slower and less intense pace to the Red System. When in control, the Blue System has the power to steady us and align our actions to the purpose in hand. (See: the astronaut conducting a delicate satellite repair during a spacewalk.)

Meanwhile, sport stars, like everybody else, are exposed to adversity all the time and it arrives in different guises. Athletes are dropped for important games, they miss out on qualification and are sidelined by injuries. Sometimes they become stuck in a poor run of form or feel frustrated because their coach doesn't *get them*. Equally, in business, people can be overlooked for promotion or passed up for a pay rise. Stress levels also rocket when a new leadership arrives and changes the working practices of a team or organisation. These events can then cause a person to spiral, especially if their Red System is leading the charge. Therein lies the duel, the battle between our mind and emotions, and we enter it every day. To win, we must:

- Train the mind to recognise our emotions without being ruled by them.
- Accept that the mind should be the leader, not the follower in guiding our actions.

MANAGING THE MOMENT PT 2: THE DUEL WITHIN

- Calm the storm without suppressing our emotions. We should respond with intent, not react impulsively.
- Master the mind by taking control of our attention (by redirecting it) and taking control of our thoughts (by reframing them).

During high-pressure moments, good and bad, the most important thing isn't the resulting emotions. *It's about how we manage our reaction to those emotions.* For example, the injured athlete might become angry. If they use that anger as fuel during their rehabilitation, then it's a positive. But if it causes them to lash out or sulk for long periods, then it's a problem.

When I first began my journey into sports psychology in the late 1980s, I referred to this process as the Red Track v Blue Track Challenge. I presented it to athletes and, later, businesspeople as a way of helping them to win the duel that kicks off when pushing through a difficult challenge where the threat levels are high. To illustrate this concept, I created a flow chart to show the choices that confront a person when they're presented with a problem or test. The chart was then placed on the wall or the floor in different locations around the team's environments (business or sport), so that a person could figure out how to walk the right track as they faced their latest moment of pressure.

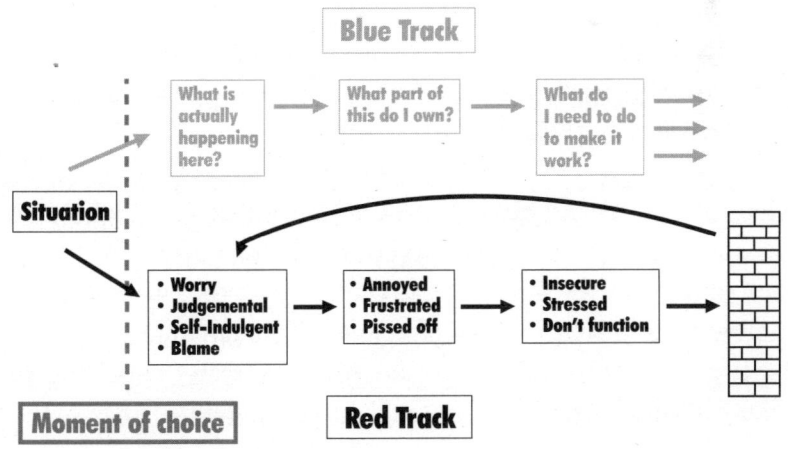

When encountering a challenging situation, we all experience a moment of choice where one of two *tracks* become available – the Red or Blue. The individual choosing the Red Track will experience emotional turbulence. Rather than relying on rational thought, they'll instead listen to and be ruled by their emotions. This then causes them to worry. As a result they can become judgemental (about themselves and others) and self-indulgent, and it's not uncommon for a person in such a situation to blame others for whatever's happening to them, rather than looking inward for a more productive solution. These emotions trigger feelings of annoyance and frustration that can manifest as insecurity and stress. Eventually, the individual hits a brick wall, which restricts their ability to function effectively. Their unpleasant feelings intensify, and they become increasingly worried, triggering a doom loop of anxiety. It's not a fun place to be.

However, if an individual can get onto the Blue Track, then an entirely different process kicks in. Faced with their moment of choice, they can apply rational thought and ask three questions:

- *What is actually happening here?* The facts of the situation are assessed and rationalised, which strips away any disruptive emotional reactions. Emotions are our worst advisers.
- *What part of this do I own?* The individual establishes what parts of the situation are within their control, and what parts aren't.
- *What do I need to do to make it work?* They then rise to the challenge by identifying proactive steps in the areas that will benefit them most.

When an athlete – All Black, Black Cap, Silver Fern – or businessperson was faced with a difficult test or situation, I often encouraged them to stand by the flow chart, to clarify where they were at, at that point in time. *The Red or the Blue Track.* This physical act brought clarity and was extremely powerful. It helped many a stuck person to move. (I also used this process to help an individual analyse their behaviour after a fast-moving event to see if they were on the Red or Blue Track.) This is very important because when a person is stuck on the Red Track, they enter a *Red Head state,* and they will either fight, flight or freeze. This can cause them to go off task, become results-orientated, panicked and ineffective. The *Blue Head state* is the optimal state to be in. They will be on task and performing to the best of their ability, while feeling expressive, calm and in the moment. They will have clear thought and clear talk. Blue Head on the Blue Track is the goal and the place to be.

> **Reflection Time:** Identify a moment from the last seven days when you could have benefited from understanding the Red Track/Blue Track state. How would you have managed your responses differently? If it helps, place your version of the flow chart on page 231 somewhere it can be referred to at all times.

Frustration Tolerance

I've experienced both sides of the brain taking control when working with the All Blacks, most notably with our two games against Argentina in 2020 in the Tri-Nations, during the height of the Covid pandemic. Argentina was a team that thrived in a niggly environment. In animalistic terms, they were most like the Chihuahua: lots of bluster, plenty of bark and very annoying. They liked to aggravate their opponents with cheap shots, mouthy comments and the 'dark arts', such as time wasting and borderline illegal tackles. Their M.O. was built around causing frustration, because a team was never penalised for frustrating their opponents and we fell into their trap. In the first match, their aim was to provoke us into retaliation in the hope that we might go rogue, which we did over and over again. We were caught in the worst of both worlds: hurtling along the Red Track with a Red Head and we were beaten 25–15 in the Western Sydney Stadium, our first defeat against them in 30 matches.

Luckily, we were playing Argentina again two weeks later. That gave us some time to reflect, review and reset. As we nursed our bruised egos, the MMA group went about their work and presented the squad with one simple question:

Argentina got under our skin: what caused it?

When the results came back, we collated the most common answers and presented them to the group.

1. Cheap/illegal shots; pushing and shoving — 52 per cent
2. Mistakes/skills errors — 21 per cent
3. Gameplan not working — 9 per cent
4. Teammates overtalking, or 'going Red' — 9 per cent
5. The referee — 9 per cent

Clearly, Argentina had done an excellent job in winding us up. Pushed to frustration by their behaviour, our reactions had become a problem, and we'd self-destructed. The answer to avoiding a repeat performance was to work on our *Frustration Tolerance* – during an intense event, such as an international rugby match, a tense business meeting or a legal dispute, a person's tolerance will move up and down a Frustration Tolerance scale from high to low, depending on what's happening at the time. When a person was high on the scale, they relied on techniques that settled their emotions, cleared their heads and calmed the mind. In that moment, they were winning the duel. When a person's frustration tolerance was low, they became aggressive, passive or sulky. In that moment, they were losing the duel. Clearly our Frustration Tolerance had been low during that Argentina game, but we set about implementing several strategies that would help increase our mindset moving forward. It's my belief they can be used by anyone in any setting to help maximise their mental performance.

MANAGING THE MOMENT PT 2: THE DUEL WITHIN

STRATEGY ONE: *Identify Your Triggers*

We focused on prevention and identified the moments, or 'triggers', from the Argentina game where we had been annoyed by our opponents and reacted recklessly, sulked or became passive as a result. We then ranked these events into three levels of aggravation.

LEVEL 1 LIGHT NIGGLE: An irritation designed to provoke an ill-disciplined response. Examples included jersey-pulling, cheap shots off the ball, and verbal abuse. This was an area Argentina excelled in.

LEVEL 2 BORDERLINE NIGGLE: On the edge, but not clear cut. A late hit or an obstruction.

LEVEL 3 UNACCEPTABLE NIGGLE: An action that crossed the line, such as a high tackle or a punch to the head.

Once we'd identified the three levels, every player was asked to plan an effective response for themselves, so they could stay calm in the face of provocation. Some chose to laugh. Others to refocus and fire themselves up for the next tackle. The aim was to prime the mind for all three levels of niggle, meaning our responses would be clear and decisive, and we would remain on task.

STRATEGY TWO: *Create Niggle Scenarios*

It's long been an All Blacks tradition that the team skipper leads the Friday training session, in what's called The Captain's Run. Ahead of the next Argentina game, the MMA group encouraged the players to sit with their journals for 15 minutes and visualise the type of emotionally challenging and/or downright annoying scenarios that might show up when in the Newcastle International Sports Centre – the venue for our next clash. We wanted to put the players into a position where they wouldn't feel surprised.

The benefits of visualisation in sport have been well documented: in short, by imagining a future situation (in which they are playing in a high-pressure event, or executing a skill at a key moment) an athlete will ready the body and mind for when the moment arrives. In these sessions, it helps if the individuals then picture some of the action going on around them, such as their teammates, the opposition and the TV cameras. Smelling the grass and the sweat and hearing the roar of the crowd can also amplify the experience. Basic visualisation can be done anywhere – in a chair, lying down in bed, or while cleaning your teeth or making a cuppa. I liked the players to take the process to another level by first *feelising* the situation, by standing up and miming the moments, before introducing them to situation training and squeeze drills.

Situation training does exactly what it says on the tin – we shoved the players into uncomfortable and annoying scenarios that they would likely experience against Argentina. During practice drills we grabbed at their jersey as they ran with the ball. We tripped them up. We barged into them as they walked away during a water break. The challenge for every All Black was simple: to not go rogue. Ahead of the 2023 Rugby World Cup we even reworked these tests into *squeeze drills* – sessions which replicated the way our opponents would heap pressure or put the *squeeze* on us. In one situation, we worked on the way the ball moved out of the base of the scrum, and when our scrum-half, Aaron Smith, reached down for the ball, it was my job to disrupt his flow by slapping his hands with two long polystyrene 'noodles' – the type you might see floating around in a swimming pool. Whenever Aaron reached in, I slapped and poked him according to how aggro I wanted to make the situation, so that he had to manage his emotions for when an opponent was interfering with his actions for real. I must have done OK because he later nicknamed me *The Noodle Man*.

All of us can set up similar squeeze drills to replicate moments of pressure or emotional turbulence. Rather than practising a speech or pay rise request in front of the mirror, run it past an audience of critical friends. When working on your negotiating skills, ask someone to play the role of the opposing party and ask them to be demanding or unreasonable. Or when preparing to launch a new system, practise how you would react during any incidents of pressure, such as a software crash or a member of staff getting sick at a key moment.

STRATEGY THREE: Build Reset Routines

Finally, we set the players a challenge: to create a three-part reset routine for when they felt their emotions winning the duel in the battle between the Red Head and Blue Head states. The role of the mental game is to keep our feelings level, but that can be difficult, even for the most level-headed of people, as evidenced by the way Argentina had previously got under our skin and every All Black in the Western Sydney Stadium had felt niggled and frustrated. What was needed in those moments was a circuit breaker, of the type outlined in Chapter Thirteen.

These strategies, when brought together, allowed the All Blacks to win the duel within. When we faced Argentina in the next match, we remained composed. Our levels were controlled. And when an opponent pulled on our jersey, or jammed a teammate's face into the ground, we didn't retaliate immediately. Instead, we looked them in the eye and gave them a simple warning: *You'll keep, mate.* We stalked our prey patiently, like a panther, and the next time they picked up the ball (and we had the opportunity) we were lethal in the tackle. In doing so, we kept our Frustration Tolerance at a high level and won the game 38–0.

Te Puna o te Kī: Playing on the Edge

Some players, such as our hooker Dane Coles, ran hotter than others. A World Cup winner in 2015, he performed best when the fire was burning in his belly. But that passion could sometimes overrun. Throughout his career, one or two opponents, like Argentina, targeted Dane hoping his temper would flare up. When we played England in 2014, Dylan Hartley yanked at Dane's jersey; the red mist came down and he lashed out. Luckily, he only received a yellow card.

'I've always been a guy who plays on the edge,' said Dane afterwards. 'But I learned a valuable lesson in England. I probably let little things get to me and at the end of the day that probably cost me. Since then, people have been doing stuff to me, but I've just been getting on with my job. I don't want to make the same mistake.'

Moving forward, a strong self-awareness and several specific training activities helped Dane to prepare for anything our opponents could throw at him. As he recalled of those matches in 2020:

We got sucked into it against Argentina – they brought a lot of passion in that first game and targeted a lot of our players, me included. We'd been staying in Manly which had a nice beach, and some of us might have still been there, mentally. Argentina sniffed blood. They've always been big on winning scrums, and we used to hear them shouting, 'No scrum, no win.' It was in their DNA and if they felt they could get a bit of dominance in there, they would come up to us and celebrate. I remember when we won a penalty, one of their guys got into my face and I slapped him, right in front of the ref. In that moment I'd got caught in a Red Head state, and the penalty was reversed. Then they put the squeeze on us which pressured us emotionally, the red mist came down and it took us off task. Argentina were a team that could spot weakness. With ten minutes to go, they sensed they were in with a chance, and they lifted considerably. This made it very difficult for us to claw anything back. We couldn't regain focus and lost the game 25–15.

Bert got us to work on our mental game afterwards and we identified and then visualised pressure situations where we reacted calmly in the moment. I was a player who operated on the edge – I ran hard, tackled harder and loved nothing more than dominating my opponent. I needed a controlled Red Head state, not a reckless one to get me there. That's how I got my edge. But because I was a forward who threw the ball in during lineouts, which involved a very technical skillset, I also needed a touch of Blue.

I took defeats personally – the loss to Argentina hurt big time. I've always believed that if an All Black didn't feel that way, they shouldn't have been an All Black. For the next game I came up with a reset structure like the one outlined in this book. If someone pulled at my jersey, or chipped away at me verbally, my first reaction was to smile at them. Sure, I sometimes threw a bit of verbal back, but in those first few seconds it was important that I didn't do something that might cost the team. I only played 20 minutes off the bench that day, but I remember one of their guys coming at me. I gave him a few words, laughed and watched as his red mist came down. He couldn't focus after that. I reset, checked in with my teammates and moved onto my next task.

Every player was different. We all had different styles of operating and mine was to perform with a little bit of the Red. OK, probably with more than a little bit. Some coaches didn't like it. There were people who would say, 'Oh, you can't play him. He's a wild guy. He does dumb stuff.' But Bert and the coaches took a different view. They wanted me to be myself and recognised the fact that aggression was what made me. They also knew that I had to control my emotional state, if I was to help the team. I had to play my edge, and I grew into this as my career progressed. Bert's work helped me to get there, and to win the Rugby World Cup with the All Blacks in 2015 was something I'll cherish for the rest of my life. Yes, there was pressure every day, but because we had solid processes in place that dealt with the duel between mind and emotions, we got the job done.

The Wero: Find the Knot

As I stated earlier, complacency is a dangerous state of mind. It can cause us to underestimate our opponents and overestimate our capacity to win when we're not at our best. This often showed up in the All Blacks when we were playing a team that was perceived as being 'easy', or in a game where the stakes were relatively low. Often, I was able to spot a dangerously relaxed player from a mile off. But to make sure, we often started our MMA meetings by asking the group to rate the nerves in their stomach – *the knot* – ahead of the upcoming game, on a scale of 1 to 10, with 1 being as still as a lake and 10 being knotted with anticipation. If the group's average came in at a low 2 or 3 – even early in the week – I felt worried. My fear was that they were in a place of comfort and unprepared for the pressures ahead. (Because to perform well on Saturday, a player and their teammates must do Monday right.) If their opponents found an extra gear to their game, there was a chance our players would be surprised and react emotionally, which could cost us the game.

I remember going through this process during the 2019 Rugby World Cup. Ahead of the quarter-final against Ireland, the players were at a 7 or 8 and we won 46–14. But during the build-up to our semi-final against England our average scores were much lower, and we were beaten 19–7. They surprised us, did what they needed to do, and we never recovered. In doing this work, a simple fact was underlined: if the knot is missing then a team or individual's ability will be compromised. This is why some athletes struggle to reach their optimum levels after winning a league title, or major competition. It's the same for people who have aced an exam, earned an employee of the year award, or completed a massive deal at work.

The trick in such circumstances is to *find the knot*, and to do so we have to look internally and locate a level of discomfort that will inspire us to success. With the All Blacks, the coaches sometimes mixed the starting XV by replacing a seasoned player with a younger one, or someone who had a point to prove. Elsewhere, they might change tactics or remind the group of the consequences of failure. (This was why the Class of 2007 were so important to the teams of 2011 and 2015 – they were a living echo of what could go wrong.) These actions, while small, added a layer of discomfort and helped to bring the knot to a lot of players' stomachs. It also helped when the players measured their performances against an internal standard rather than obsessing over an external one, like the scoreboard, or the latest result. Some of these internal standards included:

- My effort is my trademark.
- Be the example for others to look towards.

- What would the legacy expect of me?
- Never lower the standards – no matter what.

The next time you have something that's important to you, ahead of time make sure you check in on your knot.

The Library of Learnings

- The battle of thought over feelings exists in just about every walk of life, and a team/person can only win when their mind is stronger than their emotions.
- When faced with a pressurised situation, we all experience a moment of choice when one of two *tracks* becomes available – the Red or Blue. The individual choosing the Red Track will experience emotional turbulence. The individual choosing the Blue will turn to rational thought.
- While we can't predict every moment in life, we can predict our responses to them. To retain emotional control, we should identify our trigger points, prepare for them with visualisation, *feelisation* and squeeze drills, and then establish a reset structure for when they arrive.

CHAPTER 15

Winning the Energy Battle

Whenever the All Blacks went on tour, whether that be for a Test series, Bledisloe Cup or Rugby World Cup, it was my job to help create the Team Room – a private space within our hotel HQ that played sanctuary to our legacy and spirit. With the help of massage therapist George Duncan, the walls were decorated with photos from our history and an honours board featuring significant events, including our Rugby World Cup wins, a list of All Blacks with 100 Test caps, and the names of our past team captains, club captains and presidents. The aim was to create a place in which the players could draw inspiration and, most importantly, feel a sense of connection and belonging. Our hope was for every player to walk into the Team Room, see the House of Black (see page 121), stare at the photos on the wall and think, *I'm part of something special*.

Life on tour as an All Black was very much a fishbowl experience. The players and coaches were always *on* and over time this strain took an emotional toll. For this reason, the Team Room served as an area for everyone to restore and recharge, a social hub where the players could decompress and reconnect with one another, and with only one rule: *no work talk*. The players organised a weekly club night every Tuesday, an evening where everyone wore the jersey of their club of origin. As we came together for an hour or so of fun and laughter, this symbolic dress code reminded the players to stay close to their roots. Elsewhere, there were DJ nights and 'pig racing' sessions, where a short racetrack, occupied by several mechanical pigs set on runners, was laid out. Organised by a 'bookmaker', the boys threw down bets and gathered round the table-sized racetrack. Within the intense atmosphere of an international rugby tour, it was important that everyone switched off and had a little fun.

Having accepted that pressure was a lifestyle, the All Blacks also had to acknowledge that the three challenges of expectation, scrutiny and consequence were inevitable, and that they would likely take their toll at some point. No one was immune to pressure, least of all an international rugby player, and it was here that the concept of *The Energy Battle* came into play. All of us have an internal battery – a power source that's either *drained* by negative emotions (a defeat, homesickness) or *recharged* through positive ones (a win, some time spent with family or friends). When someone becomes overly drained, their emotional wellbeing is compromised, which can be concerning because the long-term mental health implications of living a life under excessive strain, without respite, are well known.

To provide a suitable level of *performance care* for the players and staff we categorised a person's emotional state into two distinct categories:

1) Mental health – an individual's overall mental and emotional wellbeing.
2) Mental strength – an individual's ability to withstand discomfort while taking constructive and courageous action under pressure.

An athlete needs to pay attention to both if they're to perform at their optimum levels and stay healthy, as does every single one of us. That's because the modern world has locked us into a constant Energy Battle where our internal batteries are being drained by excessive stress. Emotional discomfort is everywhere – in the workplace, at home and outside our front door. It's even on our phones. And it takes a heavy toll. When I appear at business events, I jokingly describe the perfect 'anti-stress kit' as a large circle, drawn on a piece of paper. In the middle are the words: *Bang head here*. And in times of anxiety, the user should place the paper on a hard surface and headbutt away until they feel some relief. The anti-stress kit is meant to be a joke, but as with a lot of humour, the comedy is rooted in truth.

The Stress Continuum

Of course, it's sometimes difficult to recognise when our mental health and strength is taking a beating, and there are a lot of different scales out there to help us track this. Inside the All Blacks we used *The Stress Continuum* – a visual guide that helped a person to register where they were in terms of their psychological wellbeing.

The beauty of this visual is its simplicity. *The Stress Continuum keeps things real.* When we're in a good place and everything is going well, we flourish. When life throws rocks at us, we falter. When things are just OK, the acceptable middle ground sees us getting by. By checking *The Stress Continuum*'s parameters, it's possible to assess how we're doing when a wave of stress hits us. We only need to ask one simple question.

Where am I on the continuum?

The results can then determine our next steps . . .

- If the pressure is on and we're somewhere in the middle, and just getting by, that's OK. We only need to shift our mindset or recharge our energy levels to move into a positive space.
- In moments when we're flourishing, we should stick to what we're doing, while paying attention to our structures, processes and behaviours. That way, we can repeat them in the future.
- If we're faltering, it's time to lean into a recharging strategy. (And we'll get to that shortly.)

Sometimes, just the act of looking at the continuum can be enough to inspire a faltering person to act. Equally, someone already in a strong location will feel reaffirmed. When the All Blacks were playing during the Covid pandemic, we used *The Stress Continuum* a lot – it helped the players to navigate a world of uncertainty and volatility.

Having assessed our position on *The Stress Continuum*, the next step requires us to lock in a suitable period of recovery that will negate the pressure in our lives and replenish our depleted energy levels, if necessary. We encouraged the All Blacks to use one, or all, of the following strategies.

STRATEGY #1: Powering Up Our Internal Batteries

An All Black who displayed physical strength might not carry the same power emotionally or mentally. To rebalance these areas, we exposed the players to waves of pressure in training so that they could deal with the challenges they'd face in the big moments, building resilience along the way. They were then encouraged to rejuvenate themselves with compensatory waves of recovery, which we called *emotional recovery activities*, or ERAs. These ERAs were deliberately scheduled activities during which a person, or persons, could fill their emotional bucket with an activity that was both pleasurable and/or restorative. Some people liked to read. Others liked to connect with nature. Whatever the activity, the priority was to *switch off* – no performance-related component was allowed. The goal was for the All Black to disengage their mind.

I like to think of the brain as an energy pack. When negative stress builds up, this power source becomes drained, sometimes dangerously so, and it's important to recharge it. When I was studying at university, I used this idea to help me navigate exam season where my days were ruled by a revision plan and test schedule. My aim was to restore my internal power reservoir throughout this tough period by plugging into one of three imaginary batteries – the AAA, the AA, and the D.

The AAA Battery: These are short, daily activities that are simple, soul-enriching and pleasurable. They are unique to you and your situation and should last no more than 10 to 20 minutes. During busy periods in my life, I like to schedule three or four a day, because they give me a lift. Examples include: a cup of coffee in the sun; 20 minutes with a mindfulness app or journal; reading a book; listening to a playlist; a quick walk in the park with the dog. No matter what a person is doing, their day can be broken up with several restorative AAA batteries, and at any time. They are also things that a person can only give to themselves – they cannot be dependent on another individual doing a task or performing an action for them.

The AA battery: Like the AAA battery, these activities power us up, but they differ slightly in time, frequency and intensity. These AA recharges are performed two or three times a week during tough times and should last for a couple of hours. Each session should help us recover from the cumulative stresses of our day-to-day lives. Some people go to the movies for their AA battery. Others perform yoga, do meditation, get a massage, engage in a creative activity, such as painting, pottery or knitting, do online learning or run through an exercise programme. Each to their own. A person should always schedule an AA ahead of time, so it gives them something to look forward to.

The D Battery: These are intensely pleasurable activities that a person will only do once or twice a year. Part of their enjoyment comes from their infrequency – they must feel special and unique, and indicative that we are in a period of focused recovery. The classic D battery is a holiday, active or inactive, but other examples might include a pleasurable workshop, course or learning day, a digital detox, or a staycation where a person takes a day at home to fully relax, by sleeping in, binge watching their favourite shows, and the like. Just knowing that a D battery is on the calendar can act as a light at the end of a tunnel.

Quick sidebar: It's not easy to switch off. Many of us take an afternoon, or day, away from whatever it is we're doing, and we drift through our decompression time, wasting energy by texting people at work, or scrolling through social media for hours on end. But this is an exhausting waste of mental calories. However, to assist in fully engaging with the disengagement process, a person can either *fill* their mind, or *still* it. For example, I have a very busy brain. When it comes to a rest day, I'll often do a session of Bikram yoga because it stills my thinking in a healthy way. On the morning of a Test match however, when the brain is buzzed and wired with lots of different thoughts, I'd fill my mind by watching a succession of movies, one after the other, knowing that I wouldn't have to engage with any work-related processes until the team got together later that afternoon.

To truly relax, it helps to first name the activity that we're going to engage in, whether that be meditation, a coffee break, or even a spa day. Then we should time it. Note exactly how long you will engage in the intended activity. This is a simple but very powerful piece of the rejuvenation process because a person will never get the full benefits, if they allow distractions to infect their designated periods of re-energising. So, name it, time it, and set aside a focused moment, or moments, throughout the day, or week, to practise some important performance self-care.

STRATEGY #2: Reframe the 'Drain'

In the 2024 National Rugby League Grand Final, Melbourne Storm was beaten 14–6 by the Penrith Panthers, and the very next morning the Storm's head coach Craig Bellamy gathered his team together. This was very unusual, most clubs would have given their players a day off to lick their wounds, but Craig wanted to capture the experience and embed the feelings in a time capsule that could be revisited the next time the team reached a Grand Final. As everyone shared their thoughts, team captain Harry Grant delivered an important message to the group: 'Sometimes when you're in a dark place, you think you're buried, when, actually, you've been planted.' Grant recognised that his teammates would have been feeling incredibly low at that point, and that this emotional slump might linger and drain their energy levels if left unchecked. Rather than wallowing in the pain of defeat, he'd reframed their situation as a positive event that, when used appropriately, would energise the group for the opportunities ahead.

As I mentioned earlier, adversity is an equal opportunity employer. It doesn't believe in the concept of fair and unfair, but it will come for everyone at one point or another. If we're unable to handle those moments when bad news or challenge comes knocking on our door, then we'll find that our energy levels are depleted very quickly. However, one way to win The Energy Battle is to conserve our mental calories by reframing the issue in hand, because if we're able to change the way we look at things, *the things we look at change.*

A question all of us can ask ourselves when looking to conserve or preserve energy is: *What things in our lives could we reframe to our benefit?* It might be that we can't stand our boss, or our job. In which case we can view them as motivating forces, ones we can use to inspire us to seek out a new role. Maybe a loved one is very sick, and while this is incredibly sad, it can also serve as a reminder to spend as much quality time as we can with them, while making new memories. Very few situations are beyond reframing, a truth I was reminded of while watching *America's Got Talent* in 2021. When a 30-year-old singer called Nightbirde (real name: Jane Marczewski) auditioned for the show, she explained how she was battling cancer and that it was 'important that everyone know that I'm so much more than the bad things that have happened to me.'. Her performance was so incredible that Simon Cowell sent Nightbirde all the way through to the quarter-final stages when he pressed 'the golden buzzer'.

When she was later told that there was only a 2 per cent chance that she might survive the disease, she had responded that at least it was better than 0 per cent. Though she died in 2022, Nightbirde's voice is the one we need to hear when we are battling through adversity. She stands as a reminder that the world we work in will always bombard us with waves of stress. If we're to win the energy war, we must learn to swim in them.

STRATEGY #3: Stay Connected to Your Positive Influences

When New South Wales defeated Queensland in Suncorp Stadium to win the 2024 State of Origin series, my old mate Wayne Smith watched from the stands as a supporter. Before the game, I went up to his seat for a catch-up because Wayne was the man that started it all for me. Our fateful meeting in the staffroom at Hillmorton High over 40 years earlier had set me on a path that led me to writing this book today. But Wayne is so much more than an opening chapter in my story. His is an enduring friendship that I cherish dearly, and it's kept me going in some tough times. Whenever my levels are running low, I'll check in with a friend like Wayne for a boost. I find the connection works wonders.

When looking to win the energy battle, it's vital we lean on our allies – and not just any old friends, either. They must be positive influences; they must understand you; they must be happy for your wins and pained by your defeats; they must have stood by you during difficult moments. Healthy friendships act like charging stations. They can power us up, and I've found that strong social support networks are vital when looking to maintain our mental health and mental strength. This is particularly so for men, who are notoriously bad at reaching out for connection, especially when things are not going so well.

My own journey has presented me with a bottom line: a person's definition of success must include an assessment of their personal relationships. *Other people matter.* You can succeed in both your work and personal relationships, they are not mutually exclusive, and getting the balance right is life's sweet spot. If our days are full of people who can put up a shield for us, then we're in good shape. But if we only experience connection when another person needs something from us, then it's likely our social life is an extra drain on the internal battery.

> **The 'One Thing' Intervention:** Identify one person that would have a significant and positive impact on your energy levels, if you connected with them differently. Over the next week, set a small, concrete action that will implement some change in this situation.

Te Puna o te Kī: Diagnose the Fevers

All sorts of fevers can afflict a person or team when they're attempting to work to their optimum levels. In a medical fever, the symptoms usually show up as a high temperature, muscle aches and shivery, flu-like body sweats. In mental performance terms, they usually look like emotional extremes such as depression or a short temper, and like a physical fever, they drain our internal battery. For example, with the All Blacks, it wasn't uncommon for some, or all, of the boys to experience cabin fever at some point during a tour, especially if the squad had been bunkered down in the same location for a good period of time. There was also gate fever, a time when the team was on the verge of going home. This usually kicked in at the end of a tour, as the attention becomes divided between the final game and what is around the corner – *normal life*. Food fever occurs when an athlete has been living to a strict nutritional plan and begins craving junk food like chips or chocolate bars.

To maintain the players' energy levels, the All Blacks acknowledged that these fevers occurred, and we worked on techniques for either preventing them, or managing them. In the case of food fevers, we sometimes treated everybody to a saveloy sandwich after a gruelling training session. This acted as both a reward for a hard day's graft and a nod to the fact that the players needed a lift. Though the team's nutritionists might have grumbled at the time, they knew that one saveloy wrapped in a piece of white bread wasn't going to derail a player. As with most things, moderation was key – one or two saveloys were fine, five or six were not. Elsewhere, we planned activities and day trips to assist with cabin fever, and we encouraged players to stay in touch with their friends, family and loved ones online, or in person, if we were competing at home. When the All Blacks won the Rugby World Cup on home soil in 2011, some individuals were allowed to stay with their families for a short period of time mid-tournament, because it was agreed that they would be recharged by some home time.

But fevers can exist outside of sports too. In the business realm *control fever* can take hold, where excessive micromanagement slows execution and leads to disengaged teams. *Perfection fever* is where nothing is ever good enough and so decisions are delayed and projects drag on, and a fear of making mistakes can cripple progress. Most people experience a fever in one way or another and they're usually triggered once their batteries have been drained. The resulting chaos often ends in burnout, poor decision-making or a loss of perspective.

As with moments of extreme pressure, we've found that when a person brings their horizon forward (see Chapter Eleven), they can often find some clarity inside the feverish brain fog. Food fever, cabin fever and homesickness can be relieved when we have our next 24 hours mapped out for us, with activities designated for every hour – even if those activities are named as 'decompression' or 'recovery' and given a set window of time. Likewise when we apply The Lethal Cocktail of discipline and structure to our maladies, and use them to nourish ourselves in some way, it's possible to build energy rather than lose it.

The Wero: The Rule of Three Bastards

This exercise is a simple warning sign that can alert us to the fact we might be losing the energy battle and in doing so we become less effective in our endeavours. It works like this . . .

If the morning is going badly, and we've seen three 'bastards' before breakfast – someone that annoys us in the gym, a person that brasses us off on the phone or email, or a colleague who rub us up the wrong way when we meet them in the lift – it's time to assess and reset. That's because the problem likely isn't them. *It's in our world.* And only we have the power to correct it. In such a situation, when working away from home with the All Blacks or on the road with a business or organisation, I'll take a moment to reset by having a quiet word with myself. I'll go to the nearest bathroom or return quietly to my hotel room, look at myself in the mirror and adjust. Your reset technique might be completely different, but whatever it is, I'd encourage you to use it. As a self-management tool, it works pretty much every time. It's certainly saved me from one or two tricky situations over the years.

The Library of Learnings

- All of us have an internal, psychological battery. It can be drained by day-to-day pressures, including work deadlines, family issues, health matters, personal relationships and financial anxiety.
- Mental health is our overall psychological and emotional wellbeing; mental strength is our ability to withstand discomfort and take constructive and courageous action under pressure. Both are impacted when our internal batteries are drained.
- In times of uncertainty and high emotion, we should check in with *The Stress Continuum* to assess our energy levels.

Simply taking the time to check can provide reassurance and keep us in a positive space.
- Lean into recharging strategies to win *The Energy Battle*. Power up your internal batteries, reframe the 'drain' and stay connected to your positive influences for support.
- Acknowledge that fevers exist in high-pressure environments. Know your personal tendencies and ensure you have strategies in place to mitigate any negative effects.

Concluding Thoughts

The Golden Wellspring

In 2016, during the week of my birthday, and following on from the All Blacks' Rugby World Cup success of the previous year, my efforts were recognised by the New Zealand government in the New Year's Honours list, when I was awarded a New Zealand Order of Merit for my services to rugby and sports psychology.

'He is well respected and educated in the mental health area,' said the official document. 'And after 15 years continues to find new ways to communicate with the players and team management, providing a unique psychological element to aid the physicality requirements. He has the trust of the players and ensures he is accessible to them to address their needs.'

I'm presenting this to you, not for the accolades, but because the acknowledgement was a *we* award and not a *me* award, one to be shared with those people I had lived, loved and worked with over the years. They stood strongly in my corner, challenged me to keep improving, and to keep believing. They always had my back, no matter what. To amplify this truth, amid the clamour and attention of the New Year's Honours list, one message put everything into perspective. It was a note written by my daughter which she gave on the day of my investiture. It read:

What a fantastic week it is. Not only do we get to celebrate another birthday and reflect on another spectacular year of accomplishments, laughs and togetherness, but we also get to formally acknowledge your achievements with the ONZM ceremony. Thank you for showing us what passion is. For showing us how to wear greatness lightly. You once told me that sport has taught you everything you need to know. I hope you know that watching you do it has taught us everything we need to know. I can't express how proud I am of you. The world is finally getting close to seeing you through my eyes and I couldn't be more thrilled. I hope you leave your pride at the door today, dad, and join us in celebrating everything that makes you you.

We love you so much, Officer, but your greatest title will always be 'Dad'.

Love, Jess.

More than any player or coach, fan or critic, my beautiful daughter had affirmed the belief that it was possible to break boundaries and swim against the tide without losing sight of the most important thing in life. Family.

In a journey full of achievements, that was my greatest of all. It's such a far leap from that little boy in the photograph, feeling lost and alone at the children's home on Tutaenui Road in Marton. Back then I had no choice about where I was born or how I was nurtured. It was the kind of life that hardens you and makes you think that you don't need anyone else, that you can do it on your own. But I learned early on that I'd never achieve everything I was capable of alone, without the support of others, so over time, I let other people in and built a network of positive influences that have all contributed to the making of me.

Most important of all was my wife, Michelle. In a world that celebrates the ones in the spotlight, you have been the quiet force behind everything I have achieved, the steady presence that has lifted me without ever asking for recognition. You have been my anchor in storms, my compass in doubt, and my greatest champion. Your wisdom (offered in perfectly timed moments) has guided me when I needed it most. There is no me without you. And without you, there is no journey, only a path half walked. Through every triumph and every trial, you have been the one constant. You are the reason this journey has meant anything at all. In your quiet, unwavering way, you not only shaped me but have helped me shape others – to stand strong, to believe, to become unstoppable.

To Ben and Jess: A father's love for his children is undefinable – such is the impact they have on your life from the moment they enter it. To then create a canvas, illuminated with so many unforgettable moments, has been a gift beyond measure for me. And inside each of these moments, you two are always there. You were there in the highs and the triumphs, the lows and the heartbreaks. Through it all, you stood with me, each in your own unique way. Alongside your mother, you have made my life whole. My greatest gifts, my proudest purpose. And in the end, the true success isn't just in what I achieved, it's in who I shared it with. You are the reason it matters and the greatest success of all.

To Andrew and Claire – what a gift both of you have been to our wider family and along with George, Louis and Sawyer your additions have enriched us in so many ways.

To my brothers, Roger, John, Bernard, Dudley and Tony (and their wives): our beginnings were challenging but we all made up for it as we forged our paths in life. Thank you for your love and support.

To Smithy, you stand alongside my family as you are truly my brother from another mother. Meeting you (and Trish) were the best pieces of luck I received in my life. Truly one of my life's true blessings.

To the warriors who contributed to the writing of this book – Richie, Dan, Kevy, Reado, Colesy, Smithy and Steve – your willingness to share your stories has created a solid experiential backbone.

To Leigh Gibbs and Keith Mair who along with Smithy had the courage to back a burgeoning young adventurer cutting tracks in the mental space which were unchartered waters at the time. And to Ron Hair who gave a young and raw teacher the chance he needed.

To my volleyball stalwarts where it all kicked off: thank you, Tony Barnett and Mike Dudson – you two were part of a special group of men that had a huge influence on me.

To the coaches I worked with along the way that always had my back – Smithy, Steve, Ted, Fozzie, Crono, Tewey in rugby; Stumpa, Tristy, Denis, Shotty and Braces in cricket.

To the rugby legends that I felt privileged to work with and that helped shape me – Tana, Richie, Dezzy, Reado, Kevy, Colesy, Ma'a, Beaudy, the two Sams – Cane and Whitelock. Each of you are special in your own way.

To the other champions that I had the privilege of working with that taught me so much – Stephen Fleming, Dion Nash, Daniel Vettori, Lesley Rumball (née Nicholl), Bernice Mene, Steven Adams – your examples were inspirational.

To some people that have been more than just good mates – George Duncan, Phil Duns, Mereana Selby, Paul and Jacqui Wright, Mike and Irene Green.

To Ceri and Derek – two experts in their areas that helped me grow my understanding and become a more effective practitioner.

In the making of this book, I'd like to thank my publishers – Géraldine and all the team at Penguin.

Matt Allen for his help in writing this book – you weaved your magic, guided me through a path of understanding that helped me to refine my thinking in a way that ensured my learnings weren't just told, but could be truly heard. There was never a terse word between us. You've been terrific. Thank you.

Dave Dixon – you appeared out of nowhere and as well as being a superb agent, we have forged a friendship that has blossomed. Meeting Arthur along the way was special.

And a special mention to some wonderful people that are no longer with us – Jock Hobbs, Christopher Doig, John Reid, DJ Graham, BJ Lochore, Mike and Joan Lydon. Your memories are a constant inspiration.

Finally, in these closing pages I'd like to leave you with one last lesson.

Years ago, Porsche produced an advert that began with a digitally altered video in which the legendary heavyweight boxer Muhammad Ali sparred with himself in the boxing ring. The next scene showed tennis champ Maria Sharapova, slamming an aggressive serve over the net. Waiting to return it on the opposite baseline was another Maria Sharapova. And in the final images, the chess prodigy Magnus

Carlsen ruminated his next move against the most testing of opponents. Magnus Carlsen. The campaign was never released, but its message struck a chord with me. It stated, very clearly, that when it comes to life, it's you against you.

Yes, our everyday existence is tough, and so much of it is beyond our control. But at some point, we must take ownership of the things we can influence. That was my decision when, at the age of 16, I left home in Palmerston North to start a new life in Christchurch. The decision to rewrite my story put me on a collision course with the All Blacks, and in doing so I realised another truth. Sure, if we're lucky, life can be a long race. And ultimately all of us are like those digitally altered sports stars in Porsche's advertising campaign: Muhammad Ali, Maria Sharapova and Magnus Carlsen. The stars of our own show, locked into a titanic duel with the self. But every moment in that battle, every jab, volley, and checkmate, is an action that affects only one person. *Us*. So, to succeed, we need to make sure we give that moment everything.

Because *that's* the key to becoming unstoppable.

References

CHAPTER 7

'How Winning Organizations Last 100 Years', *Harvard Business Review*, 2018 <https://hbr.org/2018/09/how-winning-organizations-last-100-years> [accessed 14 April 2025]

CHAPTER 8

Ali, Muhammad, 'Me, We', 1975

CHAPTER 12

Thomas, Gordon, *Teacher Effectiveness Training* (New York, 2003)
Lencioni, Patrick, *Five Dysfunctions of a Team* (2012)